Overview Map Key

D1262681

Other cities in the 60 Hikes Within 60 Miles series:

Albuquerque

Atlanta

Baltimore

Boston

Chicago

Cincinnati

Dallas and Fort Worth

Denver and Boulder

Harrisburg

Houston

Los Angeles

Madison

Minneapolis and St. Paul

Nashville

New York City

Philadelphia

Phoenix

Pittsburgh

Richmond

Sacramento

Salt Lake City

San Antonio and Austin

San Diego

San Francisco

Seattle

St. Louis

Washington, D.C.

60 HIKES WITHIN 60 MILES

CLEVELAND

Including
AKRON and CANTON

THIRD EDITION

Diane Stresing

MENASHA RIDGE PRESS
Birmingham, Alabama

60 Hikes Within 60 Miles: Cleveland

Cataloging-in-Publication Data is available from the Library of Congress.

Cover design, cartography, and elevation profiles: Scott McGrew
Text design: Annie Long
All cover and interior photographs by Diane Stresing unless otherwise noted
Cover: Hach-Otis State Nature Preserve
Back cover (left to right): Gorge Metro Park, Edgewater Park, Dix Park (courtesy of the Portage Park District), and Viaduct Park

 MENASHA RIDGE PRESS
An imprint of Keen Communications, LLC
2204 First Ave. S, Ste. 102
Birmingham, AL 35233
menasharidge.com

Visit **menasharidge.com** for a complete listing of our books and for ordering information. Contact us at our website, at **facebook.com/menasharidge,** or at **twitter.com/menasharidge** with questions or comments.

DISCLAIMER

This book is meant only as a guide to select trails in the Cleveland area and does not guarantee hiker safety in any way—you hike at your own risk. Neither Menasha Ridge Press nor Diane Stresing is liable for property loss or damage, personal injury, or death that result in any way from accessing or hiking the trails described in the following pages. Please be aware that hikers have been injured in the Cleveland area. Be especially cautious when walking on or near boulders, steep inclines, and drop-offs, and do not attempt to explore terrain that may be beyond your abilities. To help ensure an uneventful hike, please read carefully the introduction to this book, and perhaps get further safety information and guidance from other sources. Familiarize yourself thoroughly with the areas you intend to visit before venturing out. Ask questions, and prepare for the unforeseen. Familiarize yourself with current weather reports, maps of the area you intend to visit, and any relevant park regulations.

For all those who dedicate their time to preserving Ohio's natural beauty so that we all may enjoy it

Table of Contents

Summit (north), Lorain, and Medina Counties 202

Acknowledgments

IN WORKING ON the third edition of this book, I was extremely fortunate to work with essentially all of the teammates at Menasha Ridge Press who worked on the previous two editions. Thanks to Amber Kaye Henderson for managing the many files I sent into a manageable text, to Scott McGrew for dealing patiently and politely with my lack of spatial skills, and to Molly Merkle and Tim Jackson for handling the business stuff in an always friendly manner. Here at home, my family and friends were supportive and encouraging. I appreciate my husband, who, after a long day at work, put up with my moaning when I tried to explain that I'd had a hard day on the trail. I am grateful that my daughter, busy building her adult life, and my son, creeping toward those terrifying teens, took time to visit a few trails with me. I hope, and I believe, that along the way they caught a case of extreme enthusiasm for all that Cleveland and northeast Ohio have to offer. It is a magical region.

I thank my father for giving me the hiking gene, the inclination to hit the trail for no other reason than to see whatever may be waiting there to be seen. (Thanks, Dad!) I am also grateful for decades of my mother's advice. Because of it, I was careful, wore sunscreen and good shoes, always carried a snack, and drank plenty of water along the way. (Thanks, Mom. See, I was listening.) Bekah Cotton, Michelle Schultz, and Kara Skora deserve extra credit for being the best of cheerleaders, telling me I could meet another book deadline (among other things) even when it didn't seem possible.

I am also indebted to dozens of people in the field, so to speak, who shared with me their time, enthusiasm, and incredible knowledge as I worked on this book. I thoroughly enjoy those brief and casual conversations with people I meet along each trail. Hikers are the best kind of people. Thank you for sharing your thoughts along the path. Until we meet again, happy trails!

—*Diane Stresing*

Foreword

WELCOME TO MENASHA RIDGE PRESS'S *60 Hikes Within 60 Miles,* a series designed to provide hikers with the information they need to find and hike the very best trails surrounding metropolitan areas.

Our strategy is simple: First, find a hiker who knows the area and loves to hike. Second, ask that person to spend a year researching the most popular and very best trails around. And third, have that person describe each trail in terms of difficulty, scenery, condition, elevation change, and other categories of information that are important to hikers. "Pretend you've just completed a hike and met up with other hikers at the trailhead," we tell each author. "Imagine their questions; be clear in your answers."

An experienced hiker and writer, author Diane Stresing has selected 60 of the best hikes in and around the Cleveland metropolitan area. This third edition includes new hikes, as well as additional sections and new routes for some of the existing hikes. Stresing provides hikers (and walkers) with a great variety of hikes—all within roughly 60 miles of Cleveland—from urban strolls on city sidewalks to aerobic outings in the Cuyahoga Valley.

You'll get more out of this book if you take a moment to read the Introduction, which explains how to read the trail listings. The "Maps" section will help you understand how useful topos are on a hike and will also tell you where to get them. And though this is a where-to, not a how-to, guide, readers who have not hiked extensively will find the Introduction of particular value.

As much for the opportunity to free the spirit as to free the body, let these hikes elevate you above the urban hurry.

All the best,
The Editors at Menasha Ridge Press

Preface

WHAT'S THE DIFFERENCE BETWEEN a hike and a walk? I love to ponder this question. Refer to your dictionary and you'll find that *hike* comes right after *hijack,* begging a word-association game. Is a hike just a walk, hijacked by wanderlust? Perhaps.

Merriam-Webster defines *hike* as "a long walk especially for pleasure or exercise" and also "to travel by any means." But walking is a mode of transportation too. Clearly, the difference between a hike and a walk is subject to individual interpretation.

My interpretation, then, is that walking is *primarily* a means of transportation, a point-A-to-point-B kind of thing. Hiking is more a means of *exploration*—even when the ground you're exploring lies between point A and point B. When you define hiking as a means of exploration, you can turn a walk into a hike by altering your perspective. Your perspective will be different than mine, even on the same trail. That's part of the fun of hiking—finding out where the trail takes you.

Land of Plenty (of Variety)

Every hiker has a favorite topography, or three. When I began writing the first edition, I was a hill lover—the steeper and rockier, the better. A view from on high was a bonus, but I was really in it for the climb. I grew to love lake loops, recognizing that they have a serene quality, and forests offer a comfort of their own. And somewhat surprisingly (to me), I've also developed a genuine appreciation—fascination, really—for wetlands. The sticky goo of a bog and the temporary squishiness of a vernal pool create something like a giant petri dish, growing the strangest stuff!

Whatever land type is your favorite, you can probably find it here in northeastern Ohio. Between the gluey bogs and slippery marshes and the edge of Lake Erie, you'll find pretty waterfalls, steep outcrops of shale and Sharon conglomerate, boreal forests, and glacial formations, including kames and kettle lakes.

Most of these hikes travel over Ohio's glaciated Western Allegheny Plateau, and a few tread along the Great Lakes eco-region. When you consider an eco-region, you must take into account both land and water systems. The land in the Western Allegheny Plateau is dotted with short, gravelly, dome-shaped hills called kames. These bumps in the landscape were formed by converging glacial lobes. Some of the cool cavelike spots, such as those found at Nelson-Kennedy Ledges State Park and Gorge Metro Park, even support species native to Canada. The Western Allegheny Plateau also boasts some remaining wetlands, most of which are protected as state nature preserves, such as the Tom S. Cooperrider–Kent Bog and Herrick Fen.

In considering our water systems, the crooked Cuyahoga River gets a great deal of attention, but the Chagrin River, Grand River, and Tinkers Creek watersheds are of equal importance, hosting a significant number of rare and endangered plants and animals.

To learn more about Ohio's eco-regions and the unique species they shelter, spend some time at The Nature Conservancy's website, **nature.org,** or call the Ohio chapter office at 614-717-2770.

History Underfoot: From Terrible Fish to Trains

About 360 million years before the glaciers made their mark on Ohio's landscape, there was no landscape. All of Ohio was underwater. When you visit the Rocky River Reservation, you can see *Dunkleosteus terrelli,* the "terrible fish" that was considerably larger than a shark—it probably ate sharks for breakfast! The nature center at Rocky River is a great place to learn about Ohio's ancient history and more recent events as well.

The first white settlers in northeastern Ohio came here to create the Connecticut Land Company's Western Reserve. Those hardy Easterners built homes, churches, colleges, roads, and railroads when they arrived, and many of these original structures can be seen along the trails described in this book. These settlers also built stations on the "invisible" Underground Railroad—you can take a glimpse into the lives of the abolitionists when you visit Austinburg in Ashtabula County (see page 82).

The folks who settled here made their mark in other ways too. Life Saver candies were invented in Garrettsville, for example, and artist Henry Church Jr. of Chagrin Falls left his "signature" on Squaw Rock (see page 76). Many famous Ohioans are buried at Lake View Cemetery and in dozens of smaller, but equally historical, burial sites in the area. In traipsing and researching these trails, I learned more about Ohio's history than I did in all of my school days. What's more, I found these lessons fascinating. I hope you do too.

Seasons on the Trail

"Winter hiking? Are you crazy?"

All four seasons offer scenic sights on northeastern Ohio trails. Don't let a little number (such as –4°) keep you inside. Properly outfitted, you can be comfortable, have fun, and enjoy something that's hard to find on the trail in the summer months: solitude.

Hike the same trail in each season and you'll discover that it has multiple personalities. What was a serene lake in June is the scene of a raucous party of migrating waterfowl in November. If you think that the woods look dead and drab in the winter, look again. As soon as the leaves fall off the trees, they already have their spring buds. Look closely and you'll see how much tree bud structures differ from each other. And you don't have to look closely in the winter months to spot other features: bird, squirrel, and insect nests (galls) are easy to notice on bare limbs. So are the unusual shapes and growth patterns of many branches.

Before spring officially arrives, many wildflowers poke through the snow to reach for the sun. Get out and see if you can identify them by their leaves, before they bloom.

In the summer, poison ivy, black flies, and mosquitoes may make you think twice before you leave home. Don't let them ruin your fun; the proper repellent will deter them. And here's more good news: Poison ivy is just about the only plant you have to fear in northeast Ohio. Learn to identify its distinctive leaves and habits (it climbs trees as much as it creeps along the ground), and you'll be able to avoid it. Poison oak usually isn't a problem in Ohio, and if you stay away from the mushiest parts of a bog, you're almost certainly safe from poison sumac as well.

People, unfortunately, are far more dangerous to plants than plants are to people. As tempting as it may be, never pick anything along the trail. Even the seemingly innocent action of picking a wildflower on one part of a trail and leaving it on another can hasten the progression of a hostile species. Many nonnative species are aggressive (purple loose-strife and garlic mustard, for example) even though they are also pretty. Leave them where they are. In some places, wildlife management experts have decided to control or eradicate the aggressive plants; in others, they remain under observation. In any case, the hiker is bound to follow the trail mantra: "Take only pictures; leave only footprints."

What Do Timberdoodles Do, and Are Nuthatches Really Nutty?

You don't have to be a bird guru to find bird-watching fascinating. The common robin has one of the most beautiful songs of all North American birds. The often-heard catbird can imitate the songs of more than 200 other birds. It can also do impressions of other noises, such as a rusty gate hinge or a crying baby. At Tinkers Creek, I had a rather eerie feeling as I listened to a repeated, panicked call: "Wah! Wah!" If I hadn't been watching the catbird as he called, I would have been certain that I was hearing a human infant! Another time, walking along a city sidewalk, I spotted a backyard-variety blue jay flying very low. He was weighted down by his catch: a fat mole. (Imagine the feast in that nest!)

Birds, both common and rare, offer great entertainment. If you want to learn about them but are overwhelmed by the volumes of bird-watching books, I recommend picking up a chart that identifies a few local varieties for starters. Or visit the children's section of your local bookstore, where you'll find the thinner books an easy starting point. (Several examples are listed in Appendix E. It was from one of these children's books that I learned nuthatches, unlike other birds, can walk both up *and* down tree trunks and branches. Now, I'm always on the lookout for a bird walking the "wrong" way down a tree.) It doesn't take much effort—or much information—to get hooked on birds.

Another great way to learn about our feathered friends is to attend a naturalist-led outing. The rangers and naturalists I've met over the years have all been great sources of information, as well as patient and not the least bit stuffy. Watch your local park listings for events and go, ask questions, and delight in the answers.

Several years ago, I had the good luck to enjoy my first eagle sighting on a group hike hosted by Summit Metro Parks; at several other park programs, I've learned a tremendous amount from many wonderful naturalists, volunteers, and fellow hikers. So if you are able to attend any similar programs, by all means, go! And don't worry that you'll be surrounded by experienced ornithologists—chances are, you won't be the only new bird-watcher in the group.

"Bearly" Mentioned Mammals

Are bears back in Ohio? Are coyotes really common in the greater Cleveland area? Probably more so than you think. Do you need to worry? No.

Even if you hike each of these trails several times, it's unlikely that you will see a bear or a coyote. On the other hand, you are quite likely to spot deer, raccoons, and even foxes along these trails. You can also see beavers at work and watch bats zigzagging about in the early evenings.

For more information about bears that occasionally explore our neck of the woods or the coyote population around us, visit the Ohio Department of Natural Resources website (**ohiodnr.gov**) or that of Cleveland Metroparks (**clevelandmetroparks.com**). And try to avoid making snap judgments about either of these "dangerous" animals. After all, if Floridians reside with alligators and crocodiles, we can probably live in harmony with our native species too.

Here a Park System, There a Park System, Everywhere . . .

In northeastern Ohio, we enjoy the benefits of many strong park systems and conservation-minded organizations. Most of the hike descriptions in this book include contact information, so you can learn more about the area and the park system that manages it. But if you're really interested in learning about a particular area, the *best* way is to volunteer in it.

Volunteers in parks have increasingly important positions. There's a role for every person and personality too. Whether you're inclined to lead a hike, ring up sales in a nature shop, create posters, build a trail, or file paperwork, you'll be greatly appreciated. I have volunteered in city and county park systems and also in the Cuyahoga Valley National Park. Each experience has proven extremely rewarding. Volunteers have the opportunity to learn from a talented pool of workers and other volunteers, and then share their knowledge with others. No matter how much or how little time you may offer, a creative volunteer coordinator can help you find your niche. Start by calling your local parks and recreation offices, listed in Appendix D.

Finally, no matter where you hike or visit, take the time to learn where you are and to understand the rules that govern that particular trail. Rules vary. State nature preserves, for example, prohibit pets and anything with wheels, while most state parks welcome pets (on a leash) and even bikes (on some trails). Some city parks do not allow pets; others welcome canine visitors. The rules of the trail are created for a reason; following them makes outings more pleasant for everyone.

Take a Hike

In assembling a variety of hikes for this book, I walked through parks and creek beds, on city sidewalks and around the zoo. Everywhere I went, I discovered something. In the hike descriptions, I've tried to convey some of the wonder I felt in those discoveries. Now it's your turn. I hope that this book serves as a list of good suggestions, a set of starting points from which you'll discover many pleasures of your own.

60 Hikes by Category

Hike Categories

- distance (mi)
- difficulty*
- urban
- wheelchair/ stroller-friendly
- kid-friendly
- solitude
- mountain biking
- running

*Difficulty: **E** = easy, **M** = moderate, **D** = difficult

REGION Hike Number/Hike Name	page	distance (mi)	difficulty	urban	wheelchair/ stroller-friendly	kid-friendly	solitude	mountain biking	running
CUYAHOGA COUNTY									
1 Acacia Reservation	14	1.75–2.7	E–M		✓				✓
2 Bedford Reservation: Bridal Veil Falls & Tinkers Creek Gorge	17	2.0	E			✓			
3 Bedford Reservation: Viaduct Park	21	0.5	M			✓			
4 Brecksville Reservation	24	3.5–4.9	E–D		portions		✓		✓
5 Cleveland Metroparks Zoo	29	2.75–3.25	E	✓	✓	✓			
6 Cleveland West Side Wanderings	34	1.8	E	✓	✓				
7 Downtown Cleveland Highlights	39	3.2	E		✓				
8 Garfield Park Reservation & Mill Creek Falls	45	2.0–5.0	E		✓	✓			✓
9 Lake Erie Nature & Science Center & Huntington Reservation	49	1.3	E		portions	✓			
10 Lakefront Reservation: Edgewater Park	53	2.5	E		portions	✓			
11 Lake View Cemetery & Little Italy	57	3.5	E		portions				
12 The Nature Center at Shaker Lakes	62	1.5	E		portions	✓			
13 North Chagrin Reservation: Squire's Castle	67	5.0	M		portions	✓			✓
14 Rocky River Reservation: Fort Hill Loop Trail	72	1.2	M–D			✓			
15 South Chagrin Reservation: Squaw Rock	76	2.2	M–D			✓			

REGION Hike Number/Hike Name	page	distance (mi)	difficulty	urban	wheelchair/ stroller-friendly	kid-friendly	solitude	mountain biking	running
LAKE, GEAUGA, AND ASHTABULA COUNTIES									
16 Ashtabula: The Underground Railroad & Covered Bridges	82	1.5-6.0	E		portions	✓			
17 Beartown Lakes Reservation	87	2.9	E		portions	✓			✓
18 Fairport Harbor Lakefront Park	91	2.0	E	✓					
19 Hach-Otis State Nature Preserve	96	1.5	E						
20 Lake Erie Bluffs	101	3.2	E–M		portions	✓			
21 Mason's Landing Park	105	1.2	E						
22 Mentor Lagoons Nature Preserve	108	3.4	E		portions		✓		
23 Orchard Hills Park	112	1.6	M		portions	✓			
24 The West Woods	117	4.5	M			✓			
SUMMIT (SOUTH), STARK, AND PORTAGE COUNTIES									
25 Canal Fulton: Ohio & Erie Canal Towpath & Olde Muskingum Trails	124	5.9-10.6	M		portions			✓	✓
26 Dix Park	128	2.2	E				✓		
27 Headwaters Trail	132	6.3–12.6	E				✓	✓	✓
28 Herrick Fen State Nature Preserve	136	1.6	E		portions		✓		
29 Hiram College: James H. Barrow Field Station	141	5.0	M			✓	✓		
30 Nelson-Kennedy Ledges State Park	145	2.0	D						
31 Portage Lakes State Park	151	1.5, 1.0	E			✓			
32 Quail Hollow State Park	156	2.2	E			✓	✓		
33 Riveredge Trail & City of Kent	161	2.5	E	✓		✓			✓
34 Seneca Ponds	167	1.1	E						
35 Sippo Lake Park	171	2.0	E			✓			
36 Sunny Lake Park	174	2.0	E		portions	✓		✓	✓
37 Tinkers Creek State Nature Preserve	178	2.8	E			✓	✓		

REGION Hike Number/Hike Name	page	distance (mi)	difficulty	urban	wheelchair/ stroller-friendly	kid-friendly	solitude	mountain biking	running
SUMMIT (SOUTH), STARK, AND PORTAGE COUNTIES *(continued)*									
38 Tom S. Cooperrider–Kent Bog State Nature Preserve	182	0.5	E		✓		✓		
39 Towner's Woods	186	5.8	E–M			✓	✓		✓
40 Walborn Reservoir	190	2.6	E				✓		
41 West Branch State Park	194	3.0	E				✓	✓	✓
42 Wingfoot Lake State Park	198	1.5	E		✓	✓			
SUMMIT (NORTH), LORAIN, AND MEDINA COUNTIES									
43 Bath Community Activity Center & Bath Nature Preserve	204	4.25	M						✓
44 Cascade Valley Park: Oxbow & Overlook Trails	208	1.7	M			✓			
45 Cuyahoga Valley National Park: Beaver Marsh Boardwalk & Indigo Lake	212	4.0	E		portions	✓		✓	
46 Cuyahoga Valley National Park: Blue Hen Falls Trail to Buttermilk Falls	217	1.3	M			✓	✓		
47 Cuyahoga Valley National Park: Haskell Run, Ledges, & Pine Grove Trails	221	4.0	M–D						
48 Cuyahoga Valley National Park: Plateau Trail	226	4.8	M				✓		✓
49 Cuyahoga Valley National Park: Salt Run Trail	231	3.3	M–D				✓		✓
50 Cuyahoga Valley National Park: Stanford & Brandywine Gorge Trails	235	1.5	M	✓		✓			
51 F. A. Seiberling Nature Realm	239	1.4	E		✓	✓			
52 Gorge Metro Park: Gorge, Glens, & Highbridge Trails	243	6.5	M–D			✓			
53 Hinckley Reservation: Whipp's Ledges	248	1.0	D	✓		✓			
54 Hudson Springs Park	252	1.9	E			✓		✓	✓
55 Indian Hollow Reservation	256	2.5	E			✓		✓	✓

REGION Hike Number/Hike Name	page	distance (mi)	difficulty	urban	wheelchair/ stroller-friendly	kid-friendly	solitude	mountain biking	running
56 Liberty Park: Twinsburg Ledges	260	1.4	M		portions	✓			
57 Munroe Falls Metro Park	264	2.3	E–M			✓			✓
58 Ohio & Erie Canal Towpath & Quarry Trails & Peninsula History	267	3.1	E–D		portions	✓			✓
59 Rising Valley Park	272	1.5	E–M			✓			
60 Spencer Lake Wildlife Area	276	2.0	E			✓	✓		

More Hike Categories

- scenic views
- wildflowers
- wildlife
- waterfalls
- lakes
- steep
- nature center
- historical interest

REGION Hike Number/Hike Name	page	scenic views	wildflowers	wildlife	waterfalls	lakes	steep	nature center	historical interest
CUYAHOGA COUNTY									
1 Acacia Reservation	14								
2 Bedford Reservation: Bridal Veil Falls & Tinkers Creek Gorge	17		✓		✓		✓		
3 Bedford Reservation: Viaduct Park	21	✓			✓				✓
4 Brecksville Reservation	24	✓	✓	✓			✓	✓	
5 Cleveland Metroparks Zoo	29			✓				✓	
6 Cleveland West Side Wanderings	34								✓
7 Downtown Cleveland Highlights	39					✓			✓
8 Garfield Park Reservation & Mill Creek Falls	45		✓		✓			✓	
9 Lake Erie Nature & Science Center & Huntington Reservation	49	✓				✓		✓	

REGION Hike Number/Hike Name	page	scenic views	wildflowers	wildlife	waterfalls	lakes	steep	nature center	historical interest
CUYAHOGA COUNTY *(continued)*									
10 Lakefront Reservation: Edgewater Park	53	✓		✓		✓			
11 Lake View Cemetery & Little Italy	57					✓			✓
12 The Nature Center at Shaker Lakes	62		✓	✓		✓		✓	
13 North Chagrin Reservation: Squire's Castle	67			✓				✓	✓
14 Rocky River Reservation: Fort Hill Loop Trail	72	✓	✓	✓			✓	✓	✓
15 South Chagrin Reservation: Squaw Rock	76	✓	✓		✓		✓		✓
LAKE, GEAUGA, AND ASHTABULA COUNTIES									
16 Ashtabula: The Underground Railroad & Covered Bridges	82								✓
17 Beartown Lakes Reservation	87		✓	✓		✓			
18 Fairport Harbor Lakefront Park	91					✓			✓
19 Hach-Otis State Nature Preserve	96	✓	✓						
20 Lake Erie Bluffs	101	✓	✓	✓		✓			
21 Mason's Landing Park	105	✓		✓					
22 Mentor Lagoons Nature Preserve	108	✓	✓	✓		✓			
23 Orchard Hills Park	112	✓							
24 The West Woods	117	✓	✓	✓				✓	
SUMMIT (SOUTH), STARK, AND PORTAGE COUNTIES									
25 Canal Fulton: Ohio & Erie Canal Towpath & Olde Muskingum Trails	124		✓						✓
26 Dix Park	128		✓	✓					
27 Headwaters Trail	132		✓	✓					
28 Herrick Fen State Nature Preserve	136		✓	✓					

REGION Hike Number/Hike Name	page	scenic views	wildflowers	wildlife	waterfalls	lakes	steep	nature center	historical interest
29 Hiram College: James H. Barrow Field Station	141		✓	✓		✓		✓	
30 Nelson-Kennedy Ledges State Park	145	✓	✓	✓	✓		✓		
31 Portage Lakes State Park	151								
32 Quail Hollow State Park	156		✓	✓					
33 Riveredge Trail & City of Kent	161		✓						✓
34 Seneca Ponds	167		✓			✓			
35 Sippo Lake Park	171			✓		✓		✓	
36 Sunny Lake Park	174			✓		✓			
37 Tinkers Creek State Nature Preserve	178		✓	✓					
38 Tom S. Cooperrider–Kent Bog State Nature Preserve	182		✓	✓					
39 Towner's Woods	186		✓			✓			
40 Walborn Reservoir	190		✓	✓		✓			
41 West Branch State Park	194		✓	✓		✓			
42 Wingfoot Lake State Park	198	✓				✓			
SUMMIT (NORTH), LORAIN, AND MEDINA COUNTIES									
43 Bath Community Activity Center & Bath Nature Preserve	204		✓						
44 Cascade Valley Park: Oxbow & Overlook Trails	208		✓				✓		
45 Cuyahoga Valley National Park: Beaver Marsh Boardwalk & Indigo Lake	212	✓	✓	✓		✓		✓	
46 Cuyahoga Valley National Park: Blue Hen Falls Trail to Buttermilk Falls	217		✓		✓				
47 Cuyahoga Valley National Park: Haskell Run, Ledges, & Pine Grove Trails	221	✓	✓	✓			✓		
48 Cuyahoga Valley National Park: Plateau Trail	226		✓	✓		✓			

REGION Hike Number/Hike Name	page	scenic views	wildflowers	wildlife	waterfalls	lakes	steep	nature center	historical interest
SUMMIT (NORTH), LORAIN, AND MEDINA COUNTIES *(continued)*									
49 Cuyahoga Valley National Park: Salt Run Trail	231	✓	✓	✓			✓		
50 Cuyahoga Valley National Park: Stanford & Brandywine Gorge Trails	235	✓	✓		✓		✓		✓
51 F. A. Seiberling Nature Realm	239		✓	✓				✓	
52 Gorge Metro Park: Gorge, Glens, & Highbridge Trails	243				✓				
53 Hinckley Reservation: Whipp's Ledges	248	✓				✓	✓		
54 Hudson Springs Park	252					✓			
55 Indian Hollow Reservation	256		✓	✓					
56 Liberty Park: Twinsburg Ledges	260	✓	✓				✓	✓	
57 Munroe Falls Metro Park	264	✓	✓	✓		✓	✓		
58 Ohio & Erie Canal Towpath & Quarry Trails & Peninsula History	267	✓					✓		✓
59 Rising Valley Park	272		✓	✓					
60 Spencer Lake Wildlife Area	276		✓	✓		✓			

Introduction

WELCOME TO *60 Hikes Within 60 Miles: Cleveland!* If you're new to hiking or even if you're a seasoned trekker, take a few minutes to read the following introduction. We'll explain how this book is organized and how to get the best use out of it.

How to Use This Guidebook

THE OVERVIEW MAP, OVERVIEW MAP KEY, AND MAP LEGEND

Use the overview map on the inside front cover to assess the general location of each hike's primary trailhead. Each hike's number appears on the overview map, on the map key facing the overview map, and in the table of contents. As you flip through the book, a hike's full profile is easy to locate by watching for the hike number at the top of each page. The book is organized by region, as indicated in the table of contents. A map legend that details the symbols found on trail maps appears on the inside back cover.

REGIONAL MAPS

The book is divided into regions, and prefacing each regional section is an overview map of that region. The regional map provides more detail than the overview map does, bringing you closer to the hike.

HIKE PROFILES

Each hike contains seven or eight key items: a brief description of the trail, a key at-a-glance information box, GPS coordinates, directions to the trail, a trail map, an elevation profile (if the change in elevation is 100 feet or more), a trail description, and notes on things to see and do nearby. Combined, the maps and information provide a clear method to assess each trail from the comfort of your favorite reading chair.

IN BRIEF

Think of this section as a taste of the trail, a snapshot focused on the historical landmarks, beautiful vistas, and other sights you may encounter on the hike.

KEY AT-A-GLANCE INFORMATION

The information in the key at-a-glance boxes gives you a quick idea of the statistics and specifics of each hike.

DISTANCE & CONFIGURATION The length of the trail from start to finish (total distance traveled) and a description of what the trail might look like from overhead. Trails can be loops, out-and-backs (trails on which one enters and leaves along the same path), figure eights, or a combination of shapes. There may be options to shorten or extend the hikes, but the mileage corresponds to the described hike. Consult the hike description to help decide how to customize the hike for your ability or time constraints.

DIFFICULTY The degree of effort an average hiker should expect on a given hike. For simplicity, the trails are rated as easy, moderate, or difficult.

SCENERY A short summary of the attractions offered by the hike and what to expect in terms of plant life, wildlife, natural wonders, and historical features.

EXPOSURE A quick check of how much sun you can expect on your shoulders during the hike.

TRAFFIC Indicates how busy the trail might be on an average day. Trail traffic, of course, varies from day to day and season to season. Weekend days typically see the most visitors. Other trail users that you might encounter are also listed here.

TRAIL SURFACE Indicates whether the trail surface is paved, rocky, gravel, dirt, boardwalk, or a mixture of elements.

HIKING TIME The length of time it takes to hike the trail. A slow but steady hiker will average 2–3 miles per hour, depending on the terrain.

DRIVING DISTANCE Indicates expected distance from an easily identified point—in this case, from the I-77/I-480 exchange.

ACCESS A notation of fees or permits needed to access the trail (if any) and whether the trail has specific hours.

WHEELCHAIR TRAVERSABLE Notes whether the trail is wheelchair compatible.

MAPS A list of maps for the trail.

FACILITIES What to expect in terms of restrooms, water, and other amenities at the trailhead or nearby.

CONTACT Phone numbers and websites, where applicable, for up-to-date information on trail conditions.

DESCRIPTIONS

The trail description is the heart of each hike. Here, the author provides a summary of the trail's essence and highlights any special traits the hike offers. The route is clearly outlined, including landmarks, side trips, and possible alternate routes along the way. Ultimately, the hike description will help you choose which hikes are best for you.

NEARBY ACTIVITIES

Look here for information on nearby activities or points of interest. This includes parks, museums, or other hikes.

TRAIL MAPS

A detailed map of each hike's route appears with its profile. On each of these maps, symbols indicate the trailhead, the complete route, significant features, facilities, and topographic landmarks, such as creeks, overlooks, and peaks.

ELEVATION PROFILES

For trails with significant changes in elevation, the hike description will contain a detailed elevation profile that corresponds directly to the trail map. This graphical element provides a quick look at the trail from the side, enabling you to visualize how the trail rises and falls. On the diagram's vertical axis, or height scale, the number of feet indicated between each tick mark lets you visualize the climb. To avoid making flat hikes look steep and steep hikes appear flat, varying height scales provide an accurate image of each hike's climbing challenge. Elevation profiles for loop hikes show total distance; those for out-and-back hikes show only one-way distance.

GPS INFORMATION

In addition to highly specific trail outlines, this book also includes the latitude (north) and longitude (west) coordinates for each trailhead. The latitude–longitude grid system is likely quite familiar to you, but here's a refresher, pertinent to visualizing the coordinates.

Imaginary lines of latitude—called parallels and approximately 69 miles apart from each other—run horizontally around the globe. Each parallel is indicated by degrees from the equator (established to be 0°): up to 90°N at the North Pole and down to 90°S at the South Pole.

Imaginary lines of longitude—called meridians—run perpendicular to lines of latitude and are likewise indicated by degrees. Starting from 0° at the Prime Meridian in Greenwich, England, they continue to the east and west until they meet 180° later at the International Date Line in the Pacific Ocean. At the equator, longitude lines also are approximately 69 miles apart, but that distance narrows as the meridians converge toward the North and South Poles.

In this book, latitude and longitude are expressed in degree–decimal minute format. For example, the coordinates for Hike 1, Acacia Reservation (page 14), are as follows: N41° 30.094' W81° 29.297'. For more on GPS technology, visit **usgs.gov.**

TOPO MAPS

The maps in this book have been produced with great care. When used with the route directions in each profile, the maps are sufficient to direct you to the trail and guide you on it. However, you will find superior detail and valuable information in the United States Geological Survey's (USGS) 7.5-minute series topographic maps.

Topo maps are available online in many locations. At **mytopo.com,** for example, you can view and print topos of the entire United States free of charge. Online services, such as **trails.com,** charge annual fees for additional features such as shaded relief, which makes the topography stand out more. If you expect to print out many topo maps each year, it might be worth paying for shaded-relief topo maps. The downside to USGS topos is that most of them are outdated, having been created 20–30 years ago. But they still provide excellent topographic detail. Of course, **Google Earth (earth.google.com)** does away with topo maps and their inaccuracies—replacing them with satellite imagery and its inaccuracies. Regardless, what one lacks, the other augments. Google Earth is an excellent tool, whether you have difficulty with topos or not.

If you're new to hiking, you might be wondering, "What's a topographic map?" In short, a topo indicates not only linear distance but elevation as well, using contour lines. Contour lines spread across the map like dozens of intricate spiderwebs. Each line represents a particular elevation; at the base of each topo, a contour's interval designation is given. If the contour interval is 20 feet, then the distance between each contour line is 20 feet. Follow five contour lines up on the same map, and the elevation has increased by 100 feet.

Let's assume that the 7.5-minute series topo reads "Contour Interval 40 feet," that the short trail we'll be hiking is 2 inches in length on the map, and that it crosses five contour lines from beginning to end. What do we know? Well, because the linear scale of this series is 2,000 feet to the inch (roughly 2.75 inches representing 1 mile), we know that our trail is approximately 0.8 mile long (2 inches are 4,000 feet). But we also know that we'll be climbing or descending 200 vertical feet (five contour lines are 40 feet each) over that distance. And the elevation designations written on occasional contour lines will tell us if we're heading up or down.

In addition to the places listed in Appendixes A and B, you'll find topos at major universities and some public libraries, where you might try photocopying what you need. But if you want your own and can't find them locally, visit **nationalmap.gov** or **store.usgs.gov.**

Weather

Spring, summer, and fall have obvious allure for hikers in northeastern Ohio. On average, August has the clearest days, followed closely by July, September, and October. If there is a best month to hike around here, it might be October. Most of the summer bugs are gone, but some of the late summer and fall wildflowers remain. Temperatures tend to be quite nice in the afternoons, and the trees are at their colorful best. But there is no reason to stay inside during any month. Consider your destination in terms of the day's weather. A wetland trail may be impassable on a wet spring day, yet stunningly beautiful in December. Black flies bite hard (really hard!) in August; you may want to hit an urban trail then. April–October, wear mosquito repellent when you're on the trail in the afternoons and evenings.

AVERAGE TEMPERATURE BY MONTH FOR CLEVELAND, OHIO					
	JAN	FEB	MAR	APR	MAY	JUN
High	34°F	38°F	47°F	59°F	69°F	79°F
Low	22°F	24°F	30°F	40°F	50°F	60°F
	JUL	AUG	SEP	OCT	NOV	DEC
High	83°F	81°F	74°F	62°F	51°F	38°F
Low	64°F	63°F	56°F	45°F	37°F	26°F

Water

How much is enough? Well, one simple physiological fact should convince you to err on the side of excess when it comes to deciding how much water to pack: A hiker working hard in 90° heat needs approximately 10 quarts of fluid every day. That's 2.5 gallons—12 large water bottles or 16 small ones. In other words, pack along one or two bottles even for short hikes.

Some hikers and backpackers hit the trail prepared to purify water found along the route. This method, while less dangerous than drinking it untreated, comes with risks. Many hikers pack along the slightly distasteful tetraglycine hydroperiodide tablets (sold under the names Potable Aqua, Coughlan's, and others). Some invest in portable, lightweight purifiers that filter out the crud.

Probably the most common waterborne "bug" that hikers face is *Giardia*, which may not hit until one to four weeks after ingestion. It will have you living in the bathroom, passing noxious rotten-egg gas, vomiting, and shivering with chills. Other parasites to worry about include *E. coli* and *Cryptosporidium*, both of which are harder to kill than *Giardia*.

For most people, the pleasures of hiking make carrying water a relatively minor price to pay to remain healthy. If you're tempted to drink "found" water, do so only if you thoroughly understand the risks involved. Better yet, hydrate prior to your hike, carry (and drink) 6 ounces of water for every mile you plan to hike, and hydrate after the hike.

Clothing

There is a wide variety of clothing from which to choose. Basically, use common sense and be prepared for anything. If all you have are cotton clothes when a sudden rainstorm comes along, you'll be miserable, especially in cooler weather. It's a good idea to carry along a light wool sweater or some type of synthetic apparel (polypropylene, Capilene, Thermax, and so on) as well as a hat.

Be aware of the weather forecast and its tendency to be wrong. Always carry raingear. Thunderstorms can come on suddenly in the summer. Keep in mind that rainy days are as much a part of nature as those idyllic ones you desire. Besides, rainy days really cut down on the crowds. With appropriate raingear, a normally crowded trail can be a wonderful place of solitude. Do, however, remain aware of the dangers of lightning strikes.

Footwear is another concern. Though tennis shoes may be appropriate for paved areas, some trails are rocky and rough; tennis shoes may not offer enough support. Waterproofed or not, boots should be your footwear of choice. Sport sandals are more popular than ever, but these leave much of your foot exposed, leaving you vulnerable to hazardous plants and thorns or the occasional piece of glass.

The 10 Essentials

One of the first rules of hiking is to be prepared for anything. The simplest way to be prepared is to carry the "10 Essentials." In addition to carrying the items listed below, you need to know how to use them, especially navigational items. Always consider worst-case scenarios, such as getting lost, hiking back in the dark, broken gear (for example, a broken hip strap on your pack or a water filter getting plugged), a twisted ankle, or a brutal thunderstorm. The items listed below don't cost a lot of money, don't take up much room in a pack, and don't weigh much, but they might just save your life.

> ➤ *Water:* durable bottles and water treatment, such as iodine or a filter
> ➤ *Map:* preferably a topo map and a trail map with a route description
> ➤ *Compass:* a high-quality compass
> ➤ *First-Aid Kit:* a good-quality kit including first-aid instructions
> ➤ *Knife:* preferably a multi-tool device with pliers
> ➤ *Light:* flashlight or headlamp with extra bulbs and batteries
> ➤ *Fire:* windproof matches or lighter and fire starter
> ➤ *Extra Food:* You should always have food in your pack when you've finished hiking.
> ➤ *Extra Clothes:* rain protection, warm layers, gloves, warm hat
> ➤ *Sun Protection:* sunglasses, lip balm, sunblock, sun hat

First-Aid Kit

A typical first-aid kit may contain more items than you might think necessary. These are just the basics. Prepackaged kits in waterproof bags (Atwater Carey and Adventure Medical Kits make a variety of kits) are available. Even though there are quite a few items listed here, they pack down into a small space:

- ➢ Ace bandages or Spenco joint wraps
- ➢ Antibiotic ointment (Neosporin or the generic equivalent)
- ➢ Aspirin or acetaminophen
- ➢ Band-Aids
- ➢ Benadryl or the generic equivalent diphenhydramine (in case of allergic reactions)
- ➢ Butterfly-closure bandages
- ➢ Epinephrine in a prefilled syringe (for people known to have severe allergic reactions to such things as bee stings)
- ➢ Gauze (one roll and a half dozen 4-by-4-inch compress pads)
- ➢ Hydrogen peroxide or iodine
- ➢ Insect repellent
- ➢ Matches or pocket lighter
- ➢ Moleskin/Spenco Second Skin
- ➢ Snakebite kit
- ➢ Sunscreen
- ➢ Whistle (more effective in signaling rescuers than your voice)

Pack the items in a waterproof bag, such as a zip-top bag. You will also want to include a snack for hikes longer than a couple of miles. A bag full of GORP (good ol' raisins and peanuts) will kick up your energy level fast.

Animal and Plant Hazards

TICKS

Ticks like to hang out in the brush that grows along trails. Their numbers seem to explode in the hot summer months, but you should be tick-aware during all months of the year. Ticks, which are arachnids and not insects, need a host on which to feast in order to reproduce. The ticks that light onto you while hiking will be very small, sometimes so tiny that you won't be able to spot them. The two primary varieties, deer ticks and dog ticks, both need a few hours of actual attachment before they can transmit any disease they may harbor. Ticks may settle in shoes, socks, or hats, and they may take several hours to actually latch on. The best strategy is to visually check every half hour or so while hiking, do a thorough check before you get in the car, and then, when you take a post-hike shower, do an even more thorough check of your entire body. Also, throw

Most insects you'll find outside are more fascinating than fearsome.

clothes into the dryer for 10 minutes when you get home, and be sure to check your pet for any hitchhikers. Ticks that haven't attached are easily removed but not easily killed. If you pick off a tick in the woods, just toss it aside. If you find one on your body at home, dispatch it and then send it down the toilet. For ticks that have embedded, removal with tweezers is best.

The black-legged deer tick is the culprit behind Lyme disease. Experts advocate abundant repellent containing permethrin on footwear and pant legs because the nymphal stage black-legged tick often lurks in dead leaves, and ticks rarely climb higher than 18–24 inches off the ground. They can grab on to your shoes and are quite quick to climb up. Get more information from the American Lyme Disease Foundation at **aldf.com.**

MOSQUITOES

Though it's not a common occurrence, individuals can become infected with the West Nile virus by being bitten by an infected mosquito. Culex mosquitoes, the primary variety that can transmit West Nile virus to humans, thrive in urban rather than in natural areas. They lay their eggs in stagnant water and can breed in standing water that remains for more than five days. Most people infected with West Nile virus have no symptoms of illness, but some may become ill, usually 3–15 days after being bitten.

In the Cleveland area, late spring and summer are the times thought to be the highest risk periods for West Nile virus. At this time of year—and anytime you expect mosquitoes to be buzzing around—you may want to wear protective clothing, such as long sleeves, long pants, and socks. Loose-fitting, light-colored clothing is best. Spray clothing with insect repellent. Remember to follow the instructions on the repellent and to take extra care with children.

SNAKES

Some of the venomous snakes found in the United States, including the rattlesnake, cottonmouth, copperhead, and coral snake, all live in the Cleveland area and can be found on virtually every hike in this book. However, most of your snake encounters will be with the 100-plus nonvenomous species and subspecies. Though you could spend some time studying the snakes in the area, the best rule is to leave all snakes alone and give them a wide berth as you hike past.

BLACK BEARS

It's unlikely that you will meet a bear on any of these trails; there are still very few in Ohio, and in most cases, the bear will detect you first and leave. Should you encounter a bear, here is some advice, based on suggestions from the National Park Service:

- Stay calm.
- Move away, talking loudly to let the bear discover your presence.
- Back away while facing the bear.
- Avoid eye contact.
- Give the bear plenty of room to escape; bears will rarely attack unless they are threatened or provoked.
- Don't run or make sudden movements; running will provoke the bear, and you cannot outrun a bear.
- Do not attempt to climb trees to escape bears, especially black bears. The bear will pull you down by the foot.
- Fight back if you are attacked. Black bears have been driven away when people have fought back with rocks, sticks, binoculars, and even their bare hands.
- Be grateful that it is not a grizzly bear.

POISON IVY, POISON OAK, AND POISON SUMAC

Recognizing poison ivy, oak, and sumac and avoiding contact with them is the most effective way to prevent the painful, itchy rashes associated with these plants. Poison ivy ranges from a thick, tree-hugging vine to a shaded ground cover, 3 leaflets to a leaf; poison oak occurs as either a vine or shrub, with 3 leaflets as well; and poison sumac flourishes in swampland, each leaf containing 7–13 leaflets. Urushiol, the oil in the sap of these plants, is responsible for the rash. Usually within 12–14 hours of exposure (but sometimes much later), raised lines and/or blisters will appear, accompanied by a terrible itch.

Refrain from scratching because bacteria under fingernails can cause infection, and you will spread the rash to other parts of your body. Wash and dry the rash thoroughly, applying a calamine lotion or other product to help dry the rash. If itching or blistering is severe, seek medical attention. Remember that oil-contaminated garments, pets, or hiking equipment can easily cause an irritating rash on you or someone else, so wash not only any exposed parts of your body but also clothes, gear, and pets.

Poison ivy

STINGING NETTLES

Stinging nettles are common in disturbed areas, moist woodlands, and partially shaded trails. The toothed leaves are oval, ribbed, and covered with "hairs." When you brush past stinging nettles, sharp, tiny spines covering the leaves and stems penetrate your skin and release histamine and formic acid. The result is an itchy rash relieved only with hydrocortisone creams and cool compresses.

Hiking with Children

No one is too young for a hike in the woods or through a city park. Be careful, though. Flat, short trails are probably best with an infant. Toddlers who have not quite mastered walking can still tag along, riding on an adult's back in a child carrier. Use common sense to judge a child's capacity to hike a particular trail, and always keep in mind the possibility that the child will tire quickly and need to be carried.

When packing for the hike, remember the needs of the child as well as your own. Make sure children are adequately clothed for the weather, have proper shoes, and are protected from the sun with sunscreen. Kids dehydrate quickly, so make sure you have plenty of fluid for everyone.

Hikes suitable for children are indicated in the table on pages xiv–xvii.

Finally, when hiking with children, remember the trip is bound to be a compromise. A child's energy and enthusiasm alternates between bursts of speed and long stops to examine snails, sticks, dirt, and other attractions.

The Business Hiker

Whether you're in the Cleveland area on business as a resident or visitor, these 60 hikes offer perfect, quick getaways from the busy demands of commerce. Many of the hikes are classified as urban and are easily accessible from downtown areas. Instead of eating inside, pack a lunch and head out to one of the many links in the Emerald Necklace

(Cleveland Metroparks) for a relaxing break from the office or convention. Or plan ahead and take a small group of your business comrades on a nearby hike in Cleveland Lakefront State Park or along the canal. A well-planned, half-day getaway is the perfect complement to a business stay in northeastern Ohio.

Trail Etiquette

Whether you're on a city, county, state, or national park trail, always remember that great care and resources (from nature as well as from your tax dollars) have gone into creating these trails. Treat the trail, wildlife, and fellow hikers with respect.

Here are a few general ideas to keep in mind while on the trail.

➢ HIKE ON OPEN TRAILS ONLY. Respect trail and road closures (ask if not sure); avoid possible trespass on private land; obtain all permits and authorization as required. Also, leave gates as you found them or as marked.

➢ LEAVE NO TRACE OF YOUR VISIT OTHER THAN FOOTPRINTS. Be sensitive to the dirt beneath you. This means staying on the trail and not creating any new ones. Be sure to pack out what you pack in. (Note: Some people believe that there's a special place in heaven for hikers who gather rubbish while on the trail and pack that out too.)

➢ NEVER SPOOK ANIMALS. An unannounced approach, a sudden movement, or a loud noise startles most animals. A surprised snake or skunk can be dangerous for you, for others, and to themselves. Give animals ample time and space to adjust to your presence.

➢ PLAN AHEAD. Know your equipment, your ability, and the area in which you are hiking—and prepare accordingly. Be self-sufficient at all times; carry necessary supplies for changes in weather or other conditions. A well-executed trip is a satisfaction to you and to others.

➢ BE COURTEOUS TO OTHER HIKERS, or bikers, you meet on the trails.

CUYAHOGA COUNTY

Viaduct Park (see page 21)

Cuyahoga County (Hikes 1–15)

1 Acacia Reservation

In Brief

If you've ever snickered at the old adage, "Golf is a good walk spoiled," it may be time to put aside your snark. This green oasis, surrounded by shopping centers and heavily trafficked thoroughfares, is one of several former golf courses in northeast Ohio that has recently evolved from "good walk spoiled" to "super-accessible hiking destination."

Description

If your favorite hikes make you feel as though you could be lost in Winnie-the-Pooh's Hundred Acre Wood, this one may not be for you. Nothing at Acacia looks rustic. The parking lot looks like the entrance to a catering facility. In fact, it is. Acacia Reservation is one of several properties that mark a departure from business as usual for Cleveland Metroparks. Park management is evolving, just like properties, and in the case of Acacia, that means making use of the fine facilities that existed when this was a country club. Don't worry—there's a park with trails and birds and trees around back.

At present, all of the trails at Acacia are paved, following the former golf cart tracks. If that doesn't excite you, this might: In the winter, they are plowed. Anyone who has been stuck inside walking on a treadmill during a long stretch of snowfall will appreciate the park's plowing efforts. And speaking of snow, Acacia's hilly landscape provides at least one obvious spot for sledding. Can you imagine walking on a plowed, paved path to go sledding?

Membership at Acacia, which originally opened as a nine-hole golf course in 1922, was initially limited to Freemasons. It later opened membership to non-Masons and eventually grew into a full 18-hole course, enjoying a reputation as one of northeast Ohio's top clubs. Today, it's mighty valuable to Cleveland Metroparks and the people of Cleveland.

Situated almost directly south of Euclid Creek Reservation, Acacia is a jewel that fits nicely in Cleveland's Emerald Necklace, and it has the potential to connect Lyndhurst to the lakeshore with trail systems formally linking the two park properties. For now, these trails connect visitors with the birds and animals that live in the Euclid Creek watershed.

Start from the trailhead at the northeast corner of the catering building, and follow the path north over rolling hills. As you walk, look and listen for redheaded woodpeckers and many other birds that no longer have to dodge long drives in this green corridor. At about 0.5 mile into the walk, you have an option to take a path to the left and cut your hike short. Do so and you'll miss some of the wetter, lower areas where you're most likely to see native wildflowers.

Soon after you pass the shortcut path heading west, the trail bends left and then turns right, taking you to the eastern edge of the property, where you'll have the best vantage point to see the overall lay of the land. The golf path veers left again and heads back into the middle of the property, then swings wide again to the east, looping toward the

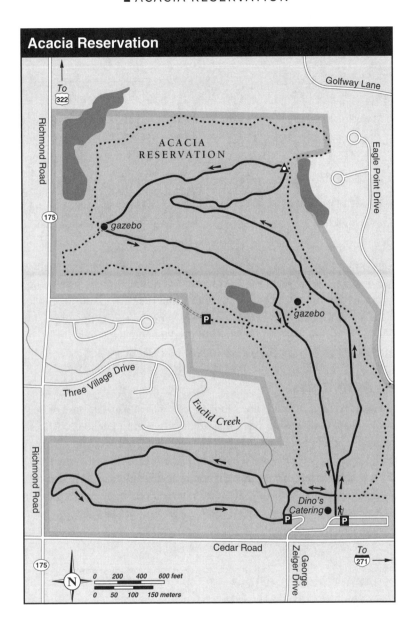

Acacia Reservation

To 322

Golfway Lane

Richmond Road

Eagle Point Drive

ACACIA RESERVATION

175

gazebo

gazebo

P

Three Village Drive

Euclid Creek

Richmond Road

Dino's Catering

P

P

Cedar Road

George Zeiger Drive

To 271

175

N

0   200   400   600 feet

0   50   100   150 meters

park's northern edge before returning you to the trailhead. To return to the park entrance and trailhead, you'll turn left, circling a gazebo before heading south.

Not surprisingly, the trails are mostly exposed to the sun; however, on this portion of the hike, you will enjoy the shade of several stands of large trees—or, if you prefer your shade designed by an architect, this gazebo's for you.

DISTANCE & CONFIGURATION: 1.75- to 2.7-mile double loop	**DRIVING DISTANCE:** 16 miles from I-77/I-480 exchange
DIFFICULTY: Easy–moderate	**ACCESS:** Daily, 6 a.m.–11 p.m.
SCENERY: Creek corridor, rolling hills, and good birding opportunities	**WHEELCHAIR TRAVERSABLE:** Yes
	MAPS: USGS *Mayfield Heights;* also on trailhead bulletin board and park website
EXPOSURE: Almost completely exposed	**FACILITIES:** Restrooms and water in main parking lot
TRAFFIC: Moderately busy	
TRAIL SURFACE: Asphalt	**CONTACT:** 216-635-3200; **cleveland metroparks.com/Main/Reservations -Partners/Acacia-Reservation-17.aspx**
HIKING TIME: 1 hour	

Because the property is in transition at the time of this writing, and likely will continue to evolve for several years, it's hard to say just how trails will develop here. That said, it's quite easy to follow the golf path, which forms the basis for the longest loop trail.

I added about 0.5 mile to the overall distance of my hike by taking the cart path just west of the catering building, heading downhill and looping back on the path that parallels Cedar Road—and I thoroughly enjoyed my good walk, unspoiled.

Nearby Activities

If you're a recovering shopaholic, don't look across Cedar Road—the lure of Beachwood Place may be more than you can bear. Instead, head north to Euclid Creek Reservation and imagine how these two jewels in the Emerald Necklace may shine even brighter if they are tied together a little more securely with a connecting trail system. Or venture south to Bedford Reservation, another Cleveland Metroparks property that, somewhat ironically, includes a golf course. Find more information about catering facilities and events at Acacia at the park's website, or reserve a tee time at Shawnee Hills Golf Course at **clevelandmetroparks.com/golf.**

GPS TRAILHEAD COORDINATES
N41° 30.132' W81° 29.365'

From I-271 N, take Exit 32 (Cedar Road), and turn right onto Cedar Road, heading west about 0.5 mile. From I-271 S, take Exit 32 (Brainard Road to Cedar Road), and turn left onto Brainard Road. After 0.2 mile, turn right onto Cedar Road, heading west about 0.6 mile. The park entrance will be on your right.

2 Bedford Reservation: Bridal Veil Falls & Tinkers Creek Gorge

Bridal Veil Falls

In Brief

This is an easy hike with a big-view payoff: Enjoy cascades and waterfalls on the way to one of Ohio's grandest canyons, nearly 150 feet deep.

Description

Cross Gorge Parkway and enter the trail, following 65 wooden steps down to the overlook. Along the way, stop and admire the water gently bathing the shale as the creek trips along to the falls.

At the bottom of the steps, the walking and bridle paths cross. Horses cross the shallow water on hoof; the rest of us use the bridge. As you look north from the bridge, notice the layers of Bedford shale that line the side of the hill.

DISTANCE & CONFIGURATION: 2-mile loop	**WHEELCHAIR TRAVERSABLE:** No, but overlook is fully accessible from Gorge Parkway.
DIFFICULTY: Easy	
SCENERY: Waterfall, gorge, lush forest, fall color, wildflowers in spring	**MAPS:** USGS *Shaker Heights* and USGS *Northfield;* also at park website
EXPOSURE: Completely shaded except for overlook	**FACILITIES:** Pay phone, water, and restrooms at Egbert Road ranger station; portable restrooms at gorge overlook; water and restrooms at Hermit's Hollow Picnic Area; emergency phones along Gorge Parkway
TRAFFIC: Moderate–heavy	
TRAIL SURFACE: Dirt and gravel on north side, paved on south side	
HIKING TIME: 45 minutes	
DRIVING DISTANCE: 9 miles from I-77/I-480 exchange	**CONTACT:** Garfield Park Nature Center: 216-341-3152; **cleveland metroparks.com/Main/Reservations -Partners/Bedford-Reservation-1.aspx**
ACCESS: Daily, 6 a.m.–11 p.m.; parking lots that close at sunset are clearly posted.	

At the bottom of the 85-foot drop, you'll find a small observation deck with benches. Stop here to enjoy the view.

Once you've had a good look, step onto the Bridle Trail, continuing west. You'll roll up and down several gentle hills, under the shade of thick maple, oak, and hemlock trees. The eastern hemlock is common in this area, often simply lumped in with the evergreen family. Hemlocks can be distinguished by their tiny opposing leaves, deep green in color, that lie flat along their branches. Look for narrow white stripes on the leaves' undersides.

The well-marked, wide dirt-and-gravel trail you're on performs double duty here: It is both the park district's Bridle Trail and a portion of the Buckeye Trail. A mile west of the falls, you'll rise up to meet Gorge Parkway again, soon reaching the gorge overlook.

The overlook itself is wheelchair- and stroller-accessible (parking is available directly off Gorge Parkway). The view is the main attraction, of course, but the history is also interesting.

Tinkers Creek, the largest tributary of the Cuyahoga River, begins in Kent, Ohio— about 15 miles southeast. Once it reaches this area, it winds its way nearly 5 miles through Bedford Reservation. In 1965 public officials planned to dam the gorge, intending to create a large inland lake called Lake Shawnee. A five-year study by naturalist William F. Nimberger, however, highlighted the valley's unique blend of plant and animal species. Public opinion, swayed in large part by Nimberger's study, convinced politicians to abandon their plans to dam the gorge. Today the gorge is a National Natural Landmark.

To return to your car, retrace your steps on the Bridle Trail or cross the parkway to the south and take the All Purpose Trail back to the parking area at Bridal Veil Falls. The difference in the two paths is negligible (about 0.1 mile).

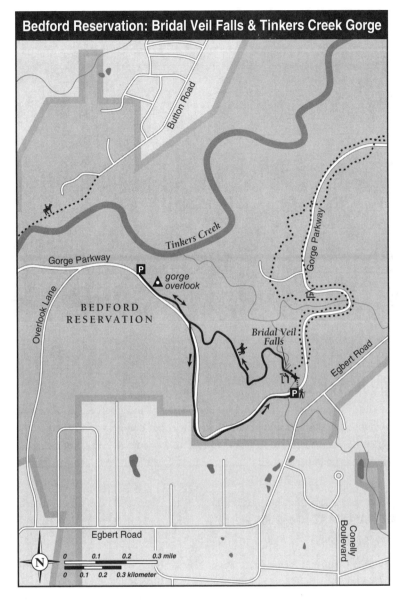

Bedford Reservation: Bridal Veil Falls & Tinkers Creek Gorge

Button Road

Tinkers Creek

Gorge Parkway

Gorge Parkway

P

gorge
overlook

Overlook Lane

BEDFORD
RESERVATION

Bridal Veil
Falls

Egbert Road

P

Egbert Road

Conelly
Boulevard

N

0   0.1   0.2   0.3 mile

0   0.1   0.2   0.3 kilometer

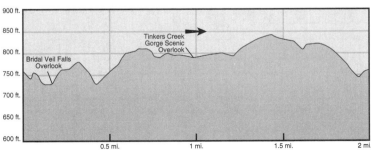

900 ft.

850 ft.

800 ft.

750 ft.

700 ft.

650 ft.

600 ft.

Tinkers Creek
Gorge Scenic
Overlook

Bridal Veil Falls
Overlook

0.5 mi.   1 mi.   1.5 mi.   2 mi.

No dam to see at this National Natural Landmark

Nearby Activities

Shawnee Hills Golf Course is just south of here; enter from Egbert Road. To arrange a tee time, call 440-232-7184. If you'd prefer to walk without clubs, head to Viaduct Park (see page 21), in the northeast section of Bedford Reservation, where another chapter of the area's history has been preserved.

GPS TRAILHEAD COORDINATES

N41° 22.313' W81° 32.936'

From I-480 E, take I-271 S to Exit 23 (Broadway Avenue/Forbes Road). Turn right onto Forbes Road and then make an immediate right onto Broadway. At about 1 mile, turn left onto Bedford Chagrin Parkway/Egbert Road, and in about 0.5 mile make a quick right onto Gorge Parkway. Head west about 2 miles to the parking area for Bridal Veil Falls Overlook, on the left.

3 Bedford Reservation: Viaduct Park

You don't have to hike far to reach the falls.

In Brief

This short trail offers a glimpse into Bedford's industrial past and the Great Falls that provided power in the city's earliest days.

Description

From the parking lot, you can see the viaduct for which this park is named, but much lies below the surface here. From the trailhead, follow the wide gravel trail as it takes you close to the creek bed. You'll hear the falls before you see them, and once you catch a glimpse, you may have a hard time being patient and staying on the trail until you can get a better look.

The main path remains wide and flat until you reach the creek bed, where it takes you almost to the water's edge via a couple of short staircases, less than 0.5 mile from the trailhead. But even before you reach those stairs, you'll have at least two opportunities to stop and gaze at the falls on your right.

DISTANCE & CONFIGURATION: 0.5-mile balloon	**ACCESS:** Daily, 7 a.m.–11 p.m.
	WHEELCHAIR TRAVERSABLE: No
DIFFICULTY: Moderate, with optional walking on creek bed and on rocks	**MAPS:** USGS *Shaker;* also posted at trailhead
SCENERY: Historic viaduct, waterfalls, rock formations, Tinkers Creek	**FACILITIES:** Emergency phone, restrooms, and water at trailhead
EXPOSURE: Almost completely shaded	**CONTACT:** Garfield Park Nature Center:
TRAFFIC: Fairly busy	216-341-3152; **clevelandmetroparks .com/Main/Reservations-Partners /Bedford-Reservation-1.aspx**
TRAIL SURFACE: Limestone and dirt trails	
HIKING TIME: Allow at least an hour	
DRIVING DISTANCE: 7 miles from I-77/I-480 exchange	

One of those opportunities comes with something of a dare: Are you willing to walk through the millrace tunnel that was used 1821–1913, when the viaduct was the site of an active sawmill, gristmill, and electric power plant? The tunnel, about 0.25 mile from the trailhead and about 4 feet high, is much less frightening inside than it may look from the entrance. Besides, it's only about 10 feet long, so you can make a quick escape if you start to feel panicky.

Most visitors are surprised that such a sweet, natural spot exists in the middle of long-developed Bedford—especially because this Cleveland Metroparks property is effectively surrounded by an industrial park. While there are no picnic shelters or other structures here, save for a few benches on the trail, the park sees a good bit of traffic during the week, as well as on weekends. During warm weather, you'll almost always catch a few folks with their feet in Tinkers Creek, enjoying splashing around on its sandy bottom. The water on the east side of the trail is fairly inviting, but closer to the falls, its power is more evident, and visitors are cautioned to stay on dry land there.

While the path indicated on the trailhead map is a balloon, several well-worn footpaths (with interpretive signage) allow you to gain a little insight into the area's history and to explore the water's edge.

When you're ready to return, you can loop back uphill to the parking lot, where a concrete deck overlooking the viaduct features a few interpretive signs that will lend a little more understanding of the falls and their contribution to Bedford's natural and industrial history.

Nearby Activities

It's easy to forget that Viaduct Park is situated inside Bedford Reservation, but it is. That means you're just minutes away from the reservation's other attractions, including hiking trails galore (see page 17), as well as Shawnee Hills Golf Course. You can book a tee time by calling 440-232-7184, or see what other attractions can be found in the reservation on the park's website.

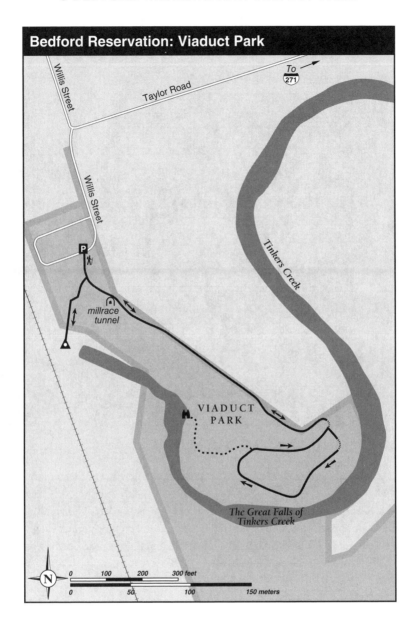

GPS TRAILHEAD COORDINATES

N41° 23.111' W81° 32.047'

From I-480 E, take I-271 S to Exit 23 (Broadway Avenue/Forbes Road). Turn right onto Forbes Road and then make an immediate right onto Broadway. After 1.3 miles, turn left onto Taylor Road, and in 0.2 mile, take another left onto Willis Street, where you'll find the park entrance.

4 Brecksville Reservation

Brecksville Reservation offers hikers great trail variety.

In Brief

Brecksville Reservation packs a lot of plant diversity into its borders. This combination of three short loops provides a good leg stretching and several picture-perfect views. Prairie fields, a vernal pond, and a forest trail to a lovely "mountain" give the budding naturalist (and casual sightseer) plenty to think about.

Description

Start the first of two short loop trails from the Harriet Keeler Memorial parking area on the south side of Chippewa Creek Drive. Follow the paved Prairie Loop Trail west to a raised prairie observation deck.

This prairie is managed so it won't become a forest. It is dominated by tall grasses and brightened by wildflowers most of the year. Foxgloves and beardtongue varieties bloom May through midsummer; pretty Shreve's irises bloom in June and July. Tall sunflowers stretch above the grasses from July through early fall, and goldenrods gild the prairie August–October.

DISTANCE & CONFIGURATION: 3.5- to 4.9-mile loops with optional connector trail	**HIKING TIME:** 1 hour
	DRIVING DISTANCE: 8 miles from I-77/I-480 exchange
DIFFICULTY: Salamander Loop Trail, moderate–difficult; other trails, easy	**ACCESS:** Daily, 6 a.m.–11 p.m., except where otherwise posted
SCENERY: Prairie with wildflowers, vernal pool, great views of Chippewa Creek and Gorge	**WHEELCHAIR TRAVERSABLE:** Harriet Keeler Memorial, yes; other trails, no
EXPOSURE: Prairie Loop Trail, exposed; other trails, shaded	**MAPS:** USGS *Northfield;* also at nature center and park website
TRAFFIC: Short trails are well traveled; Salamander Loop Trail and My Mountain Scenic Overlook offer solitude.	**FACILITIES:** Restrooms and water at nature center
TRAIL SURFACE: Prairie Loop Trail, asphalt and grass; other trails, loose dirt and gravel	**CONTACT:** 440-526-1012; **cleveland metroparks.com/Main/Reservations -Partners/Brecksville-Reservation-4 .aspx**

Continue west to the Harriet Keeler Memorial. Keeler graduated from Oberlin College in 1870 and then moved to Cleveland. She was a suffragette and a Cleveland public school teacher, and she eventually became the system's superintendent. Keeler was also a prolific nature writer. For all of these accomplishments, she is honored here. From the memorial, you'll head south on a path of short grass, through a peaceful tallgrass prairie. The path gradually turns eastward, passing an intersection with the Wildflower Loop Trail. Continue forward, and soon after the mown grass trail meets asphalt, you'll find the nature center. (*Note:* Deer Lick Cave Loop Trail is a popular 4-mile trail that leaves from the nature center; if you wish to extend your hike at this time, go inside for a map.) Walk around the nature center clockwise, and as you leave the building, you'll notice some of the trees along this paved trail are labeled for easy identification. With a bit of studying, you can learn to tell your dawn redwoods from your black cherries. Continue west on the paved trail (the north half of Wildflower Loop Trail), and you'll see that a few of the trees are not only labeled by name but also noted for their utility. For example, pioneers made chewing gum from the sap of sweet gum trees.

You'll have walked about 0.7 mile when you return to the Keeler Memorial. Start a new loop here, Hemlock Loop Trail, by crossing to the north side of Chippewa Creek Drive and walking down to the creek overlook (where you'll want to pull out your camera!). The path turns right then left again, sloping downhill. The path here is generally shady; during the fall, your feet noisily crunch over the oak leaves. You'll hear the creek before you see it; once it comes into view, you will follow its path. Eventually, you'll part ways—the creek ducks under OH 82 and out of sight.

Take a sharp left, heading back up the hill on a carpet of leaves and gravel. Turn to follow the trail southeast, back to the All Purpose Trail, which will eventually lead you to "your" mountain—My Mountain Scenic Overlook, that is—via the Metroparks's

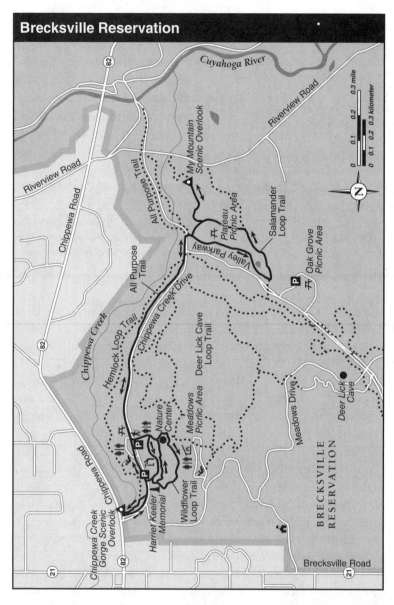

Brecksville Reservation

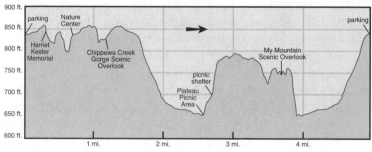

Salamander Loop Trail and the statewide Buckeye Trail. To reach the mountain, you can follow the All Purpose Trail running along the northern side of Chippewa Creek Drive to Valley Parkway and Plateau Picnic Area (about 1.25 miles away), or drive to the Plateau Picnic Area; let your legs decide.

From the Plateau Picnic Area, follow signs for the Salamander Loop Trail and the blue blazes of the Buckeye Trail and begin walking toward the shelter. About 100 yards in front of the shelter, you'll enter the rugged path. Once known as My Mountain Trail, the path is now named for the amphibians that this area supports, and it's also a simple delight for hikers who like hills. This area, like the prairie below, is managed by thinning the forest periodically to encourage the growth of rare wildflowers. Valley Parkway falls away to your right as you head up the steep path. You'll be glad that you wore your boots here—the going is slippery and uneven due to roots and gravel. The narrow path follows the ridge of the hill (it's not really a mountain) until the roadway lies 40 feet below. Then the trail bends left, looking over the picnic shelter below.

Things are pretty quiet up here, and you can imagine that it truly is your mountain, if you wish. The only sound you'll hear may be the squish of your boots as you near the vernal pool. This oak-hickory forest was thinned in the 1990s to encourage wildflower growth. Here, evidence of thinning is obvious, an aid to hikers to get a good look at the usually wet area.

Formed like puddles in contained basin depressions, vernal pools have no permanent aboveground outlets. They typically follow the water table—rising with winter and spring runoff, drying in summer, and filling and freezing in fall and winter. Because they dry out, they cannot support fish. But vernal pools support other species, such as frogs, salamanders, and fairy shrimp, which lay eggs in the pools. Depending on the species, the eggs either hatch before the pool dries out or incubate throughout the wet-dry-freeze cycle, hatching the next year. While these temporary pools look like puddles, they are important ones.

On the western side of the pool, about 0.3 mile into the trail, you'll make a sharp left and see the blue blazes of the Buckeye Trail again. (Up for a really long trek? This is part of a 16-mile section of the statewide trail.) Soon, the trails split, and Salamander Loop Trail veers left. Almost a mile into your jaunt, the trail offers you a short spur to the overlook—take it, if you're not afraid of heights. From the top end of this steep and narrow path, you'll have a bird's-eye view of Riverview Road and the OH 82 bridge.

Retrace your steps down, taking a sharp right to rejoin the loop and continue counterclockwise. This last leg of the trail offers great wildflower displays in the spring. Your legs, perhaps tired of climbing, will welcome the downhill portion of the loop at about 1.4 miles. A short set of wooden steps leads to the bottom of the picnic area driveway. Turn left to return to the parking area if you drove; if you walked, turn right and cross the parkway to follow the All Purpose Trail over a pretty bridge and Chippewa Creek.

A tallgrass prairie buzzes with life.

Nearby Activities

Brecksville Reservation offers several other trails with nice hills—Deer Lick Cave Loop Trail, for example, is about 4 miles long. Stop at the nature center, visit the park website, or call 440-526-1012 for more information.

History buffs might want to visit the Squire Rich Museum, built in 1842 using local black walnut trees. Located inside Brecksville Reservation and managed by the Brecksville Historical Association, the museum hosts annual festivals and is open for tours on Sunday afternoons, mid-May–mid-October. Call 440-526-7165 or visit **brecksville historicalassociation.org/squire-rich-museum.html** for a schedule.

GPS TRAILHEAD COORDINATES
N41° 19.099' W81° 37.152'

Follow I-77 S, and take Exit 149A (OH 82 E/East Royalton Road), merging onto OH 82/East Royalton Road. Follow OH 82 1.5 miles, past OH 21 through Brecksville, and turn right onto Chippewa Creek Drive. The Harriet Keeler Memorial/Overlook parking area is about 0.4 mile southeast of the park entrance.

5 Cleveland Metroparks Zoo

Kyle Lanzer/Cleveland Metroparks

African elephants

In Brief

Is this a hike or an amusement park? Both. And where else in Cleveland can you see elephants, camels, koalas, *and* kangaroos?

Description

The zoo dates back to 1882, when Jeptha Wade donated 73 acres in the University Circle area and a small herd of deer to the zoo. Over the years, other local animals, such as Canada geese and raccoons, were added to the collection. Eventually, plans to establish the Cleveland Museum of Art in Wade Oval meant that the menagerie must move. From 1907 to 1914, the animals were relocated to the zoo's current site, then called Brookside Park. The Works Progress Administration (WPA) completed many projects at the zoo during the Depression era. Since then, the zoo has had several caretakers: The Cleveland Museum of Natural History from 1940 to 1957, the Cleveland Zoological Society from 1957 to 1975, and the Cleveland Metroparks since 1975. Each has added to the zoo's history and attractions.

Inside the RainForest's 2-acre habitat, you'll find some of the world's strangest animals. Wolf Wilderness exposes us to a pack of gray wolves, a beaver dam, and a variety of other species both indoors and out. Australian Adventure (which may be closed in

DISTANCE & CONFIGURATION:
2.75-mile loop (add The
RainForest for a total of 3.25 miles)

DIFFICULTY: Easy, except a long hill

SCENERY: African savanna, desert,
beaver dam, greenhouse, outdoor sculptures, rain forest building

EXPOSURE: Path is mostly exposed;
exhibits provide shade and shelter.

TRAFFIC: Moderate, with crowds for
special events

TRAIL SURFACE: Asphalt and boardwalk

HIKING TIME: 4 hours to see it all

DRIVING DISTANCE: 7 miles from
I-77/I-480 exchange

ACCESS: Daily, 10 a.m.–5 p.m.; closed
January 1 and December 25. Holidays:
10 a.m.–7 p.m. Memorial Day–Labor Day,
Saturday–Sunday: 10 a.m.–7 p.m. Admission: Adults, $13.25; seniors, $12.25; children ages 2–11, $9.25; children age 1 and
younger, free.

WHEELCHAIR TRAVERSABLE: Yes

MAPS: USGS *Cleveland South;* also at
entrance gate

FACILITIES: Restrooms, water, and
phone at Welcome Plaza

CONTACT: 216-661-6500; **cleveland
metroparks.com/zoo**

inclement weather) invites visitors to venture into the outback. So lace up your boots,
mate, and walk this way.

From the Welcome Plaza, head north (right) to the African Savanna. As the path
curves to the west, you'll encounter gazelles, African crowned cranes, and, finally, the
Masai giraffes. The Masais are hard to miss: They are the tallest animals on Earth, reaching 16–18 feet. A male born here in September 2014 was 6 feet tall and weighed 140
pounds at birth! If they aren't near the fence as you round the park's northern edge, don't
worry; observation decks on both sides of the exhibit give you plenty of chances to catch
them, if only on camera. Once you've visited with the black rhinos and strolled under the
impressive Fulton Road Bridge, you'll have logged more than 0.5 mile.

Following the signs to the Northern Trek section, a right turn leads you to some of
the zoo's older exhibits. The sea lion pools were built of native stone quarried from Euclid
Creek Reservation. Climb the steps between the bear and sea lion exhibits to watch both
from above.

Continuing through the Northern Trek, you'll walk by the placid Bactrian camels (two
humps) before reaching Wolf Wilderness. Step inside the cabin-style building to see a variety of exhibits, including fish and beavers. Watch for the Mexican gray wolves from behind
the cabin's glass wall. They are hard to spot until they move; be patient and you can get a
good look. Leave the cabin for the center of the Northern Trek to visit with several bear species, tigers, and reindeer. Heading southeast, back under the Fulton Road Bridge, you'll
pass the African Savanna again. The greenhouse, at about 1.5 miles, is a must-stop spot for
plant lovers. Opposite the greenhouse is the original zoo building—Wade Hall. Relocated
from Wade Park in the mid-1970s and completely refurbished in 1992, today it is a Victorian-
style ice cream parlor.

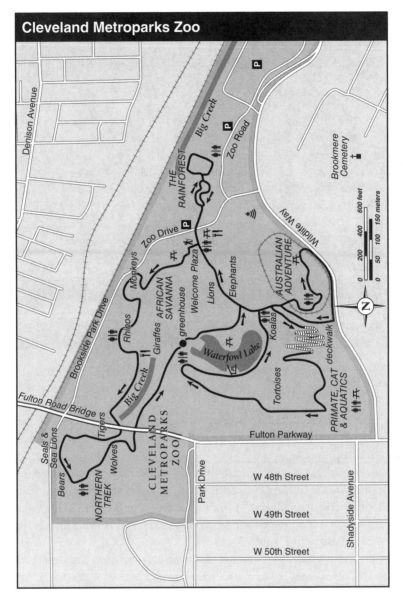

Cleveland Metroparks Zoo

Denison Avenue

Big Creek

Zoo Road

Brookmere Cemetery

THE RAINFOREST

Wildlife Way

600 feet

400

200

150 meters

100

50

Zoo Drive

Monkeys

AUSTRALIAN ADVENTURE

Elephants

Lions

Rhinos

Welcome Plaza

greenhouse

Giraffes

AFRICAN SAVANNA

Koalas

Waterfowl Lake

PRIMATE, CAT & AQUATICS

deckwalk

Brookside Park Drive

Big Creek

Tortoises

Fulton Road Bridge

Seals & Sea Lions

Tigers

Bears

NORTHERN TREK

Wolves

CLEVELAND METROPARKS ZOO

Fulton Parkway

Park Drive

W 48th Street

Shadyside Avenue

W 49th Street

W 50th Street

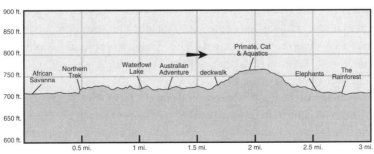

900 ft.

850 ft.

800 ft.

Primate, Cat & Aquatics

750 ft.

African Savanna

Northern Trek

Waterfowl Lake

Australian Adventure

deckwalk

Elephants

The Rainforest

700 ft.

650 ft.

600 ft.

0.5 mi.   1 mi.   1.5 mi.   2 mi.   2.5 mi.   3 mi.

Prowl around the zoo for exercise, and leave with an education.

On your right you'll find a towering birdcage. It has to be towering because it houses Andean condors, some of the world's highest flyers, along with vultures and other large birds.

Once you reach the southern edge of Waterfowl Lake, turn left and then right to visit the koalas in GumLeaf Hideout (Australian Adventure). On your right, just past the koalas, looms the only serious hill in the park: a 1,250-foot-long boardwalk climbing 800 feet up from Australian Adventure to the land of primates, big cats, and big fish above. Before you tackle that, head for the land down under.

Australian Adventure is serious fun. The animals—including lorikeets, kangaroos, sheep, and wallabies—may be the main attraction, but a 55-foot Yagga tree holds its own here. You can "climb" inside the man-made baobab tree on a swingy suspension bridge. Bats, snakes, and a creepy animatronic crocodile await your entrance. The exit is a slide, disguised as a long snake. (*Good to know:* Much of the Australian Adventure area is wheelchair accessible; the tree house isn't. Also, while some of the exhibits may be closed during inclement weather, GumLeaf Hideout, the indoor koala exhibit, is open year-round, even when the rest of the area is not.)

Next, you'll take the 1,250-foot boardwalk up 800 feet to the southwest corner of the park. (You can take the tram instead, but then you'll miss the only serious aerobic work-out of the hike. The tram, which is free, takes zoo guests from the Welcome Plaza to the top of Wildlife Way, where the Primate, Cat & Aquatics Building is located.) Steps in the middle of each zigzag along the ramp allow walkers a bit of a shortcut, while strollers and wheelchairs can roll up. At the top of the climb, you've logged about 2.5 miles and several dozen species. Pause to enjoy a shady view of the Big Creek ravine before proceeding to the Primate, Cat & Aquatics Building. You'll follow the path as it heads north, giving you another view of Waterfowl Lake, before it takes you east through the impressive African Elephant Crossing, which opened in 2011. While Cleveland Metroparks is committed to developing new and exciting exhibits that offer the best experiences for both the animals and zoo visitors, there are also nods to the area's history here. One example: Euclid bluestone was used to build many of the zoo's older exhibits and public areas. Undoubtedly, you walked by (or walked on) some of the stone as you traipsed through the zoo. To learn more about the bluestone and the industry it created in the 1800s, visit Euclid Creek Reservation, another Cleveland Metropark.

At this point you'll have more than 2 miles on your sneakers and, probably, a head full of freshly gained knowledge. If you leave the zoo and head east to The RainForest building, you'll add at least 0.7 mile to your hike, as well as a new perspective on rain forest habitats and inhabitants. The fishing cat exhibit has always been one of my favorites. While I've never seen the rare cat catch a fish, I marvel at the engineering behind the exhibit, which was built to allow the animal to catch fish as it does in the wild.

Whether the cat is fishing when you visit or not, inside the dome-shaped exhibit, you can watch as dozens of bats feed, fly, and crawl about a red-lit room. Other nocturnal creatures are here (especially on the second floor), and on the lower level, you can experience a rainstorm, complete with thunder, lightning, wind, and rain, every 12 minutes.

By the time you've covered all of the zoo's territory, it's quite possible that a zoo hike will have provided you with more information than you can process in one day. Don't worry—there's no quiz later, and you can always return to refresh your memory.

GPS TRAILHEAD COORDINATES
N41° 26.821' W81° 42.696'

Take I-480 W to Exit 16 (OH 94/State Road). Follow State Road north for 1.2 miles until it dead-ends at Pearl Road. Turn right and follow Pearl Road/US 42 approximately 0.5 mile; then turn left onto Wildlife Way, which leads to the zoo's main entrance.

6 Cleveland West Side Wanderings

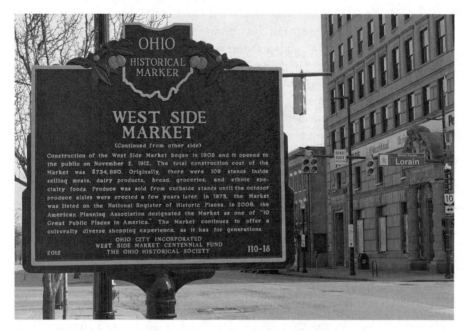

West Side Market has been in continuous operation since 1912.

In Brief

Columbus Road runs east and west through downtown Cleveland, and as any good Clevelander knows, that's enough to start a fight. It's no surprise, then, to learn that the Columbus Road Bridge has caused a few clashes between East Siders and West Siders—going back to at least the 1830s. Well, at least in this urban hike, the West Siders win.

Description

It's not the prettiest drive in Cleveland's resurging downtown, but Columbus Road on the West Side boasts several bustling, established businesses and some interesting developments underway. Rivergate Park is one of them.

The Cleveland Rowing Foundation, fueled by an incredibly passionate group of volunteers, is carving out a home for its rowers on the east bank of the Cuyahoga River. However, you're less likely to see scullers and more likely to see skateboarders in action here, as a small skateboard park is very well used on the property. Also gaining in

DISTANCE & CONFIGURATION: 1.8-mile balloon	**ACCESS:** 24/7
DIFFICULTY: Easy	**WHEELCHAIR TRAVERSABLE:** Yes
SCENERY: Cleveland skyline, historical bridge and buildings	**MAPS:** USGS *Cleveland South*
EXPOSURE: Almost completely exposed	**FACILITIES:** Emergency phone and restrooms in Merwin's Wharf parking lot and at West Side Market
TRAFFIC: Fairly busy	**CONTACT:** Rivergate Park: **rivergate-park.org;** Merwin's Wharf: 216-664-5696; **merwinswharf.com;** West Side Market: 216-664-3387; **westsidemarket.org**
TRAIL SURFACE: Asphalt	
HIKING TIME: Allow at least an hour	
DRIVING DISTANCE: 8 miles from I-77/I-480 exchange	

popularity on this small triangle-shaped green space: Merwin's Wharf, a restaurant owned and managed by Cleveland Metroparks.

With an array of new sites to see here, it's hard to know where to begin. After you've walked around the restaurant, seen the early stages of the rowing center, and watched a few feats performed at the sparkly new skateboard park, it's time for a history lesson. You'll find it right in front of you, in the Columbus Road Bridge.

A bridge has been here since the mid-1830s. West Siders apparently weren't too happy about it and tried to take it down in 1836. Three bridges and more than 175 years later, it's pretty certain that this bridge is here to stay. In fact, the current bridge underwent a major renovation in 2014. Walk across this piece of history to explore some old and new sites on the West Side.

As soon as you cross Riverbed Street, you'll head uphill, now officially on the West Side of Cleveland. This is the east side of Ohio City, which was a city, not a neighborhood, from 1836 until 1854, when it was incorporated into the city of Cleveland. In 0.5 mile from Riverbed, make a sharp right onto West 25th Street, where you'll find a mix of businesses, small and large. Many of these businesses are housed in historical buildings, such as Crop Bistro & Bar, a trendy restaurant inside the United Bank building, which dates to 1925. The exterior of the building is more or less in its original form; the inside, I'm told, has been lavishly restored.

Continue northwest on West 25th about two blocks, and it's impossible to miss the West Side Market, which has operated continuously since 1912. If you can, time your hike on a day when the market is open (see **westsidemarket.org** for hours) and get the full experience. Independent vendors sell fresh flowers, produce, meats, baked goods, and more inside; some are willing to haggle over prices. If a visit to the market doesn't convince you that Cleveland is, and always has been, an international city, nothing will.

Wandering around the blocks surrounding the market, you'll notice that the rumors about the West Side being trendy and happening are absolutely true. Here a brewery, there a coffee shop, and in between cool street art and smart new urban designs, from

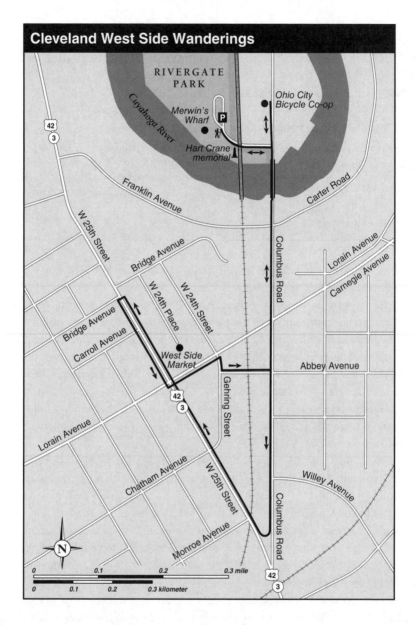

bike racks to bus stops. Yep, this is a good place to be. But you're parked on the east side of the river, so return you must. On my jaunt, I continued on West 25th Street to Bridge Avenue, and then backtracked along West 25th, turning left onto Lorain Avenue (near West Side Market) for one block before taking Abbey Avenue back to Columbus Road. Whatever route you take, find your way back to Columbus Road either on West 25th Street or Abbey Avenue.

As you return down Columbus Road, pass the entrance to Rivergate Park and explore some of the old and new businesses here. The Ohio City Bicycle Co-op, a small but

The West Side Market is one of several historical sites on West 25th Street.

The Columbus Road Bridge was renovated in 2014.

long-established nonprofit, operates here, thanks to some very dedicated volunteers. In addition to salvaging bicycles and teaching new riders about bike maintenance and riding safely in an urban environment, co-op members lead regular group rides in Cleveland's Flats and downtown. The co-op and a handful of other businesses along this stretch of road are East Siders, but just barely. In fact, so close to the river, it's really hard to understand what the rift is all about. Before you puzzle over it too long, return to the parking lot at Merwin's Wharf, being sure to stop at the base of the bridge to learn more about poet Hart Crane in the memorial to him here.

Nearby Activities

Now that you've seen the West Side, visit some landmarks on the East Side (see next page). Or head a bit northwest to reach the beach at Edgewater Park (see page 53).

GPS TRAILHEAD COORDINATES

N41° 29.371' W81° 42.136'

Take I-77 N to Exit 163 (East Ninth Street). Keep right, following signs for East Ninth Street, and merge onto 14th Street. Immediately turn right (northwest) onto US 422 W/Orange Avenue. In 0.5 mile, turn left (southwest) onto Carnegie Avenue. In 1 mile, turn left (south) onto West 20th Street. At the next block, turn right (west) onto Abbey Avenue, and then right (north) again onto Columbus Road. In 0.3 mile, turn left (west) onto Merwin Avenue.

7 Downtown Cleveland Highlights

Urban hikers can go inside many Cleveland landmarks.

In Brief

Here's a hike that's uniquely Cleveland—and it starts out at a historical landmark and shopping mall. Whether you have out-of-town guests who want to see the north coast, or you haven't been downtown for a while, this mini-tour will put you in a Cleveland state of mind, with stops at stately Public Square, the anything-but-square Rock and Roll Hall of Fame and Museum, and other highlights, including the Terminal Tower observation deck, offering panoramic views of the city. In addition to Cleveland's man-made skyline, you may also spot some of the peregrine falcons that nest on ledges of the building's exterior.

Description

From Tower City's lower lot, go inside Tower City Center, up the escalator, and wander north through the fabulous shopping center. When the Van Sweringen brothers planned the 52-story tower in the 1920s, they worked to sway both public opinion and political decisions to have it constructed to their desired specifications. Built to be the main tower

DISTANCE & CONFIGURATION: 3.2-mile loop	**MAPS:** USGS *Cleveland North* and *Cleveland South;* street maps posted at each Regional Transit Authority stop
DIFFICULTY: Easy	
SCENERY: Landmark buildings (both old and new), our Great Lake, public art, and peregrine falcons	**FACILITIES:** Public restrooms and water at Tower City and Galleria (East Ninth Street and Lakeside Avenue)
EXPOSURE: Mostly exposed	**CONTACT:** Purchase tickets for the observation deck (open April–December, Saturday–Sunday) at the information desk at Terminal Tower or online at **towercity cleveland.com/info/skylight** (choose "Observation Deck" on the left-hand menu). To learn more about the peregrine falcons at the tower, see **falconcam -cmnh.org** or inquire at the information desk. See "Nearby Activities" on page 44 for additional contact information.
TRAFFIC: Heavy	
TRAIL SURFACE: Asphalt	
HIKING TIME: 1.5+ hours	
DRIVING DISTANCE: 9 miles from I-77/I-480 exchange	
ACCESS: 24/7; most shops, museums, and attractions open daily.	
WHEELCHAIR TRAVERSABLE: Yes, except cemetery and historical ships	

in the Cleveland Union (railroad) Terminal, it was the tallest building outside of New York City from its opening in 1930 until 1967. Today, the tower cum mall-and-office space has far outlived the railroad line for which it was planned (though the Rapid Transit station is still active), yet the building remains a signature flourish on Cleveland's skyline.

Exit Tower City Center onto Euclid Avenue and find yourself on Public Square. The Soldiers' and Sailors' Monument, built in 1894, sits to your right, on the eastern side of Ontario Street. The monument to the almost 10,000 Cleveland-area soldiers who served in the Civil War is open inside; you can walk right into it, if you like.

Continue north across Public Square to the Old Stone Church. Established here on the corner of Ontario Street and Rockwell Avenue in 1834, the church has been rebuilt a couple of times since. The building you see today dates to 1855. If your timing is good (don't interrupt a wedding!), you can go in to appreciate its ornate interior. Follow Ontario north, across St. Clair Avenue, to the Cuyahoga County Courthouse. As you approach, crane your neck to take in six stately sculptures atop the building's facade. Various artists created the marble figures in 1911; each statue honors an individual for his contributions to English law. Sculpted by Herbert Adams, Simon de Montfort (1208–1265), for example, created a parliament with two houses, which became the precursor of the House of Commons. Below, bronze busts of Alexander Hamilton and Thomas Jefferson, both by Karl Bitters, grace opposite sides of the main entrance steps.

With a nod to Misters Hamilton and Jefferson, turn left in front of the courthouse and follow Lakeside Avenue southwest about a block; then turn right onto West Third Street. From the top of the hill, you'll catch a glimpse of Lake Erie. Follow West Third downhill, passing the Port of Cleveland on your left, and wind around the 31-acre site of Cleveland

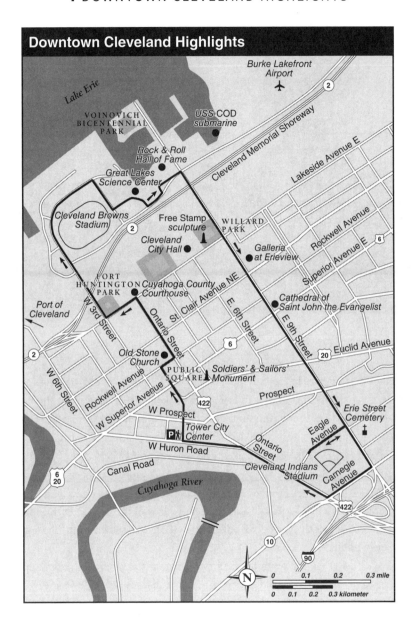

Downtown Cleveland Highlights

Browns Stadium. This may be a good place to get some landscaping ideas: The grounds-keepers focus on the field (which is heated to extend the growing season of the grass), so the rest of the area features hardy, attractive, low-maintenance plants.

Follow West Third east as it bends right, heading south onto Erieside Avenue—the 171-foot-tall stadium now stands to your right. Several sculptures, including one honoring Cleveland's firefighters, dot this part of the walk. Turn left onto North Marginal Road, walking east past the Great Lakes Science Center and the Rock & Roll Hall of Fame and

The USS COD *performed the only international submarine-to-submarine rescue in history.*

Museum. Be sure to peer behind the Science Center to marvel at the 618-foot-long *William G. Mather* steamship, a piece of history in striking visual contrast to the futuristic Rock & Roll Hall of Fame and Museum, designed by architect I. M. Pei. Here you'll also notice signs advertising tours on the *Goodtime III.* When visiting Cleveland, the *Mather, Goodtime,* and nearby USS *COD* submarine offer a comprehensive education in the city's unbreakable connection to the Great Lakes. Tours on any of the three are enjoyable, but the hands-down best choice for hikers is a walk-and-crawl-through tour of the USS *COD.* (See "Nearby Activities" on page 44.) Continue your walk from here by turning right, going south on East Ninth Street. Cross over busy OH 2, also known as the Shoreway, and begin to head uphill.

Soon you'll see the always-good-for-a-conversation-starter *Free Stamp* sculpture at Willard Park, on the north side of Lakeside Avenue. And just south of Lakeside, you'll find the Galleria. The beautiful mall, modeled to honor Cleveland's history of interior arcades, lost many retail occupants after the prestigious Tower City Center opened its mall, but the food court inside the Galleria remains popular with downtown workers and visitors.

Ahead and on your left, at the corner of East Ninth and Superior Avenue, is the Cathedral of Saint John the Evangelist. Originally constructed from 1848 to 1852, the current church is part of a complete rebuilding that took place from 1946 to 1948.

From the church, continue south about 0.5 mile (crossing Vincent, Chester, Euclid, and Prospect Avenues) to reach Bolivar Road. Progressive Field (known for years as Jacobs Field), home of the Cleveland Indians, is on your right. To see some of the

Free Stamp *by Claes Oldenburg and Coosje van Bruggen at Willard Park*

interesting sculptures designed for the new ballpark in 1994, take a brief detour and follow Eagle Avenue west. Several of the sculptures function as fashionable benches: *Who's
on First, Meet Me Here,* and the abstract *Sports Stacks.* (Between you and me, I see a
baseball bat in there, but you'll see what you want to see.) Once you've peered inside the
gates of Progressive Field, return to East Ninth and turn right, heading south again.

On the eastern side of East Ninth (on your left) is old Erie Street Cemetery. Created in
1826, when Erie Street was constructed, it was the city's first official cemetery. Many bodies
buried at church cemeteries were relocated here when the cemetery opened. And there lies
Chief Thunderwater, the most likely inspiration for the city's baseball tribe. Thunderwater
appeared in *Buffalo Bill's Wild West* show and was known as the "official" Cleveland Indian.
Today, Thunderwater shares the grounds with Cleveland's earliest permanent settlers,
Lorenzo and Rebekah Carter, and other folks notable in the city's history.

As you leave the cemetery, take East Ninth to Carnegie Avenue and head west past
the front of Progressive Field, where you'll face the oft-photographed entrance to Hope
Memorial Bridge, which opened in 1932 as the Lorain-Carnegie Bridge. Impressive stone
carvings on each entrance represent the progression of transportation. The figures hold
various icons: a covered wagon, stagecoach, car, and several trucks. Water transportation
isn't represented by the figures, but the bridge itself reminds us—it was built 93 feet above
water level to allow for shipping clearance.

With your feet now on Broadway Avenue, turn right (northwest) to West Huron
Road, and return to the parking garage at Tower City Center.

Nearby Activities

It's OK to act like a tourist here, even if Cleveland is your hometown. Grab your camera and go see the USS *COD,* for starters. Open May–September, the World War II submarine tour is only for the agile. Visitors enter and exit through original hatches and climb ladders over equipment inside. For information, call 216-566-8770 or visit **usscod.org.** Less constraining is the Steamship *William G. Mather,* the 1925 flagship of the Cleveland-Cliffs Iron Company, which is now operated May–October by the Great Lakes Science Center as a floating maritime museum; call 216-694-2000 or visit **greatscience.com** for information. You can cruise the Cuyahoga River aboard the *Goodtime III,* enjoying fabulous views of Cleveland's industrial flats and the area's many different bridges. So (ahem) for a *Goodtime,* call 216-861-5110 or visit **goodtimeiii.com.** For a hike offering a different view of the skyline, visit Edgewater Park, part of the expanding Lakefront Reservation (see page 53).

This walk abuts Cleveland's celebrated theater district and historic Gateway neighborhood. More information, including a schedule of walking tours focusing on the area's history, can be found at **clevelandgatewaydistrict.com** or by calling 216-771-1994.

GPS TRAILHEAD COORDINATES

N41° 29.811' W81° 41.635'

From I-77 N, take Exit 163 (E Ninth Street). From East Ninth Street, merge onto East 14th Street; in 0.2 mile turn right onto US 422/Orange Avenue and follow signs to Public Square/Stadium. In 0.7 mile turn left onto West Huron Road. In 0.3 mile turn right onto West Sixth Street to park at the Tower City Center parking garage.

8 Garfield Park Reservation & Mill Creek Falls

Mill Creek Falls

In Brief

Garfield Park Reservation is rich in both history and features. The nature center on the park's southeast side offers a wide variety of educational programs for visitors of all ages; the paved All Purpose Trail encircling the park offers two heart-pounding hills for joggers and in-line skaters. Look closely and you may catch glimpses of the park's former life—in the middle of it all, there are remnants of the original stonework and bridges dating back nearly a century.

Description

Garfield Park was created when the city of Cleveland purchased three farms from the Carter, Dunham, and Rittberger families in 1895. Opened in 1896 under the name Newburgh Park, the property featured tennis, swimming, and boating facilities for many years. It became a part of the Cleveland Metroparks system in 1986. Start your stroll at the historical Trolley Turn Trailhead, immediately south of Garfield Park Boulevard.

Follow the (paved) All Purpose Trail counterclockwise as it takes you uphill before looping around and taking you to the east, where you'll see a forest of maples, beeches, and elms on your left. Heading downhill along the southern end of the loop and curving

DISTANCE & CONFIGURATION: 2-mile loop, plus 3-mile out-and-back	**ACCESS:** Daily, 6 a.m.–11 p.m., except where otherwise posted
DIFFICULTY: Easy, with two steep sections	**WHEELCHAIR TRAVERSABLE:** Yes, though steep sections may be difficult
SCENERY: Natural and historical stonework, waterfall, ravines	**MAPS:** USGS *Shaker Heights;* also at nature center and park website
EXPOSURE: Mostly shaded	**FACILITIES:** Emergency phones throughout park; water and restrooms inside nature center; grills, water, and restrooms at picnic areas
TRAFFIC: Moderate–heavy	
TRAIL SURFACE: Crushed gravel and asphalt	
HIKING TIME: Allow 2 hours to explore the trails, nature center, and waterfall at the northern end of the park.	**CONTACT:** 216-341-3152; **clevelandmetro parks.com/Main/Reservations-Partners /Garfield-Park-Reservation-7.aspx**
DRIVING DISTANCE: 7 miles from I-77/I-480 exchange	

left again, you'll notice the lines of Bedford shale in the ravine walls above Wolf Creek. At this point, Wolf Creek begins to tumble over a series of stone ledges, descending nearly 50 feet. (On the northern side of the park about a mile away, Wolf Creek empties into Mill Creek and eventually into Lake Erie. We'll get to that waterfall soon enough.)

On the eastern side of the park, the All Purpose Trail is actually the old park roadway. As such, it gives wide berth to strollers, bikers, joggers, and skaters. Happily, hikers can find a narrow and slightly higher footpath just inside the loop of the All Purpose Trail that affords better views of the ravine and creek so far below.

Just north of Red Oak Picnic Area, you'll see a stone staircase leading to an old trail (Iron Springs Trail) that may be redeveloped in the future. Here, you can duck off the paved trail and head for the old boating pond, where beautiful stonework remains from the park's early days.

The pond and the stonework were part of a master park plan, developed in the 1890s by landscape architect Ernest Bowditch, who was inspired by Frederick Law Olmsted. The Iron Springs Loop Trail is an unpaved nature trail that intersects with several others nestled inside the larger loop of the All Purpose Trail. While these footpaths can be somewhat damp, especially during the spring, they're worth getting a bit muddy if you want to get a firsthand look at the Olmsted-inspired designs.

Even from the paved trail, you'll be able to appreciate nature's stonework. Once you've finished this loop, but before you return to Trolley Turn, you can follow the paved trail as it veers north past a baseball field, cuts through a residential block, and continues for almost 1.5 miles before reaching Mill Creek Falls Overlook. The nearly 50-foot-tall waterfall, also known as Cataract Falls, is the tallest waterfall in Cuyahoga County.

When the city was known as Cleaveland, in the late 1700s and early 1800s, the water powered a mill, and the industry it spawned fueled the area's continued growth. By the

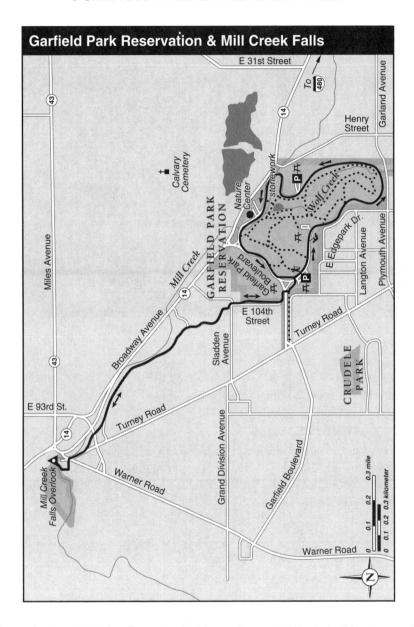

Garfield Park Reservation & Mill Creek Falls

falls overlook, you'll find Mill Creek Falls History Center. While the building is open limited hours, the grassy yard behind the center offers history lessons of its own. Interpretive signage and ironworks—paying homage to the history of men, machines, and construction—are worth a few moments' reflection.

The spur to the falls is an out-and-back, and while it's a good path to give your legs some exercise, the scenery isn't exciting until you get to the falls. So my advice, if you want to see the park and the falls, is to take your bike to the falls and back and save the walking for the rest of the reservation.

Ironwork at Garfield Reservation celebrates Cleveland's early industry.

However you decide to explore Garfield Park Reservation, you're bound to learn something about the city and its history, flora, and fauna.

Nearby Activities

Be sure to visit the nature center on the park's eastern side, where educational programs are held all year long. Call 216-341-3152 for program information, or check the park website. For more information about Mill Creek Falls, contact Slavic Village Historical Society at **slavicvillagehistory.org.**

GPS TRAILHEAD COORDINATES

N41° 25.786' W81° 36.601'

From I-77/I-480, follow I-480 E and take Exit 23 (OH 14/Broadway Avenue). Turn right and go north on Broadway for about a mile, turning left onto Garfield Park Boulevard just north of the Henry Street intersection. Turn left again onto Mill Creek Lane to reach the nature center. To reach the trailhead instead, follow Garfield Park Boulevard west and veer left onto Wolf Creek Lane to the Trolley Turn picnic area, approximately 1 mile west of the Broadway Avenue park entrance.

9 Lake Erie Nature & Science Center & Huntington Reservation

Huntington Beach is always beautiful, if not always inviting.

In Brief

Crawl through a hollow log, visit the stars, and hit the beach—all in the span of a mile.

Description

Huntington is one of the oldest Cleveland Metroparks reservations. It gets its name from English immigrant John Huntington, who purchased the land in 1880. He built a distinctive tower used to pump water from Lake Erie to irrigate his grape fields. The water tower still stands; today it is an ice cream shop (open seasonally), much appreciated by picnickers and beachgoers. A plaque on the side of the ice cream shop relates the park's history and illustrates some of the improvements made by Cleveland Metroparks after purchasing the land in 1927.

But you're probably not here to study history; you're here to make memories. Start by wandering through the Lake Erie Nature & Science Center. It is brimming with life,

DISTANCE & CONFIGURATION:
1.3-mile balloon

DIFFICULTY: Easy

SCENERY: A little creek, a Great Lake, and Lake Erie Nature & Science Center

EXPOSURE: Mostly exposed

TRAFFIC: Path lightly traveled; beach very busy during summer

TRAIL SURFACE: Asphalt, dirt, and sand trails

HIKING TIME: 40 minutes, plus playtime at the beach and Lake Erie Nature & Science Center

DRIVING DISTANCE: 20 miles from I-77/I-480 exchange

ACCESS: Daily, 6 a.m.–11 p.m., except where otherwise posted; Lake Erie Nature & Science Center: Daily, 10 a.m.–5 p.m. No pets allowed on beach.

WHEELCHAIR TRAVERSABLE: Lake Erie Nature & Science Center, yes; trails, no

MAPS: USGS *North Olmsted;* also at Lake Erie Nature & Science Center and park website

FACILITIES: Restrooms and water inside Lake Erie Nature & Science Center and on both sides of Lake Road

CONTACT: 216-635-3200; **cleveland metroparks.com/Main/Reservations -Partners/Huntington-Reservation-9 .aspx;** Lake Erie Nature & Science Center: 440-871-2900; **lensc.org;** swimming conditions: 216-635-3383

from turtles and tarantulas to pythons and piranhas. Large aquariums full of critters fascinate folks of all ages. Nimble visitors can crawl through a 15-foot-long hollow tree that lies just inside the center's front door.

The center also houses the Walter R. Schuele Planetarium, which offers regular presentations on weekends. (See the website for an events schedule—this is a busy nature center!) Outside, the center's lovely "backyard" is great for bird-watching and relaxing.

Once you've soaked up the sights inside and around the nature center, head north on the All Purpose Trail to the lake. You'll follow the paved trail past the Wolf Picnic Area (about 0.1 mile) down a slight incline and across a small bridge over Porter Creek. You'll share the way with light car traffic, so stay on the trail as you make your way back up the hill.

Just over the bridge, there's a lovely view of Porter Creek as it heads east before making its final turn to drop into Lake Erie. You'll lose sight of the creek as you climb up a small hill that serves as a sledding hill when conditions are right. There, on your left (western side of the trail), you'll see the Huntington Playhouse.

You can see the lake from here, but don't cross busy Lake Road to get there. Instead, turn right and follow signs to the pedestrian tunnel underpass. (Restrooms and emergency phones are located near the tunnel's entrance.)

Emerging on the north side of the park, you'll find a shady playground area, a large picnic shelter, and the distinctive tower. Next to the tower (ice cream shop), follow the steep stairs—about 50 of them—down to the shore. During the too-short summer season, the beach is often crowded. But on a windy late fall day, you may even find solitude along the breakwater—on such days, the lake seems more green than blue, and the gulls are the only ones playing in the waves. And if you dare to breach the shore during one

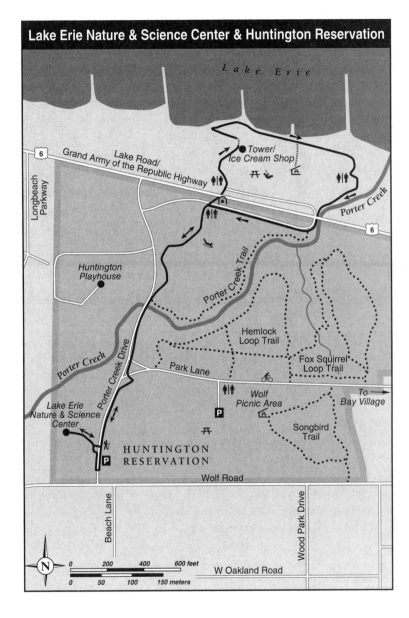

Lake Erie Nature & Science Center & Huntington Reservation

of Cleveland's extended cold snaps, you might think that you could walk across the lake to Canada. (*Note to adventurous types:* Don't do it.)

Walk east along the shore about 0.2 mile, where you'll find another set of stairs that leads up to the picnic shelter. If you continue walking east on the beach, however, you'll soon find a path that curves to the right and stays low. This narrow path along Porter Creek takes you south through the underpass—not the tunnel—under Lake Road.

You'll meet some nonnative species inside the Lake Erie Nature & Science Center.

Follow the dirt path along the side of the road as it curves west, toward the sledding hill and back to the All Purpose Trail. From here, turn left to retrace your steps back to the Lake Erie Nature & Science Center.

Nearby Activities

Huntington Beach has lifeguards on duty from the first Saturday in June to the second Sunday in August, then Saturday–Sunday until Labor Day, 11 a.m.–7 p.m.; fishing is permitted year-round.

Catch a star-studded show at the Walter R. Schuele Planetarium at Lake Erie Nature & Science Center; call 440-871-2900 or visit **lensc.org** for a schedule or for information about other programs at the center.

Huntington Playhouse, 28601 Lake Road, is a popular community theater offering live productions for children and adults. To find out about the current season's shows, call 440-871-8333, or visit **huntingtonplayhouse.org.**

GPS TRAILHEAD COORDINATES
N41° 29.159' W81° 56.253'

Take I-480 W to Exit 7 (Clague Road to Westlake/Fairview Park). Turn right onto Clague Road. In 4.1 miles, turn left onto Wolf Road. In 2.9 miles, you'll see the entrance to Lake Erie Nature & Science Center, at the intersection with Porter Creek Drive.

10 Lakefront Reservation: Edgewater Park

Edgewater is just a few minutes from downtown Cleveland.

In Brief

Iconic Edgewater Park is experiencing new life under the management of Cleveland Metroparks. Clevelanders, as well as visitors to the city, hike along the Lake Erie shore, fish from the pier, and enjoy the 900-foot-long public swimming beach here. The beach still provides one of the best places to watch Cleveland's annual Independence Day fireworks display.

Description

Edgewater Park sits between downtown Cleveland and the city of Lakewood, perhaps not a location many would consider scenic. But it is!

Start at the western edge of the park, at the upper parking area signed as a scenic overlook. It is that! From there, follow the paved trail east. Along the way, you'll meet German composer Richard Wagner. Actually, it's just his statue, a gift to the city from many of Cleveland's German immigrants. From the base to the top of his hat, Wagner stands 18 feet tall, and he's been looking out over the lake and the skyline since 1911. If only he could talk. . . .

DISTANCE & CONFIGURATION: 2.5-mile figure eight	DRIVING DISTANCE: 14 miles from I-77/I-480 exchange
DIFFICULTY: Easy	ACCESS: Daily, 6 a.m.–11 p.m.
SCENERY: Lake Erie views, Cleveland skyline, historical markers, and bird-watching opportunities	WHEELCHAIR TRAVERSABLE: Partially; the paved trail and pier are accessible.
	MAPS: USGS *Cleveland South;* also at park website
EXPOSURE: Mostly exposed	
TRAFFIC: Moderately heavy	FACILITIES: Restrooms and water at changing area and at fishing pier
TRAIL SURFACE: Paved, beach, and dirt trails	CONTACT: 216-635-3200; **cleveland metroparks.com/Main/Aquatics1 /Edgewater-Beach-2.aspx**
HIKING TIME: 1+ hour	

Continue east on the paved path. Several unmarked paths on your left lead down to a sandy dirt trail about 25 feet closer to the lake and as many feet below you. Stay on the paved path; the path below is your return route.

The paved trail offers striking lake views to the north as it continues east, growing shadier by the step as you make your way to the picnic pavilion. The Spanish-style, melon-colored pavilion is a reservable shelter. (Contact Cleveland Metroparks for information.) A memorial fountain to Conrad Mizer also lends a note on history. Mizer hosted free public concerts at Edgewater and helped support the Cleveland Symphony Orchestra. With a nod to Mizer, continue on the path that begins to slope downhill as it ventures east, toward the beach.

The swimming beach at Edgewater is 900 feet long; on warm summer afternoons, you'll hear it long before you see it. It's a popular spot for swimming and just hanging out. In the off-season, you'll hear the coos and cries of hundreds of other visitors: seagulls. They are some of the only wildlife you'll spot here most days, but they make up for lack of variety with their sheer numbers.

Continue on the path downhill, veering to the left at the triangle intersection; you'll cross this way again on your return. Walk past the bathhouse and head toward the lakeshore. The path curves to the left; from here, you'll have a great view of the city skyline and the Cleveland West Pierhead Light. The lighthouse you'll spot in the distance was built in 1911, adjacent to the fog signal building. It remains a U.S. Coast Guard facility and marks the entrance from the lake to the Cuyahoga River.

Follow the path along the shore, past the fishing pier, and as far east on the breakwater as you dare. The old, uneven sidewalk is popular with anglers; on good days, they catch perch and walleye here. The footing can be challenging, but if you are willing to take a few giant steps over breaks in the path, you can continue to the end. As always, be very careful; the wind blows hard on the breakwater. Turn your back to the wind and look south and you'll have a good view of the marina. It's a busy place, with boats coming and going almost

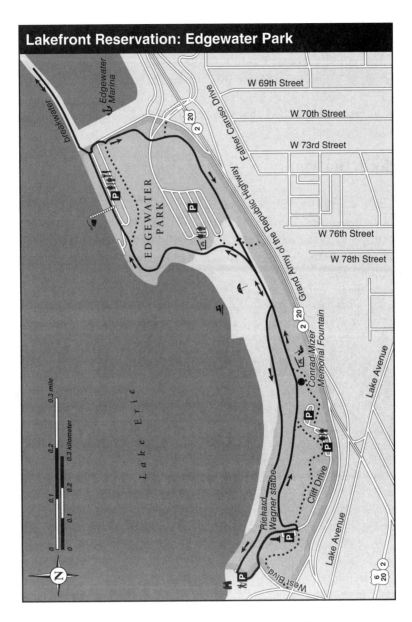

Lakefront Reservation: Edgewater Park

Edgewater Marina

breakwater

W 69th Street

W 70th Street

W 73rd Street

Father Caruso Drive

EDGEWATER PARK

W 76th Street

W 78th Street

Grand Army of the Republic Highway

Conrad Mizer Memorial Fountain

Lake Erie

Lake Avenue

Richard Wagner statue

Cliff Drive

Lake Avenue

West Blvd.

0.3 mile

0.3 kilometer

0.2

0.2

0.1

0.1

0

0

constantly during the summer; in the winter it seems eerily abandoned, and the only noise coming from the water will be the screeches and whistles of gulls.

As you return west along the breakwater, you'll notice that the rocks stuck into the side of the breakwater have strange, weather-beaten faces. Lean over the edge a bit to peer in the water, where you can see freshwater clam and zebra mussel shells.

From the western end of the breakwater, follow the paved path, which heads left (south) along the eastern edge of the main parking lot. The path soon bends right and heads west again, past Washington hawthorn trees full of bright-red berries much of the year. As you continue west, just a bit inland and away from the beach, you'll walk under the shade of deciduous trees, past several picnic spots, and eventually up a staircase to cross a drain culvert. Continue along the path, heading west, and closer to the shore. You'll get an entirely different perspective on the lake from this lower trail, which extends almost all the way to the overlook. Scenic? Without a doubt. Before you go, take the steps at the far western end of the park about 30 feet down to the beach for one last look at Lake Erie and the Cleveland skyline.

Nearby Activities

Downtown Cleveland beckons! See page 39. But it may be hard to leave Edgewater—park naturalists host activities, from live music to bird hikes, year-round. Find a calendar of events at the park website. Also, between Edgewater and downtown Cleveland, Whiskey Island and Wendy Park are rapidly becoming destinations in their own right. For more information about those up-and-coming properties, see **planning.co.cuyahoga.oh.us /whiskey.**

Special thanks to Joe Yachanin, communications specialist with Cleveland Metroparks, for keeping up with Mr. Wagner and fielding a few last-minute questions about the lakefront and recreational wonders on our scenic north coast.

GPS TRAILHEAD COORDINATES

N41° 29.314' W81° 45.051'

Take I-77 N to Exit 163 (I-90 E). Follow signs to Erie, PA, and merge onto I-90 E. Take Exit 174B to merge onto OH 2 W, toward Lakewood, which becomes US 20 W/US 6 W. In 4.8 miles, take the West Boulevard exit, and turn right, then left into the Lakefront Reservation: Edgewater Park lot.

11 Lake View Cemetery & Little Italy

The Archangel Michael stands over John Hay's grave site.

In Brief

A cemetery is an unlikely tourist attraction, but Lake View's history and incredible beauty draw thousands each year. Lake View was designed after the garden cemeteries of Victorian England and France. Adding to its European appeal, it lies next to Little Italy, one of Cleveland's tastiest neighborhoods.

Description

Hiking through a cemetery strikes some people as rather strange. But Lake View Cemetery encourages visitors—tourists, even—and throughout the year offers tours highlighting its unique architecture, geology, history, and horticulture. If you choose to stroll through sans guide, call or stop in at the office for the day's burial schedule, so you won't walk near a burial or where a family is mourning.

Established in 1869, Lake View Cemetery is a Cleveland landmark. President James A. Garfield and industrialist John D. Rockefeller are both buried here. A tour booklet available in the cemetery administration office identifies the grave sites of members of

DISTANCE & CONFIGURATION:
3.5-mile figure eight with out-and-back

DIFFICULTY: Easy

SCENERY: Splendid architecture, views of downtown and Lake Erie

EXPOSURE: Half exposed

TRAFFIC: Moderate

TRAIL SURFACE: Dirt, grass, stone steps, and city sidewalks

HIKING TIME: 1–3 hours, depending on interest and stamina

DRIVING DISTANCE: 13 miles from I-77/I-480 exchange

ACCESS: Cemetery: November–March: Daily, 7:30 a.m.–5:30 p.m. April–October:
Daily, 7:30 a.m.–7:30 p.m. Do not walk in areas where there will be a burial, and be respectful of families who are burying or mourning a loved one. Little Italy: 24/7.

WHEELCHAIR TRAVERSABLE: Cemetery, no; Little Italy, yes

MAPS: USGS *East Cleveland;* also at Euclid Avenue cemetery office

FACILITIES: Restrooms in the cemetery office, Community Mausoleum, and the Garfield Monument

CONTACT: Call for burial schedule before visiting. 216-421-2665; **lakeview cemetery.com**

The Early Settlers Association of the Western Reserve Hall of Fame who are buried at Lake View. This description highlights only a few of the famous folks buried here and offers a basic introduction to some of Lake View's treasures. When you visit, you will discover many more.

Begin at the Garfield Monument, built in 1890, where you'll enjoy views of Cleveland and the lake. On the north side of the impressive monument is a terra-cotta plate showing Garfield in action, teaching geology and other sciences. A professor, Garfield also taught ancient languages at Hiram College. The monument is open April–mid-November. Inside, you'll find stained glass windows and windowlike panels, representing the 13 original colonies, Ohio, and war and peace. Garfield's statue stands in the middle of the monument; his and his wife's crypt are on the lower level.

From the James A. Garfield Monument, head southeast on Garfield Road to the Mayfield Gate. Turn left onto Quarry Road. Along the way, you'll pass beautiful threadleaf Japanese maples on your left and the Mayfield Gate and mausoleum on your right. After crossing little Dugway Brook, you'll notice an old dirt road, closed to the public. It was once used for traffic coming and going from the quarry. In operation from the 1870s through the mid-1930s, the quarry never wasted its contents. Dust from the quarry was used as the foundation for many of the headstones placed here; rocks from this quarry were incorporated in many of the cemetery's buildings and also form the massive cemetery wall that stretches west from the Mayfield Gate to East 123rd Street.

(Visitors usually see the quarry on the cemetery's guided Geology Tour. See the website or inquire at the office about the tour schedule.) Continuing, you'll soon reach a traffic island splitting the road. Follow the road left and walk toward section 30, where the Van Sweringen brothers are buried. The Van Sweringens built Cleveland's Rapid transit system and Terminal Tower. You can cross Circle Road to visit their grave site

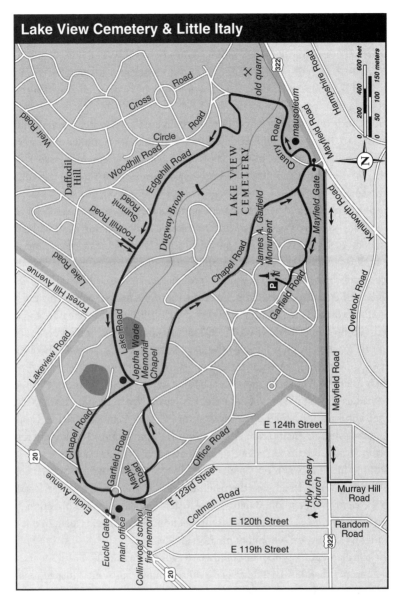

Lake View Cemetery & Little Italy

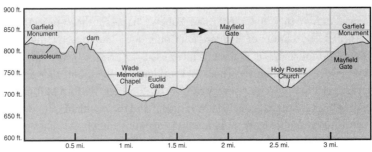

(no. 117), or continue bearing left to pick up Edgehill Road, passing section 35 on your right and the ravine on your left. You'll soon reach the dam, standing 60 feet high and 500 feet across. It can impound 80 million gallons of water. When it was built in 1978, it was the largest concrete-poured dam east of the Mississippi River. That it only has to hold back mild-mannered Dugway Brook seems odd, but suffice it to say that the waters here are well under control.

Proceed northwest along Edgehill to Summit Road. Just after Summit, turn right into section 3 to find the monument of Jeptha Wade (no. 4), cofounder of Western Union Telegraph Company and first president of The Lake View Cemetery Association. Just east of his monument is Daffodil Hill. Each spring, more than 100,000 daffodil blooms burst with color.

Return to Edgehill and head northwest until the road intersects Lake Road. Turn left and follow Lake Road as it passes between two scenic lakes. Just northeast of the lakes, on the south side of Lake Road, is a memorial to Eliot Ness. After helping bring down Al Capone in Chicago, Ness served as Cleveland's safety director from 1935 to 1942. He modernized the police department, developed an emergency medical patrol, and improved Cleveland's traffic fatality record from second-worst in the nation to receiving the National Safety Council's Safest City Award. When Ness died in 1957, he was cremated, and his ashes remained with his family for 40 years. In 1997 he was honored with a memorial service and this memorial stone. The grassy area by the lakes is graced with several pieces of sculpture, creating a good spot to sit, sip some water, and enjoy your surroundings.

When you're ready to continue on Lake Road, turn right at the intersection to follow Chapel Road as it goes north. On your right is Jeptha Wade Memorial Chapel. Stop to admire the windows, designed by Louis Comfort Tiffany. When the chapel is open, you can go in to appreciate the interior. Also on your right, in section 5-C, are the remains of Carl Burton Stokes, the first African American mayor of a major US city.

Continue heading north on Chapel Road to the Euclid Gate. Cross Garfield Road and then follow Maple Road past the cemetery office. You'll reach Office Road, which bears to the right, but keep on Maple as it bears left and circles around section 26. Look for a road/path that leads right and cut across section 25 to Garfield Road. In this section, you'll find the Collinwood school fire memorial.

When an elementary school in Collinwood caught fire in 1908, 172 students, 2 teachers, and a rescuer died inside. The tragedy caused numerous school inspections nationwide and spurred new, stricter building codes.

At Garfield Road, turn right (south). At the next intersection, turn left and then take an immediate right to pick up Chapel Road. Follow Chapel southeast to section 10, where John D. Rockefeller, founder of Standard Oil Company, is laid to rest. Other notable people in this section include Dr. Harvey Williams Cushing (no. 57), who pioneered brain surgery techniques, and John Hay (no. 73), President Abraham Lincoln's personal secretary during the Civil War and Secretary of State to President William McKinley.

Heading back toward the Garfield Monument and the Mayfield Gate, you'll appreciate the intricate gardening work and incredible planning for which Lake View is known.

In the late 1800s, many Italian stonecutters and gardeners migrated to Cleveland to work at the cemetery. When you leave the cemetery through the Mayfield Gate, turn right and walk west to the neighborhood these immigrants built.

As you amble downhill on the north side of Mayfield Road, you'll appreciate the craftsmanship on the impressive wall of Berea sandstone that runs west toward Little Italy. You'll know that you've arrived when you see many red, white, and green signs for *ristorantes*—Little Italy offers a wealth of Italian food and culture. Sample some locally made doughnuts, pizza, or Italian ice. Don't worry; you can walk off a few of those calories by climbing Murray Hill Road.

For a few days every August, part of Mayfield Road is closed to car traffic for the Feast of the Assumption. The Italian-Catholic festival is celebrated with Masses at the church and with games, music, and dancing. Like an Italian Mardi Gras, the party happens as much on the street as inside the neighborhood's shops and eateries.

Before you say "ciao" to Little Italy, stop at Holy Rosary Church, 12021 Mayfield Road. Built in 1909, the grand redbrick building is the heart of the neighborhood and of the feast. As you head back up the hill, east to the cemetery, you're likely to have a belly full of Italian food and a new appreciation for Cleveland's history.

Nearby Activities

Lake View offers an almost constant schedule of tours and special events; check the website or call the office for details. For more information about happenings in Cleveland's Little Italy neighborhood, visit **littleitalycleveland.com.**

GPS TRAILHEAD COORDINATES
N41° 30.595' W81° 35.495'

From I-77 N, take Exit 163 (I-90 E). Follow I-90 E to Exit 173B (Chester Avenue). Turn right onto Chester, going about 3 miles before turning left onto Euclid Avenue. In 1 mile, the Lake View Cemetery entrance is on the right, at 12316 Euclid Avenue.

12 The Nature Center at Shaker Lakes

The view from the north end of Lower Lake

In Brief

Located amid Shaker and Cleveland Heights, this preserved wilderness was nearly wiped out in the 1960s by a proposed freeway. Now dirt trails and boardwalks lead visitors past the nature center and its wildflower garden and around Ohio's oldest artificial lake.

Description

In the late 1800s Cleveland city dwellers escaped to the relative "country" of the city's eastside Heights area. In the 1960s it seemed like a good place to construct a freeway connecting the city and the eastern suburbs. That is, it seemed like a good idea to people who did not live in the Heights area. Residents were so opposed, in fact, that they hustled to establish a nature center and effectively prevented the freeway's placement. Good thing too—a few years later, the National Park Service named the center a National Environmental Education Landmark and a National Environmental Study Area. In short, coming here will probably make you smarter—and you'll have a good time too.

Start exploring on the short All People's Trail, a boardwalk featuring marsh and stream habitats and a small waterfall. You'll also get an interesting perspective on the park—from several spots on the All People's Trail, you're surrounded by natural beauty and, at the same time, you can hear the cars go by on North Woodland Road. That is the defining characteristic of this property: Its preserved wildness is firmly entrenched in the densely populated, long-civilized cities of Shaker and Cleveland Heights.

DISTANCE & CONFIGURATION: 1.5-mile loop; option for shorter or longer loops	**HIKING TIME:** 1 hour, plus time for inside sightseeing and education
DIFFICULTY: Easy	**ACCESS:** Trails: sunrise–sunset; Nature Center: Monday–Saturday, 10 a.m.–5 p.m. and Sunday, 1–5 p.m. Foot traffic only—no bikes, skates, or pets permitted, though a bike trail does intersect the hiking trail.
SCENERY: Birds; wetland, marsh, and lake views; wildflower and rain gardens	
EXPOSURE: Mixed sun and shade	
TRAFFIC: Rarely crowded	**WHEELCHAIR TRAVERSABLE:** Yes, nature center and one trail
TRAIL SURFACE: Wooden boardwalk, dirt, hard-packed gravel, and some asphalt	**MAPS:** USGS *Shaker Heights;* also at nature center
	FACILITIES: Restrooms and water
DRIVING DISTANCE: 13 miles from I-77/I-480 exchange	**CONTACT:** 216-321-5935; **shakerlakes.org**

From the north end of the parking lot, follow the All People's Trail north to a marsh overlook. Turn around and follow the trail clockwise. Looping around, you'll see a gate with a sign TRAIL TO LOWER LAKE. Obviously, that's your exit. Go through the gate, follow the wooden steps down to the dirt path, and follow it as it curves to the left, up a short hill, to cross North Woodland Road.

From the north side of Woodland, you can see most of Lower Shaker Lake. The bike trail splits off to the right; hikers should follow the stone steps down to a skinny dirt path along the lake. (If you aren't so sure-footed, take the high road, which in this case is the asphalt bike trail. It also offers lake views but from a wider, flatter trail several yards to the north.) About 0.2 mile north of Woodland, the bike path and walking trail merge into each other for a time and then round the northwest edge of the lake.

At the northernmost end of the lake, you'll have your choice of crossings: over a pretty wrought iron bridge or via the smaller, older bridge just north of it. The older bridge, made mostly of wide, flat fieldstone, affords an interesting perspective on the lake as seen from under the wrought iron bridge. Lower Shaker Lake is the oldest man-made lake in Ohio. It was formed from Doan Brook in the 1820s. In 1852 the Shaker community dammed Doan Brook again to create Horseshoe Lake, on the other end of the brook, to power the community's mills. *Note:* After returning to the nature center, you may decide to walk down to Horseshoe Lake; see "Nearby Activities" on page 65.

As the path circles left and heads generally south, you'll parallel South Park Boulevard for a while before crossing Woodland again. As you head back to the nature center, the path is wider, part wood and part gravel.

Soon you'll be able to see Stearns Trail, a series of boardwalks running alongside and over Doan Brook. At one point on the trail near the nature center, under the shade of beech and oak trees, you'll pick up your feet to step over a tree root and realize that it joins two trees—one on either side of the trail. It begs some rather philosophical questions: Is this a

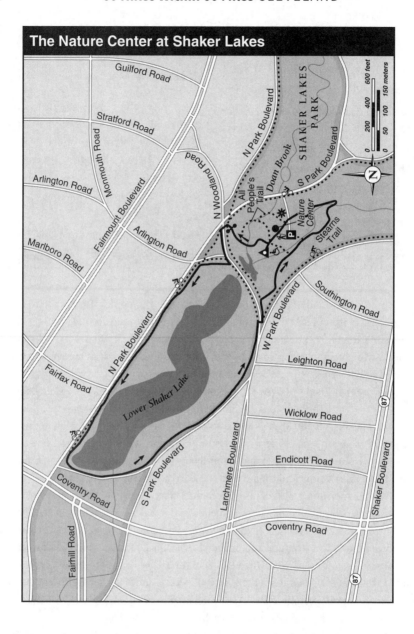

The Nature Center at Shaker Lakes

root or a branch? Is this one tree or two? You may pick one of several park benches nearby from which to contemplate the answer . . . if there is one.

Where Stearns Trail isn't boardwalk, it's hard-packed gravel. Looping and linking trails will take you back—when you're ready—to the nature center. Immediately southeast of the building, you'll find a small wildflower garden and some alarming news: Some

Visit the rain garden along the Nature for All Trail.

of these pretty flowers are intruders! Most of the flowers are planted natives for show, but purple loosestrife (which can actually be rather pinkish in color), Japanese knotweed, and goutweed have more than unusual names in common. All three are rather pretty pests. These invasive plants crowd out native flowers and vegetation, harming animal habitats and increasing soil erosion in the process. But there's good news here too—by minding what we plant, or allow to grow, and working with our natural resources, we can minimize our footprint on the land.

Visitors to the nature center can pick up many good ideas here, from the plant selection to the center's building design, which features rain barrels and swales to make wise use of water in the gardens, as well as compost bins that utilize organic waste rather than sending it to a landfill.

When you've learned all you can outside, go inside the nature center, so your education, and fun, may continue.

Nearby Activities

Add 3 miles or more to your hike here by heading east from the nature center along either North or South Park Boulevard until you reach Horseshoe Lake. It's a popular trek for dog walkers, and the bike path that runs along North Park Boulevard is busy with cyclists as well.

Many thanks to Justin Evans, naturalist at the Nature Center at Shaker Lakes, for reviewing this hike description.

This urban park is an official Wildlife Habitat site and Audubon Important Bird Area.

GPS TRAILHEAD COORDINATES

N41° 29.119' W81° 34.466'

The best way to get here is on the Rapid. Take the Shaker Heights Green Line to the South Park stop; walk north along South Park Boulevard about 0.3 mile. The nature center is on the left, at the bottom of the hill, at 2600 S Park Blvd. By car, from the I-77/I-480 exchange, follow I-480 E to I-271 N. Take Exit 29 (OH 87/US 422/Chagrin Boulevard), and then head west for 0.5 mile on OH 87/US 422/Chagrin Boulevard. Turn right onto Richmond Road, and go 1 mile north to Shaker Boulevard; turn left. In 3.9 miles, turn right onto South Park Boulevard. After going down a small hill, the road forks. Veer left; a sign and the driveway to the nature center will be on your left.

13 North Chagrin Reservation: Squire's Castle

Sanctuary Marsh Loop Trail is ideal for strollers and wheelchairs.

In Brief

North Chagrin Reservation has something for everyone. The nature center's exhibits are educational and fun for all ages. Paved trails, bridle trails, and nature trails intersect throughout the reservation, leading visitors to a gentle waterfall, through fragrant ravines, and ultimately to a castle romantically set on a sloping hill.

DISTANCE & CONFIGURATION: 5-mile loop	**ACCESS:** Daily, 6 a.m.–11 p.m. Nature center: Daily, 9:30 a.m.–5 p.m.; closed January 1, Easter, Thanksgiving, and December 25
DIFFICULTY: Moderate, with difficult sections	
SCENERY: Waterfall, deep ravine overlooks, beaver activity, historical country estate	**WHEELCHAIR TRAVERSABLE:** Sanctuary Marsh Loop and All Purpose Trails, yes; other trails, no
EXPOSURE: Mostly shaded	**MAPS:** USGS *Mayfield Heights;* also at nature center and park website
TRAFFIC: Moderate–heavy	
TRAIL SURFACE: All Purpose and Sanctuary Marsh Loop Trails, paved; bridle and hiking trails, hard-packed dirt	**FACILITIES:** Restrooms inside nature center; grills, water, and restrooms at each picnic area
HIKING TIME: 2.5 hours	**CONTACT:** 440-473-3370; **clevelandmetro parks.com/Main/Reservations-Partners /North-Chagrin-Reservation-11.aspx**
DRIVING DISTANCE: 24 miles from I-77/I-480 exchange	

Description

Start at the nature center, stepping onto the paved Sanctuary Marsh Loop Trail, which runs between Sunset Pond and Sanctuary Marsh. Sanctuary Marsh Loop Trail is perfect for strollers and wheelchairs; its boardwalk over the marsh affords a look at a beaver habitat as well as a variety of waterfowl.

Head north on Sanctuary Marsh Loop Trail, connecting with Buttermilk Falls Loop Trail. The falls overlook, on the western side of Buttermilk Falls Parkway, is about 0.5 mile from your starting point. The pretty falls tumble over Cleveland shale, which has fractured in such a way to make the stairsteps of Buttermilk Falls look as if they were carved by a stonemason, though, in fact, natural forces created them.

Leave the waterfalls and head east (right), crossing the parkway, where you'll find a trailhead sign pointing to the Hickory Fox Loop Trail (marked by a squirrel symbol), the Hemlock Trail (marked by a bird symbol), and the Bridle Trail. Follow the Bridle Trail right, down a hill and heading east. The trail is hilly, rising up to parallel Ox Lane before intersecting with Castle Valley Trail (marked by a castle symbol).

From here you may choose to follow either the Bridle Trail or Castle Valley Trail to the castle. They cover approximately the same distance and connect several times. While a sturdy pair of sneakers will do on the Bridle Trail, you'll certainly want boots on the Castle Valley Trail, as it is rocky, narrow, and, in places, quite steep. *Note:* The wider, flatter Bridle Trail is more popular with runners because of its surface. Regardless of the trail you take to the castle landmark, be courteous in sharing the trail.

If you're up for a bit of a challenge, head north (left) onto Castle Valley Trail. Hugging the side of the ravine, you'll take 38 steps down the valley and cross a little wooden footbridge into the woods. Poison ivy and jewelweeds grow along the trail here. Continue to drop down into the valley (you may notice the temperature dropping a bit too), bottoming

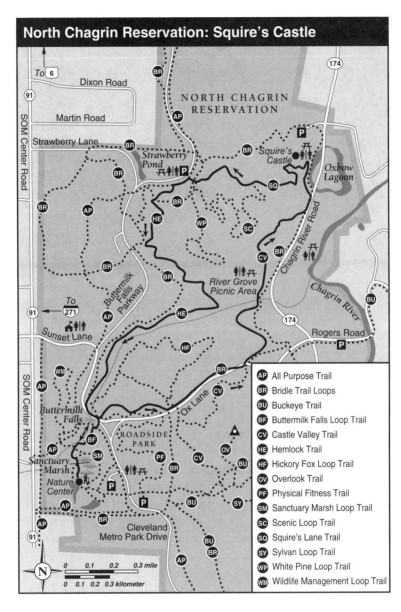

North Chagrin Reservation: Squire's Castle

AP	All Purpose Trail
BR	Bridle Trail Loops
BU	Buckeye Trail
BF	Buttermilk Falls Loop Trail
CV	Castle Valley Trail
HE	Hemlock Trail
HF	Hickory Fox Loop Trail
OV	Overlook Trail
PF	Physical Fitness Trail
SM	Sanctuary Marsh Loop Trail
SC	Scenic Loop Trail
SQ	Squire's Lane Trail
SY	Sylvan Loop Trail
WP	White Pine Loop Trail
WM	Wildlife Management Loop Trail

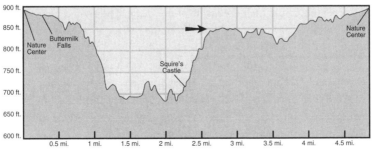

The former caretaker's cottage, better known as Squire's Castle

out at about 1.8 miles to cross a creek on widely spaced sandstone steps. Rising up on the left (east) side of the trail is River Grove Picnic Area. The Bridle Trail is on your right.

Heading north from here, you'll spot at least three connector trails to the Bridle Trail, now running parallel to Chagrin River Road. As you approach the castle, Castle Valley Trail meanders over a ridge; the Bridle Trail runs about 10 feet below, level with the road.

Squire's Castle isn't really a castle, but it's pretty enough to earn the name. In fact, the building was a gatehouse (though one that included bedrooms, a library, and a trophy room). Feargus B. Squire, vice president of the Standard Oil Company, owned 525 acres of land here, and he planned to build a vast estate. In the 1890s he, his wife, and their daughter summered in the gatehouse. As it happened, Mr. Squire never built his estate, and the Cleveland Metroparks purchased the land in 1925. To thwart vandals, the park filled in the basement and gutted the inside of the castle. They could not, however, stop reports of Mrs. Squire's ghost. Though folks from the Metroparks explain repeatedly that no one has died in the castle, local legends abound, most of which feature Mrs. Squire carrying a red lantern through the cottage; some claim that screaming can be heard along Chagrin River Road on cool, dark nights. What you believe is up to you, of course, but one way to avoid such encounters is to visit the castle in the sunshine.

No matter when you visit, you'll surely have company, as the castle and surrounding picnic area are quite popular with the area's living population.

After your tour of the "castle," exit through the back door, heading west on Squire's Lane Trail. The path rolls uphill as it leaves the castle behind. The trail is well marked, which is good, because it intersects several times with the Scenic Loop Trail and other trails—so mind the signs. At about 3.5 miles into the hike, Squire's Lane Trail ends. Follow the Hemlock Trail signs and travel south along the eastern side of the All Purpose Trail. Hemlock Trail is narrow and pretty, zigzagging over several tributaries to the Chagrin River. This trail offers amazing fall colors, thanks to a mighty mix of deciduous trees and evergreens. At least once along here, venture to the edge of the ravine and watch a leaf fall or a bird dive until you can no longer see it. The ravine is deep, fragrant, and peaceful. In my experience, Hemlock Trail is lightly traveled compared to the other trails here. Its beauty alone makes it worth the trip; stretches of solitude are a bonus.

Hemlock crosses the Bridle Trail before heading down steep railroad-tie steps to cross a wooden footbridge over another trickle of water. Go up, then down again, twice, and you'll meet the Bridle Trail once more. Briefly plod along next to the Bridle Trail, passing Sunset Lane on your right. Hemlock winds down 16 railroad-tie steps for a final foray into and out of the valley. The path widens and levels out in time to return to the trailhead across from Buttermilk Falls. If you time your trip right, returning to Sanctuary Marsh at dusk, you may get to see some beavers at work.

Nearby Activities

Why leave? North Chagrin Reservation and the nature center offer programming for all ages and interests, such as campfires, dog hikes, and photography clubs. You can check the schedule at the park website, or call 440-473-3370 for information.

Also nearby is one of Cleveland's prettiest golf courses, which sits at the north end of this Metroparks property. Call 216-635-3673 to request a tee time at Manakiki Golf Course. From North Chagrin Reservation, you're also about a 15-minute drive from Orchard Hills Park (see page 112), just over the border in Geauga County.

GPS TRAILHEAD COORDINATES

N41° 33.706' W81° 26.119'

Take I-271 N to Exit 36 (Wilson Mills Road). Head east on Wilson Mills Road about 0.5 mile, and turn left (north) onto OH 91/SOM Center Road. Go north about 2 miles, and turn right onto Sunset Lane into the park. In 0.3 mile, turn right onto Buttermilk Falls Parkway, and follow the signs 0.5 mile south to the nature center.

14 Rocky River Reservation: Fort Hill Loop Trail

Dunkleosteus terrelli *doesn't swim here . . . anymore.*

In Brief

While the initial climb might make your legs wobble, this hike provides spectacular views of the Rocky River that will leave you breathless. There's plenty for natural history fans too, including a nature center, a "terrible fish," and ancient American Indian ceremonial grounds. This hike is not recommended for those with a fear of heights. Others will find it gorgeous, a trip not to be missed.

Description

The earthworks on the Fort Hill Loop Trail are considerably less impressive than the better-known mounds of southern Ohio. But what these ridges lack in size, they make up for in location. To reach the earthworks, you'll have to do some climbing—135 steps of climbing, to be precise—but the view is worth it. From the top of the stairway, you'll look upon the east branch of the Rocky River, more than 100 feet below, where it bends like a fishhook and snatches the breath from your mouth.

However, before experiencing the climb and the view, you might find yourself a bit breathless in front of the nature center. There, approximately where a welcome mat should be, you'll be greeted by a model of the "terrible fish" known as *Dunkleosteus terrelli.* The huge hunter swam the oceans that covered Ohio millions of years ago, eating

72

DISTANCE & CONFIGURATION:
1.2-mile figure eight

DIFFICULTY: Moderately difficult, with lots of stairs to climb

SCENERY: River views, earthworks

EXPOSURE: Mostly shaded

TRAFFIC: Can be busy, especially on warm weekends

TRAIL SURFACE: Dirt trail, wooden boardwalk, and stairs

HIKING TIME: 45 minutes

DRIVING DISTANCE: 15 miles from I-77/I-480 exchange

ACCESS: Daily, 6 a.m.–11 p.m. Nature center: Daily, 9:30 a.m.–5 p.m.; closed January 1, Easter, Thanksgiving, and December 25. The steps leading to Fort Hill Earthworks are closed when icy; if in doubt, call ahead to check on weather conditions.

WHEELCHAIR TRAVERSABLE: No

MAPS: USGS *North Olmsted;* also at nature center and park website

FACILITIES: Restrooms, phone, and water at nature center

CONTACT: 440-734-6660; **cleveland metroparks.com/Main/Reservations-Partners/Rocky-River-Reservation-13 .aspx**

sharks and probably terrorizing other ancient sea critters. The well-preserved specimen was discovered nearby, in the shale cliffs above the riverbed, making it difficult to retrieve. The fossil remains were moved to the Cleveland Museum of Natural History, but you'll find more information about the beast, including a full-size 20-foot replica, inside the nature center.

Before beginning your hike from the back of the nature center, you can relax for a moment by watching for birds in the feeding area to your left and around West Channel Pond on your right. From here, you may choose to follow two dirt paths: West Channel Pond Loop or the Wildlife Management Loop. But the biggest bang for your buck—and the best views in my opinion—await at the top of the stairs to your left.

After you've scaled this steep section of the trail, you'll find yourself about 100 feet higher, likely taking another deep breath. There, at the top of the trail, you'll notice a sign explaining what researchers understand about the earthworks in front of you.

The earthworks' ridges lie like mussed-up blankets under the shade of pin oaks. Almost 2,000 years ago, American Indians formed these earthworks, probably for ceremonial purposes. The mounds they left here are small, but the mystery is great: Who were these people? What, besides the view, was so special about this spot? Inside the nature center, you can learn more about these American Indians and the earthworks they left behind.

Here, an alternate, slightly shorter trail allows you to walk on both sides of the earthworks; however, following it will cheat you out of more breathtaking views of the river below. Continue on the main trail instead, following the bright yellow markers of the Fort Hill Loop Trail.

Along the way, you might stop to read interpretive signs describing how the river has changed, and continues to change, the landscape. Approximately 360 million years ago, all but the southeast portion of Ohio was under ocean. While the ocean is long gone, the

Rocky River Reservation: Fort Hill Loop Trail

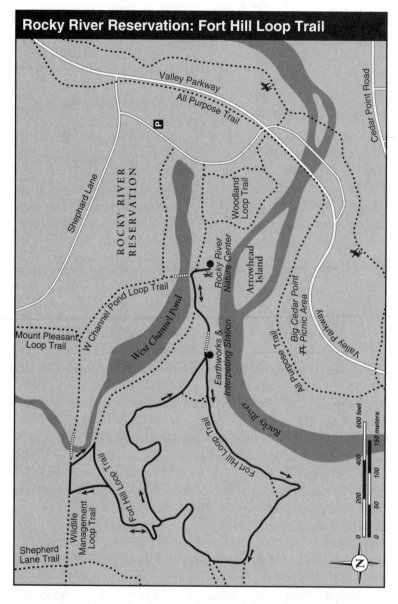

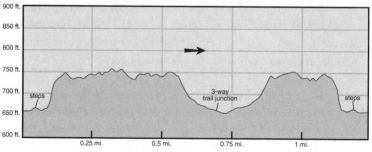

Rocky River continues to cut away at the land. It's obvious as you look at the trees clinging to the cliff sides, the soil that once supported them having eroded and washed into the river below. The soil and other sediment has formed islands in the river, and the trees that grow there—sycamores, cottonwoods, and willows—are ones that can survive the silt and changing water levels. The story is a compelling one about the power of nature. The dirt path leaves the ridge and curves clockwise, descending slowly into thick woods. Wildflowers and a variety of trees, including hemlocks, are sprinkled along this portion of the trail.

As you bottom out near the northern edge of West Channel Pond, you'll find an interpretive station explaining the rusty red color in the groundwater. When Ohio was covered with seawater, minerals, such as iron pyrite, were trapped in the silt. Gradually, the rust sediments formed a new rock known as bog iron. It was mined extensively in the 1800s, and several large pig iron furnaces were constructed between Toledo and Cleveland. (One of the largest was in nearby Westlake.)

As you head back to the nature center, the trail is mostly boardwalk. You'll complete the clockwise loop, walking up a slight incline to return to the back of the nature center.

Before returning to the parking lot, stop in at the wildflower garden in front of the nature center. Even in the dead of winter, you'll find that you can identify some flowers— wild leek and wild ginger, for example—just by their stalks. A single dogwood stands in the center of the garden. A plaque explains that there's more to the tree than its pretty spring blooms. In that way, it's rather like the earthworks here in the park—there's much more to both than meets the eye.

Nearby Activities

Don't leave the park without a good look around inside the nature center. There, children can wander through a tree-shaped activity center filled with fun, educational displays, including a water feature with fish and turtles. Then explore the rest of the Rocky River Reservation—it offers more than a dozen hiking trails, plus bridle trails, a fitness trail, and the paved All Purpose Trail.

The Frostville Museum, also located inside Rocky River Reservation, honors the history of the local area from the 1800s. Restored buildings include a church, barn, several homes, a general store, and an outhouse. The museum building, open 9 a.m.–1 p.m. most Saturdays, is located at the corner of Cedar Point and Lewis Roads. For more information about the museum, see **olmstedhistoricalsociety.org** or call 216-501-3345.

GPS TRAILHEAD COORDINATES

N41° 24.558' W81° 53.051'

From I-77/I-480, take I-480 W to Exit 7 (Clague Road). Turn left off the ramp, and follow Clague south 0.3 mile, when it ends at Mastick Road. Turn right, heading west 0.4 mile to Rocky River Reservation. Turn left onto Shephard Lane; follow it 0.6 mile to Valley Parkway. Turn right on Valley Parkway and go 0.2 mile; park in the nature center lot, on the right at 24000 Valley Parkway.

15 South Chagrin Reservation: Squaw Rock

Henry Church carved images on this rock by lantern light.

In Brief

A rocky ravine, gentle rapids, and a bit of a mystery are waiting for you in the Cleveland Metroparks South Chagrin Reservation. While you're there, you can enjoy a shady stretch of the Buckeye Trail and views of the scenic Chagrin River. Good hiking boots are highly recommended for this hike.

Description

Start on the Squaw Rock Loop Trail at the eastern edge of the parking lot, where you'll also see the blue blazes of the Buckeye Trail. The path veers right and then down a wide stone staircase to the banks of the river and a small waterfall. Though they are shallow, the falls can be rather boisterous after a rain. (And the steps can be slippery!) As you head south and upstream, the noise tapers off to a mere gurgle. Beautiful, picturesque rock formations rise 25–30 feet above you on the right. Continue south, hugging the skinny path about 12 feet above the Chagrin River.

DISTANCE & CONFIGURATION: 2.25-mile figure eight	**DRIVING DISTANCE:** 15 miles from I-77/I-480 exchange
DIFFICULTY: Moderate; steep, uneven stairs and uphill portions of All Purpose Trail are challenging	**ACCESS:** Daily, 6 a.m.–11 p.m.; parking lots that close at sunset are clearly posted. Steps to Squaw Rock are closed when icy.
SCENERY: Curious old carvings, a waterfall, Chagrin River rapids, deep ravine overlooks	**WHEELCHAIR TRAVERSABLE:** No
EXPOSURE: Almost entirely shaded	**MAPS:** USGS *Chagrin Falls;* also at park website
TRAFFIC: Moderate on Squaw Rock Loop Trail; heavy on the All Purpose Trail	**FACILITIES:** Restrooms at Squaw Rock parking area; public phone at the sledding hill parking lot south of Miles Road
TRAIL SURFACE: Squaw Rock Loop Trail, dirt trail and stone steps; All Purpose Trail, paved	**CONTACT:** 440-247-7075; **clevelandmetro parks.com/Main/Reservations-Partners /South-Chagrin-Reservation-14.aspx**
HIKING TIME: 1 hour	

You'll cross a stone footbridge at 0.1 mile and a wooden walkway just a few steps later, arriving at famous Squaw Rock at 0.2 mile. The rectangular sandstone rock is about 10 feet high. On its south face are several carvings, including a bundle of quivers, a tomahawk, an American Indian maiden, a rattlesnake, an infant, and a bird in flight.

Henry Church carved the images in 1885. Born and raised in Chagrin Falls about 2 miles east of here, Church was a blacksmith by trade. He also enjoyed painting and sculpting. Though his art was considered unusual at the time, in 1980 (72 years after his death) his work was featured in a special exhibit at the Whitney Museum of American Art in New York City.

Church reportedly walked from his home to Squaw Rock every night to carve by lantern light. He quit when his neighbors found out what he was doing. On the east face of the rock are unfinished carvings of a log cabin and the U.S. Capitol. What Church intended by the carvings is unknown. Some speculate that the collage is a celebration of American history; others believe that it was meant to be an artistic condemnation of our government's policies in the late 1800s. This much we know: His work continues to lure many people to this trail.

Step back onto the path, again heading south. Climb up another staircase, where you'll see and hear a gentle waterfall about 12 feet high. If you're feeling adventurous, you can walk underneath it—but don't try unless you have good balance and good boots. A bit farther south, you'll climb up another long set of stone stairs.

At the top, turn right. Though you may be winded from climbing the steps, you've only covered a little less than 0.3 mile. Head north through a thick forest of hemlock, beech, and oak trees. You'll see an alternate path that heads west from here to Arbor Lane. Go straight instead to cross two sturdy wooden bridges. From either one, you can watch as thin tributaries bounce down to the river more than 50 feet below. The woods

South Chagrin Reservation: Squaw Rock

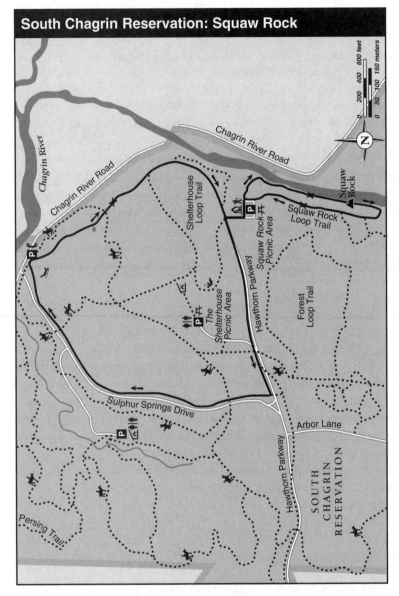

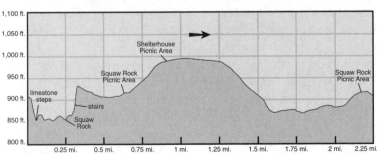

are thick here, so even with a faint wind, the rustling of leaves drowns out the river's sounds. Continuing north, you'll notice the blue blazes of the Buckeye Trail along this path before you return to the southeast corner of the parking lot.

(*Note:* The higher portion of this loop is flat and offers great views of the ravine. It makes a nice, easy stroll for those who aren't sure-footed enough to attempt the steps and lower trail. In dry weather, the surface is hard-packed enough for most strollers.)

Cross the parking lot, turning left from its northwest corner onto the All Purpose Trail that parallels Hawthorn Parkway. You'll notice that you're following the blue blazes of the Buckeye Trail as the path continues uphill for nearly a quarter of a mile. The hill will get your heart thumping before you reach the Shelterhouse Picnic Area.

Follow the All Purpose Trail west, then north as it bends right along Sulphur Springs Drive. The Buckeye Trail turns into the woods along with the Bridle Trail, but you'll stay on the now paved All Purpose Trail that parallels Sulphur Springs Drive. During the winter you're likely to hear howls of laughter coming from the sledding hill to your right.

Rounding the bottom of the hill, the trail curls to the east, past a small pond full of frogs and ringed with jewelweeds. The path rises gently and then crosses a wide stone bridge where you can peer into the river ravine again. You'll climb up just a few more feet before returning to the northwest corner of the parking lot where you began.

Nearby Activities

A sledding hill sits at the south end of Sulphur Springs Drive, and additional parking is available there. Fishing is allowed at Shadow Lake, located on Hawthorn Parkway about 2.5 miles southwest of OH 91. South Chagrin Reservation also offers seven picnic areas. Look About Lodge, just north of the sledding hill, hosts a wide variety of programs throughout the year. Check the park website for upcoming events, which range from concerts and movies to educational workshops.

To visit Church's hometown, the quaint village of Chagrin Falls, travel about 2 miles east on Miles Road. There's a waterfall on the western side of Main Street, as well as several shops and restaurants that are worth a visit.

GPS TRAILHEAD COORDINATES
N41° 24.987' W81° 24.911'

Take I-480 E until it ends at I-271/US 422, and exit right onto US 422 E. Follow US 422 E for 3.8 miles, and exit onto OH 91 (toward Solon). Turn left onto OH 91 N/SOM Center Road. In 1.5 miles, turn right onto Hawthorn Parkway. Follow Hawthorn east about 1.5 miles. The road ends at the bottom of the hill; Squaw Rock Picnic Area and parking are on your right.

Lake, Geauga, and Ashtabula Counties

David Stresing

Mason's Landing Park (see page 105)

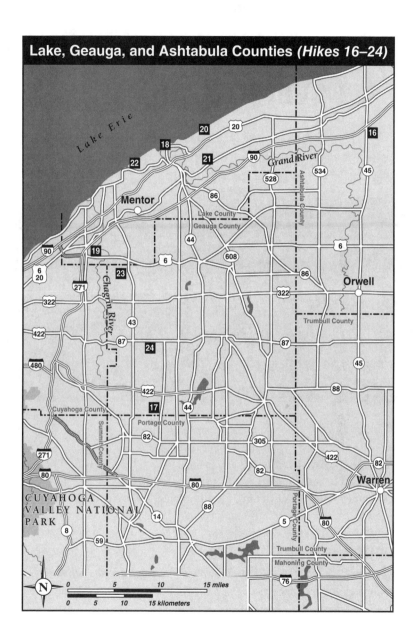

Lake, Geauga, and Ashtabula Counties *(Hikes 16–24)*

16 Ashtabula: The Underground Railroad & Covered Bridges

The Grand River runs beneath Ohio's third-longest covered bridge.

In Brief

Ohio's largest county has a lot of secrets. Consider these two short hikes a teaser: The first introduces you to some of Austinburg's most notable Underground Railroad sites; the second takes you across Ohio's third-longest covered bridge.

Description

Travel light. On foot. At night. Leave behind your family, friends, and all that is familiar. Depend on the kindness of strangers to hide you from those who would capture you, beat you, and return you to a life of slavery.

Would you trust your life to an invisible thing called the Underground Railroad (UGRR)? The UGRR operated from the 1780s until about 1862. During that time, an estimated 40,000 freedom-seeking slaves passed through Ohio. Many were spirited through Austinburg along the UGRR, courtesy of the fervent abolitionists who lived here. This hike gives you a small taste of what they experienced.

DISTANCE & CONFIGURATION: 4.5-mile loop (Austinburg); 1.5-mile balloon (Harpersfield)	**ACCESS:** 24/7; Harpersfield parking may not be plowed November–March
DIFFICULTY: Easy	**WHEELCHAIR TRAVERSABLE:** Austinburg, yes; Harpersfield, no
SCENERY: Underground Railroad sites, cemeteries, Ohio's third-longest covered bridge, river	**MAPS:** USGS *Ashtabula South* and USGS *Geneva;* **ashtabulacountymetroparks .org/pockettrailmap.pdf**
EXPOSURE: Austinburg, exposed; Harpersfield, shaded	**FACILITIES:** Restrooms, concessions, and picnic shelters open April–October at Harpersfield; phone, restrooms, and food at Exits 223 and 218 off I-90
TRAFFIC: Both moderately busy	
TRAIL SURFACE: Sidewalks, dirt	
HIKING TIME: 1+ hour in Austinburg; 15 minutes driving between trails; 30+ minutes at Harpersfield	**CONTACT:** Ashtabula County Metroparks: 440-576-0717; **ashtabulacounty metroparks.org**
DRIVING DISTANCE: 56 miles from I-77/I-480 exchange	

Enter the Western Reserve Greenway near Austinburg Town Hall, and follow it south about 1.5 miles. During warm weather, you'll share the trail with bicyclists; if the trail is covered in snow, you may find yourself in the company of snowmobiles. Heed them, with this perspective: A run-in with either vehicle could be dangerous, but it would be nothing compared to meeting up with bounty hunters or your owner if you were a runaway slave in the 1800s. Admire the natural beauty along the trail, or if you prefer, imagine where you might hide if you were running away to protect your life. Today this hike is just a walk in a park, but 200 or so years ago, it was an escape route.

When you reach the Lampson Road trailhead, turn right and follow the grassy berm along the north side of the road for about 0.5 mile, when you arrive at Austinburg Center Cemetery, also known as the Cowles Cemetery. Many of the burial plots here date to the first half of the 19th century. Look across OH 45 to see the Cowles family homestead. The northernmost house was the home of Betsey Mix Cowles, born in 1810. The family, headed by Giles Hooker Cowles, the minister at First Congregational Church of Austinburg, was progressive for the times, to say the least. The Cowles family values included education and freedom for all (including women and African Americans). Betsey Cowles grew up to be a teacher, educating both black and white children in Austinburg's Sabbath Schools. She graduated from Oberlin College, served as the first female dean of the women's department at Grand River Institute, and became one of the first female public school superintendents in the state. At a time when women were discouraged from public speaking, Cowles was nationally known for her very public presentations against slavery and discriminatory laws.

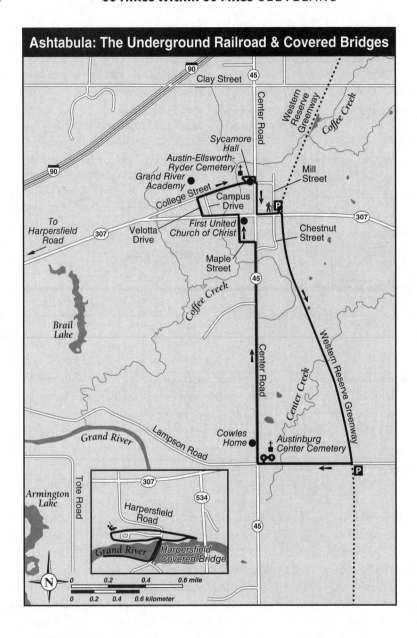

Ashtabula: The Underground Railroad & Covered Bridges

Turn right (north) onto Center Road/OH 45 and follow it 1.2 miles to Maple Street, where you'll turn left and follow it as it heads west and then veers north, past the First United Church of Christ in Austinburg. The church is one of the oldest churches in Ohio, and the building, erected in 1874, is listed on the National Register of Historic Places.

When Maple meets OH 307 in 0.2 mile, head west and follow the sidewalk another 0.2 mile to Velotta Drive. Velotta will lead you onto the campus of Grand River Academy, where many abolitionists probably heard Cowles speak.

When Velotta meets College Street in 0.1 mile, turn right and head west and uphill 0.3 mile, past the Austin-Ellsworth-Ryder Cemetery, which dates to 1803. A few abolitionists from Austinburg and throughout Ashtabula County, mostly from the Austin family, are buried there. Continue on College to find Sycamore Hall, which is enjoying new life as a garden center and nursery.

If buildings could talk, Sycamore Hall would have much to divulge. Built by Eliphalet Austin in 1813, the expansive house features a secret compartment that the Austin family used to hide fugitive slaves. Historical accounts abound, and the secret compartment doesn't figure in all of those stories. Once, when a slave master had pursued his "property" to the Austin home and Mr. Austin reluctantly permitted the man inside to search the home, the master combed every room in the house. When he opened the door to one room and found Mrs. Austin sleeping, he apologized for the intrusion. The master left, empty-handed. Once he left, the runaway slave slid out from under Mrs. Austin's bed and continued on his way north.

From Sycamore Hall, you can turn and head south 0.2 mile on OH 45 and then east on OH 307 for 0.1 mile to return to the Western Reserve Greenway parking lot. From there, you can drive to Harpersfield to discover a very different but notable spot in Ashtabula County.

Harpersfield Covered Bridge Metropark is about 4 miles west on OH 307. Drive past OH 534 and turn left onto Harpersfield Road/County Road 154. Harpersfield Road winds down a steep hill and bottoms out at the small but popular county park.

Park in the lot at the bottom of the hill, where you can wander along the northern banks of the Grand River. The river, designated a Wild and Scenic River by the state of Ohio, bisects the small park and runs under the third-longest covered bridge in the state. The bridge measures 228 feet long and is just 1 of 18 covered bridges in the county. The newest of those, West Liberty Covered Bridge on West Liberty Street in Geneva, was completed in 2011; at 18 feet, it may be the shortest covered bridge in the country. In comparison, the Smolen-Gulf Bridge, on County Road 25 in Ashtabula township, is the longest covered bridge in the United States. Regardless, it's probably accurate to say that the Harpersfield Covered Bridge is the longest *historic* covered bridge in the state. (Located in Knox County, the Bridge of Dreams, the second-longest bridge in the state, was built in the 1920s, but it wasn't covered until 1998.) Ashtabula celebrates them all, new and old, during the annual Covered Bridge Festival, held the second weekend of October.

From the parking lot on the north side of the park, you can walk east on a dirt-and-gravel path to the riverbanks and a boat launch, or walk west to find play equipment and picnic shelters.

Cross the bridge on the cantilevered walkway and, when you emerge, read the historical marker detailing the bridge's history. It was originally built in 1868, but a 1913 flood washed away the northern section of the bridge. Later that year, a 140-foot steel extension was added; in 1992 the bridge was rehabilitated (the walkway was added at that time) and eventually added to the National Register of Historic Places.

The bridge is popular with photographers and artists, so bring your favorite tools to capture its likeness. Picnic tables abound, but perhaps the best spot from which to contemplate the bridge is a giant, flat rock planted on the riverbank, just southwest of the bridge. It's not the driest spot, but it offers great ambience.

Though the park's concessions and main parking lots are closed November–March, the river (and the park) is a popular year-round destination. It is also a good fishing spot; anglers here lure bass, trout, crappie, and bluegill onto their hooks.

Nearby Activities

The Western Reserve Greenway is a paved, mixed-use trail running 43 miles from Ashtabula to Warren—hop on your bike to experience it firsthand. A couple of local liveries rent boats and organize seasonal canoe trips. For more information about Ashtabula-area outfitters, as well as the county's covered bridges and many award-winning wineries, visit the county's convention and visitors bureau website at **visitashtabulacounty.com.** Special thanks to Charlie and Pam of Ashtabula County Metroparks for their careful review of this description, and also to the historians at the Hubbard House Underground Railroad Museum for offering greater insight into the area and its historic importance. To learn more about the museum, see **hubbardhouseugrrmuseum.org,** or visit in person Friday–Sunday, Memorial Day–Labor Day. The museum is located in Ashtabula, about a 15-minute drive from Austinburg.

GPS TRAILHEAD COORDINATES

Austinburg: N41° 46.336' W80° 51.132'

Harpersfield: N41° 45.421' W80° 56.609'

Take I-90 E from Cleveland, and take Exit 223 (OH 45). Go south on OH 45 about 1 mile to OH 307. Turn left (east) and go one block to park across from Town Hall, at the corner of OH 307 (River Road) and Mill Street/Chestnut Street. Parking for the Western Reserve Greenway is off Lampson Road/County Road 194, about another 1.5 mile south on OH 45. Turn left onto Lampson Road, and go 0.5 mile. Parking is on the right. *Note:* Directions from Austinburg to Harpersfield are in the hike description.

17 Beartown Lakes Reservation

You'll see more fish than bears at Beartown Lakes.

In Brief

Mature beech and maple forests, a small pine grove, and three lakes comprise this 149-acre park in southern Geauga County. Beavers, herons, hawks, and deer are prevalent. But will you see a bear?

Description

Bainbridge township was settled in the early 1800s. At the time, the area was simply awash in bears. Local lore tells of a time when one of the McConoughey boys killed five bears in a single day. Not surprisingly, residents began calling the area Beartown.

In the late 1950s, three interconnecting lakes were constructed, and the surrounding land was operated as a private fishing club. In 1993 Geauga Park District purchased the land; Beartown Lakes Reservation was dedicated in 1996.

The park is a mixture of water (22 acres), wetlands (20 acres), and forest (93 acres). Three trails encircle the park. Each has distinct characteristics; yet, like the wetlands, woods, and water they visit, all three are closely related. The trails also share a common trailhead area, under the shade of tall maples and oaks, just north of the parking lot.

LAKE TRAIL (0.7 MILE)

Lake Trail heads west from the trailhead and quickly bends left, crossing a wooden footbridge that overlooks the sledding hill. Lake Trail is exposed on the north-to-south stretch. As you head south, you'll be able to peer into Lower Bear Lake to catch a glimpse of a

DISTANCE & CONFIGURATION: 2.9-mile loops	**DRIVING DISTANCE:** 23 miles from I-77/I-480 exchange
DIFFICULTY: Easy	**ACCESS:** Daily, 6 a.m.–11 p.m.
SCENERY: Tall beech forests, three lakes, fish, wildlife; bear sightings unlikely!	**WHEELCHAIR TRAVERSABLE:** Lake Trail, yes; other trails, no
EXPOSURE: Beechnut and Whitetail Trails, mostly shaded; exposed by the lakes	**MAPS:** USGS *Aurora;* also usually posted at park welcome sign and park website
TRAFFIC: Moderately busy, especially on warm weekend afternoons	**FACILITIES:** Restrooms and water at North Point Shelter in the middle of the park and at Minnow Pond Shelter on the east side of the park
TRAIL SURFACE: Lake Trail, paved, boardwalk; Beechnut and Whitetail Trails, packed gravel	**CONTACT:** 440-286-9516; **geaugapark district.org/parks/beartown.shtml**
HIKING TIME: 1 hour	

bluegill. I'm told they're easy to catch here, as long as you use short, live bait. Any bait dangling off the end of your hook will be nibbled away; the fish is then free to go, having enjoyed a safe snack. (It really is a game, isn't it?) In addition to the small bluegill, bass and northern pike are found in Lower Bear Lake. The park district encourages releasing all catches.

Cattails and duckweeds are plentiful at the south end of the lake. A boardwalk bridge runs across the corner of the lake; from it you'll head east through the woods. Avoid the unmarked paths that wander off from the south side of the Lake Trail, which lead to private residential areas.

Continue east until you reach the southeastern edge of Lower Bear Lake, where the woods open to reveal a boardwalk that spans the dam separating Middle and Lower Bear Lakes. Turn left, crossing the boardwalk, where in the summertime you'll enjoy an amazing array of dancing dragonflies. Wildlife photographers could spend hours here. (*Note to shutterbugs:* Bring sunscreen and extra memory cards.) From the north end of the walkway, turn left and follow the shoulder of the park roadway back to the parking lot.

BEECHNUT TRAIL (0.6 MILE)

The Beechnut and Whitetail Trails are not paved, and they run north together for a few yards before they split.

The Whitetail Trail veers to the left; follow the Beechnut (trail signs are marked by two beech leaves) to the right. The sandy dirt-and-gravel trail is flat, but it winds about as it leads you through the woods. You'll cross four small footbridges in the first 0.25 mile.

As you wind your way to the observation point at Upper Bear Lake, you might amuse yourself by watching for, or imagining you see, bears. Or maybe that's not so amusing. A bear—or two—seems to have made the rounds (and the local news) in Geauga and Portage Counties each year in recent memory. Black bears, typically young males in search of

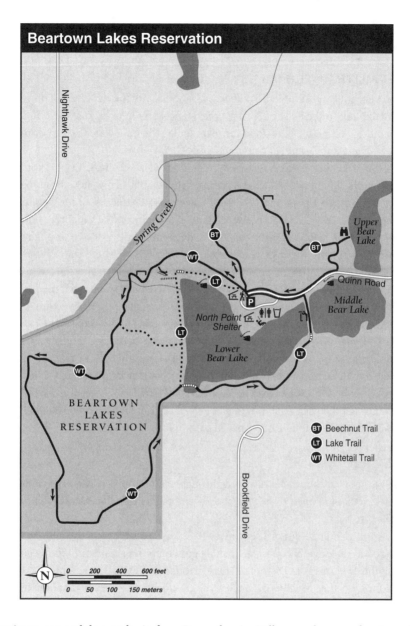

Beartown Lakes Reservation

BT Beechnut Trail
LT Lake Trail
WT Whitetail Trail

a territory, can and do wander in from Pennsylvania. Still, your chances of seeing a deer or a rabbit are much greater than that of seeing a bear.

Your chances of seeing a turtle, water snake, or frog from the observation deck at Upper Bear Lake are pretty good too. You can relax and watch on the western side of the lake before getting back on the path and heading south.

Before you leave the woods, you'll cross a fifth and final footbridge. The trail curves to the left and then goes up a short incline; its 5-foot rise is the only "climb" you'll have on this trail. The path ends at the park road, directly across from a fishing pier on Middle

Bear Lake. Turn right, following the road back to the parking lot (the same return path you follow for Lake Trail).

WHITETAIL TRAIL (1.5 MILES)

From the Beechnut and Whitetail Trailhead, head west with the sledding hill on your left, following the trail to the edge of Spring Creek. The water here is quite clear and pretty, but remember: No matter how good a stream looks, the only water safe to drink is the stuff you brought from home, in your own bottle.

Crossing the creek is easy; relatively stable rocks lead the way. Even if you slip in, you'll find yourself in only 2–4 inches of water. Trudge uphill a few steps from the creek, where you'll come to a park bench, a great place to watch and listen for woodpeckers. Soon, the trail bends to the left. Whitetail Trail is the only one of the three trails designated for horseback riding, and you're likely to encounter a rider or two through here.

About 0.5 mile into the hike, you'll cross a small tributary where you may spot some spring peepers. Enjoy the fragrant pines as you go up a little hill and follow the trail as it skirts the edge of some private farmland. Enjoy it while it lasts. Subdivisions abut the park on all other sides. Though cut-through trails have been created in places here, take care to stay on the main trail. (It's well signed.) There's also a sign indicating a connector to the Lake Trail. Ignore it; you want to enjoy the rest of the scenery that the woods and farmland offer.

Still skirting the farm fields, the trail ventures east, meandering through an old sugar bush (a narrow strip of sugar maples) and then heads northeast. At about 1 mile, Whitetail approaches the southwest corner of Lower Bear Lake. From here, you can follow the trail left, through the prairie, as Whitetail circles back onto itself, or you can jump onto Lake Trail and finish your hike on its paved path.

Nearby Activities

The park's picnic areas can be reserved through the park office. Much of Middle and Lower Bear Lakes are open to fishing, and several piers make it easy to get a line in the deep-water areas.

The small sledding hill north of Lower Bear Lake provides young children a gentle introduction to the downhill sport. (Groaning grown-ups will appreciate the steps on the side of the hill!) Geauga Park District offers year-round educational programming. Call 440-286-9516 for a schedule of activities, or view the calendar online at **geaugaparkdistrict.org.**

GPS TRAILHEAD COORDINATES

N41° 21.298' W81° 17.777'

Follow I-480 E to Exit 26 (US 422 E). Continue on US 422 E for 9.1 miles, and take the OH 306 exit. Turn right, following OH 306/Chillicothe Road south 1.2 miles. Turn left (east) onto Taylor May Road, and go 2.7 miles. Then turn right onto Quinn Road. Follow it south 1.4 miles to the park entrance, at 18870 Quinn Road.

18 Fairport Harbor Lakefront Park

The Perry Nuclear Power Plant, seen in the distance, opened in 1986.

In Brief

Summer is too precious in northeastern Ohio. Visit Fairport Harbor for its postcard-worthy vistas and a frolic on the beach to create memories you can relish when winter's dreariness descends.

Description

At the top of the town stands a small stone lighthouse, originally built in 1825. Behind the lighthouse sits the keeper's house, now the Fairport Harbor Marine Museum, packed with nautical exhibits as well as a mummified cat. But of course there's more to that tail. Er, tale.

In fact, the lighthouse harbors many tales. Step inside the museum (open seasonally) to begin your hike, tour, and history lesson.

Samuel Butler was the first lighthouse keeper and an abolitionist. Under his watch, the lighthouse was a stop on the Underground Railroad, offering a new life for many escaped slaves who were able to reach Canada via Lake Erie. Later, Civil War veteran Joseph Babcock became keeper of the lighthouse, newly rebuilt in 1871. He and his wife,

DISTANCE & CONFIGURATION: 2-mile balloon

DIFFICULTY: Easy beach stroll; lighthouse requires some climbing

SCENERY: Lake Erie, lighthouse, beach, stacks of nuclear power plant

EXPOSURE: Almost entirely exposed, except in lighthouse and museum

TRAFFIC: Moderately heavy, especially on warm weekends

TRAIL SURFACE: Pavement, beach

HIKING TIME: 45–50 minutes

DRIVING DISTANCE: 39 miles from I-77/I-480 exchange

ACCESS: Fairport Harbor Marine Museum and Lighthouse: May–October, call for hours; adults, $5; seniors, $4; children ages 6–12, $3; children age 5 and under, free. Park: Daily, 6 a.m.–11 p.m.; $3 parking fee ($2 for Lake County residents)

WHEELCHAIR TRAVERSABLE: No; surf chair available at beach in summer

MAPS: USGS *Mentor OE N*; also posted at park entrance

FACILITIES: Restrooms, water fountains, and concessions (in summer) at park

CONTACT: Lake Metroparks: 440-639-9972; **lakemetroparks.com/parks /fairport-harbor.shtml;** Fairport Harbor Marine Museum and Lighthouse: 440-354-4825; **fairportlighthouse.com**

Mary, had three children, two of whom were born in the keeper's house. Unfortunately, their youngest son, Robbie, died of illness at the age of 5, and Mary spent several years afterward in bed—sick, depressed, or both.

Reportedly, Mary loved cats and had several, including a gray one. After Mary died, numerous people reported seeing a ghost cat playing in the kitchen and elsewhere on the grounds. When HVAC repair workers found the mummified body of a cat inside a crawl space, it seemed to confirm the stories, and tales of the feline apparition live on.

After a new lighthouse was constructed in Lake Erie in 1925, the original lighthouse was ordered demolished. But local residents managed to save it; today volunteers continue to maintain the lighthouse and operate the popular museum.

If you come here during the summer on a day the lighthouse is open, pay the small fee that grants access to climb the 69 steps to the top of the light and look upon Lake Erie, where you will see the new light, Fairport Harbor West Breakwater Lighthouse.

The newer, oft-photographed red-and-white building sits on the breakwater, where it was operated and maintained by the U.S. Coast Guard until 2011. An individual has since purchased the property and restored it into what may be the coolest residence on the lake.

Below the pretty panorama on the surface, a busy salt mining operation provides the road salt that drivers are so dependent on during the winter months. In the summertime, it's easy to forget about that, especially as you watch boaters zipping along on the surface, enjoying the too-short summer season on the lake.

Once you've twisted down the skinny spiral staircase and returned to the sidewalk, follow Second Street west to Water Street. On the way, you'll surely see a few yachts cruise by on their way to the club just past the sand and gravel operations. Turn right

The lighthouse at Fairport Harbor

(north) onto Water Street, passing a bait shop and—on warm afternoons, at least—a line of cars awaiting entry (or admission) to the port. A launch fee is charged for boaters here, but pedestrians are allowed to walk out onto the breakwater, though the public is not permitted to access the newer lighthouse. When you've appreciated the beauty, industry,

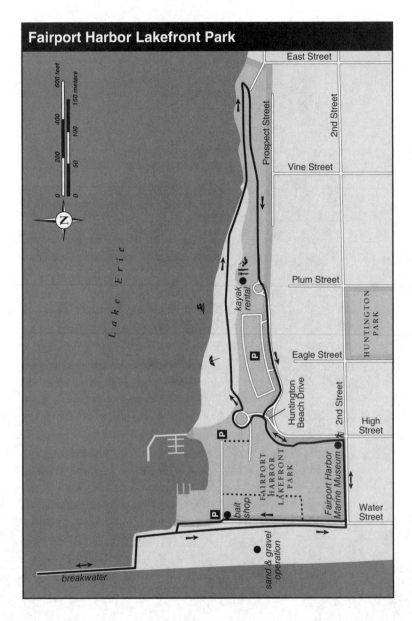

and recreation that this great lake offers residents of Fairport Harbor, turn and retrace your steps to the original lighthouse site.

Once back at the historical marker, look northeast and down the hill toward Fairport Harbor Lakefront Park, which sits like a beacon for summer-lovers of all ages. Follow the sidewalk as it curves down to the right, and you'll probably spot beach umbrellas and families enjoying the lake well before you reach the park's entrance.

Before heading to the beach, you should know that, while there's no admission fee for visitors walking on the beach, a nominal parking fee is charged. A surf chair, or all-terrain wheelchair, is available for visitors with physical disabilities; call 440-639-9972 for more information. Dogs are allowed only on the paved parking lot and in the designated dog swim area, and all dogs must be leashed.

Stroll on the sand or take off your shoes and wade into the shallowest of the Great Lakes. The park offers very little shade, but the beach is dotted with all the amenities that make a visit, well, a day on the beach. Two small playgrounds, food concessions, kayak rentals, volleyball courts, and several picnic tables are sprinkled on the south side of the park.

You can walk about 0.3 mile along the beach before you reach the end of the park, all the while eyeing the two thick, silent stacks of the Perry Nuclear Power Plant perched on the horizon. Standing in odd juxtaposition to this picturesque landscape, they're quiet and easy to ignore but, at the same time, hard to resist snapping with your camera.

Once you've soaked up some sun and stored a few images in your mind, camera, or both, return to the top of the village of Fairport Harbor, where your visit began.

Thanks to John Venen of Lake Metroparks for his review of this property description.

Nearby Activities

During the summer months, there's plenty to do right here. Besides swimming, active visitors can rent kayaks at the park to enjoy Lake Erie's waves. Lake Metroparks hosts seasonal events throughout the year. History buffs can visit the Finnish Heritage Museum, just down the street from the lighthouse (440-352-8301; **finnishheritagemuseum.org**). If you'd like to explore another part of Erie's shore, consider Mentor Lagoons Nature Preserve (see page 108), less than 10 miles from Fairport Harbor.

GPS TRAILHEAD COORDINATES

N41° 45.410' W81° 16.633'

Take I-77 N to Exit 163, and merge onto I-90 E, following signs to Erie, Pennsylvania. Go 10.9 miles to Exit 185, and merge onto OH 2. Go 15.6 miles, following signs to Painesville, and exit at OH 283/OH 535/Richmond Street toward Fairport Harbor. Turn right (northwest) on Richmond and then continue straight on Fairport Road/High Street. Continue following the road for a total of 2.2 miles. The lighthouse is at the corner of High and Second Streets; the park is down the hill, where High Street becomes Huntington Beach Drive.

19 Hach-Otis State Nature Preserve

Chagrin River in Lake County

In Brief

This hike is not for folks who have a fear of heights. Please read this hike description before you decide whether this trail is right for you. That's good advice for all of the hikes in the book (and in general), but it's more applicable for Hach-Otis State Nature Preserve than for most other trails. Warnings aside, this spot offers some of the most breathtaking views in northeast Ohio.

Description

Since 1944, the 81-acre Hach-Otis State Nature Preserve has been protected as a bird sanctuary. The Hach, Otis, and Clark families who are primarily responsible for its preservation should be commended—their foresight and generosity have benefited not only the wildlife but also countless people who enjoy the land's remarkable scenery.

The parking lot is completely shaded, thanks to a thick beech-maple-oak canopy. The boardwalk trail is adjacent to a kiosk, where a trail map is posted. An unmarked (but oft-used) dirt path meanders north and tempts you to step off the boardwalk; don't. While it meets up with the official trail in about 0.25 mile, the footing and scenery are

DISTANCE & CONFIGURATION: 1.5-mile figure eight	**ACCESS:** Daily, 8 a.m.–4 p.m.
DIFFICULTY: Easy, with one hill and some very precarious edges	**WHEELCHAIR TRAVERSABLE:** No
	MAPS: USGS *Mayfield Heights;* also at trailhead and park website
SCENERY: Forest, ravine, stunning river views	**FACILITIES:** None
EXPOSURE: Mostly shaded	**CONTACT:** Audubon Society of Greater Cleveland: 216-556-5441; **cleveland audubon.org;** Ohio Department of Natural Resources: **naturepreserves.ohiodnr .gov/hachotis**
TRAFFIC: Light	
TRAIL SURFACE: Dirt, grass	
HIKING TIME: 1 hour	
DRIVING DISTANCE: 28 miles from I-77/I-480 exchange	

better on the sanctioned path. Even if your curiosity is piqued, hiking etiquette and legitimate concerns about erosion should keep you on the right track.

To complete the loops in a clockwise fashion, follow the wooden boardwalk, where you have hardwood trees for company; soon after the boardwalk ends, you'll meet a few hemlocks. As you continue on a dirt trail, you'll start to notice how busy this corridor is with a variety of birds. You may catch a glimpse of a pretty little gully on the property's northern border; you will almost certainly encounter some of the many birds that crisscross the woods. Pileated woodpeckers, aptly named bank swallows, and owls are often sighted here; sometimes turkeys surprise visitors too. As you continue following the trail northeast, you can appreciate the rustic nature of the preserve in general and this trail in particular. Several tree falls have been cut away to allow you to pass, and the woods are thick. (You'd be smart to wear bug spray whenever you visit.)

While the trail is rustic, it is relatively level and easy to follow. It's almost like a bit of teasing—the calm before the storm—as it leads you to the edge of the preserve. And let's be clear: The emphasis belongs on *edge.*

About 0.5 mile from the trailhead, you'll reach the periphery of the preserve and its stunning view of the Chagrin River, about 150 feet below. As fantastic as the view is, hikers must not lose themselves in the moment—the edge is quite obviously eroding, day by day, minute by minute. The exact location of a safe boundary is questionable—and constantly changing. I recommend allowing a safety zone of 4–5 feet away from the edge.

Along this picturesque portion of the preserve, the trail is hard to follow. One worn path continues northeast and approaches a gully; others skirt the precarious edge. When you turn away from the rim, looking south and into the woods again, you'll see what is almost certainly the intended path. Follow it and soon daylight bleeds through the canopy; you'll emerge from the woods and stand overlooking the Chagrin River again.

The trail here is shaded, with a few opportunities to gaze at the river below.

From this point, you can turn to consider the northernmost overlook you just left. The erosion on the banks, where you were probably just standing, will likely give you pause and convince you that staying away from the brink is the right thing to do.

The lesson is important, but don't let it overshadow the beauty here. I believe that this is the most picturesque spot on the trail—if not for pure scenery, then for its sweeping view. Looking directly west, you can see OH 91 in the distance; to the southeast, you can appreciate just how high you are above the fields and homes on the other side of the river.

As the trail bends to the southwest, you follow it within spitting distance of the edge again. Notice the ravine that defines the southern portion of the trail and the preserve. Soon you return to the boardwalk trail, just a couple hundred feet from the parking lot. You can end your visit here, of course, if you're very time-pressed. But continue, and you'll see a different side of this preserve.

Continue on the South Loop of the boardwalk trail, veering left and east. This portion of the boardwalk isn't long either. After you step onto the dirt trail, the path takes you once again to a narrow overlook area, where common sense is your best friend— there is no fence rail or other warning sign. Because of the primitive nature of this trail, I strongly recommend that you bring your better judgment on this hike and leave dogs and young children at home for this outing.

Now and again your feet will find boardwalk trail, likely put in where needed to help hikers across softer spots on the path. As the loop fans out to the east, you'll start to see that you're circling around a gully, also eroding, but shored up by a variety of plants, including several types of ferns and a thicker population of hemlocks.

On the southern loop, too, it's hard to stay on the trail, but obvious clues help guide you. In some areas, trees have noticeably been cleared away with the help of chain saws and volunteers.

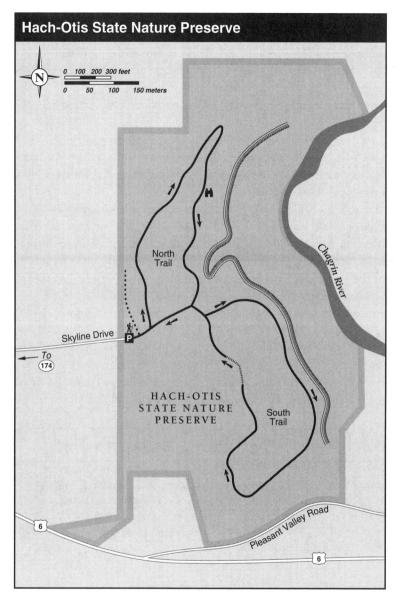

Hach-Otis State Nature Preserve

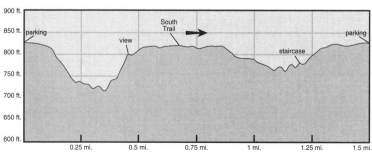

Because the woods are insulating, even in the hottest months, I recommend long pants and long sleeves on this hike—it's cool and very buggy. Hey, you may not like the bugs, but they're a big draw for the many birds you probably came to see.

Also, because of the cool, shady nature of this area, you're likely to spot mayapples along the trail, long after their season is over on other trails.

With so many warnings in this description, why did I include these trails? There are several reasons. The dense bird population, wildflowers, and stunning scenery certainly earn high marks. Yet Hach-Otis offers even more. While the top half of the property features those fantastic views, the southern loop's less dramatic ravine gives hikers a chance to feel as if they are immersed in nature, even though they are actually still within earshot of passing cars on OH 91 and I-271.

In other words, we need to be able to let nature take our breath away, and to get away, in the middle of it all. You can do that here.

As the trail curves to the north, you're heading once again back to the parking lot, your car, and your cares. But first you have to cross that gully you've been flirting with since you first saw it from the northern loop. A rustic but lovely set of stairs leads down, into, and across the gully.

Once across, you're out of stairs. A series of about a dozen railroad ties—the most strenuous and demanding part of the trail—helps you climb back up and out. If you need a distraction from your exertion, don't worry; the birds will likely be entertaining you all the while, as they're even more active on the south side of Hach-Otis than they seem to be on the north. Soon, you're returned again to the boardwalk, leading you back to the parking lot, likely more enthused than exhausted by the ground you've just covered.

GPS TRAILHEAD COORDINATES

N41° 35.486' W81° 24.694'

Take I-480 E to Exit 26, and merge onto I-271 N. Go about 13 miles, continuing on I-90 E, and take Exit 189 to OH 91/SOM Center Road in Willoughby Hills. Follow OH 91 south about 1 mile, and turn left (east) onto US 6/Chardon Road. In 1.2 miles, turn left (north) onto OH 174/River Road, and then make an immediate right (east) onto Skyline Drive to the preserve parking lot.

20 Lake Erie Bluffs

One of Lake County's newest parks, Lake Erie Bluffs is a good place to spot eagles.

In Brief

Hike in the company of various shorebirds, gaze across Lake Erie, and stick your toes in the water, if you wish, at one of Lake County's newer park properties.

Description

In 2012, 139 acres on Lake Erie's shore—tucked behind established industrial and residential developments, yet relatively unspoiled—were officially opened to the public as a Lake (County) Metropark and were later expanded to 600 acres. In addition to nearly 3 miles of hiking trails, Lake Erie Bluffs boasts several scenic overlooks, a natural beach, fishing, and fantastic birding opportunities. The land mix includes coastal marshes and prairies, plus lake access.

No lifeguards are on duty, so swimmers assume all risk. There are also no boat ramps. Kayaks may enter and exit the lake from the beach, but you must carry your equipment to and from the parking lot. The beach access here is chiefly that: access, so we can soak up and savor the lake at its natural best. Now, where to start? The stunning overlook beckoning from the east end of the parking lot seems like a good place.

DISTANCE & CONFIGURATION: 3.2-mile figure eight	**ACCESS:** Daily, 6 a.m.–11 p.m.
DIFFICULTY: Easy–moderate	**WHEELCHAIR TRAVERSABLE:** Yes, Eagle View Loop, Bluff Loop, and Lakeview
SCENERY: Lake Erie's shore, natural bluff habitat	Trails are densely packed gravel; Shoreline and Forest Edge Trails, no.
EXPOSURE: Mostly exposed	**MAPS:** USGS *Perry*; also at trailhead and park website
TRAFFIC: Moderate	**FACILITIES:** Restrooms, water, and reservable picnic shelter
TRAIL SURFACE: Crushed gravel, dirt, sand	**CONTACT INFORMATION:** Lake Metroparks: 440-358-7275; **lake**
HIKING TIME: 1 hour	**metroparks.com/parks/lake-erie-bluffs**
DRIVING DISTANCE: 47 miles from I-77/I-480 exchange	**.shtml**

Go ahead and stop and stare. The lake is the main attraction here and deserves your attention. When you are ready, turn away to follow Eagle View Loop Trail as it rolls to the east over several small hills. You really could see an eagle here; active adults are in the area. Of course, you are also likely to see (and hear) several varieties of shorebirds on this short loop. A handful of benches dot the trail, so you can stop and see who swoops in to take a look at you.

Instead of returning to the parking lot trailhead, continue straight and follow Lakeview Trail about 0.25 mile west to Bluff Loop Trail. The two flat trails give you what their names suggest, a good chance to enjoy views of the lake and its habitat from a vantage point atop the bluffs.

Both Lakeview and Bluff Loop Trails are bike-, wheelchair-, and stroller-friendly; however, Shoreline Trail isn't. So if you plan to ride, bring a lock too, so you can leave your bike behind to enjoy a sandy stroll. Once you've completed Bluff Loop (avoid the shortcut trails to spend more time appreciating the views), from the western end of Lakeview, you'll follow Shoreline Trail to its namesake. Before you head to the beach, however, take a moment to appreciate the fabulous vista that the lone campsite provides. The unique and lovely site is reservable and likely to be very popular; more campsites are planned for the park.

As you start on Shoreline Trail, you'll traipse downhill under the shade of mature trees, probably hearing the lake before you see it. Once you arrive on the thick silvery sand, head east and pick your way across a fairly wide expanse of beach. While the point of this trail (and the park itself) is to allow us to enjoy our Great Lake, this particular spot is not especially inviting for swimming. Dip your toes in the water, so you can say you did; then continue your walk on shore. As in the rest of the park, birding opportunities abound here. And on this trek, you'll see something else that is distinctly Erie.

When you reach the eastern end of the beach trail, you can't help but notice the stacks of Perry Nuclear Power Plant. Of the 61 nuclear power plants in the United States, 2 sit on the Lake Erie shore: Perry, here, and Davis-Besse, in Oak Harbor. The structures

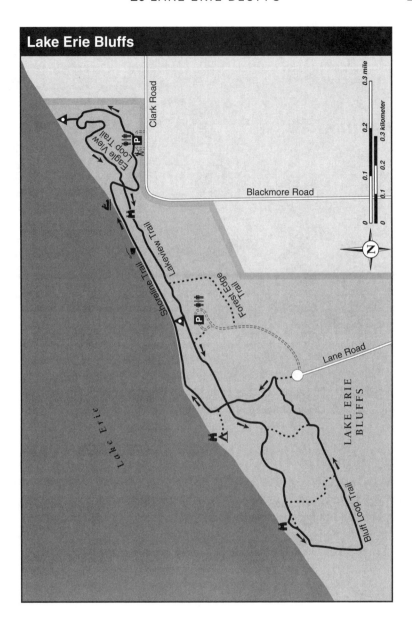

are awesome, if unnatural, sites along the shore, off in the distance but still adding interest to the overall picture. They are a reminder that we leave our mark here, sometimes intentionally, sometimes absentmindedly.

As you walk along the beach, you'll certainly appreciate the colorful assortment of rocks and driftwood, piles of which are peppered with pretty, fragile white shells and, unfortunately, a few items your fellow humans have left behind. A gentle nudge: It doesn't have to be Earth Day for you to carry a small trash bag and pick up debris from the trail.

The aptly named Shoreline Trail

Future generations will appreciate it, even if they don't know your name. To return to the parking lot, climb back up to meet the Eagle View Loop Trail.

Thanks to John Venen of Lake Metroparks for reviewing this description.

Nearby Activities

Even more so than other parts of the very green and lush Lake County, Perry is dotted with nurseries and greenhouses. If you're seeking a specific tree or plant, or advice on growing almost anything, you're likely to find what you're looking for within a mile or two of Lake Erie Bluffs. And if your return trip takes you west along OH 2, you'll be very close to Fairport Harbor, where you can stop to swim or tour a lighthouse museum (see page 91).

GPS TRAILHEAD COORDINATES
N41° 47.315' W81° 10.457'

Take I-77 N to Exit 163, and merge onto I-90 E, following signs to Erie, Pennsylvania. Go 10.9 miles to Exit 185, and merge onto OH 2. Continue on OH 2 E for 19.7 miles, when it ends and becomes OH 20. Follow OH 20 1.1 miles to Blackmore Road in Perry township. Turn left (north) and follow Blackmore 1.3 miles until it ends. Turn right (east) onto Clark Road. The park entrance will be on the left (north).

21 Mason's Landing Park

David Stresing

Bring your canoe.

In Brief

This short hike meanders along the banks of the Grand State Wild and Scenic River. The trail, wisely, lets the river be its guide.

Description

From the parking lot, head west up a slight hill on a sandy dirt trail. The path snakes along the north bank of Grand River and offers shade and good bird-watching opportunities. Along the trail, and high above your head, be sure to notice the large bird boxes available to sleepy owls. The trail rises and falls and wiggles and bumps over several small hills, just enough to keep you from going on autopilot. Turn south to pass within a few feet of the riverbank, and then turn north, running 20 feet or more into the woods. As a result of the trail's wending and winding, your perspective of the river changes almost constantly.

If you veer off the main trail, you can follow a fishermen's trail that runs much closer to the water. On a sunny day, you can expect to find a snake or two soaking up the rays' warmth along the sandy riverbank.

About 0.5 mile west of the starting point, a park bench waits for you, where you can watch the river as it heads south or look east to the bridge. In between, you're likely to see

DISTANCE & CONFIGURATION: 1.2-mile out-and-back	**ACCESS:** Daily, 6 a.m.–11 p.m.
DIFFICULTY: Easy	**MAPS:** USGS *Painesville;* also at kiosk and park website
SCENERY: Grand River, good bird-watching along the trail	**WHEELCHAIR TRAVERSABLE:** No
EXPOSURE: About half shaded	**FACILITIES:** Restrooms, small picnic area with grills, playground, and canoe launch
TRAFFIC: Light	**CONTACT:** 440-358-7275; **lakemetroparks.com/parks /masons-landing.shtml**
TRAIL SURFACE: Dirt, sand	
HIKING TIME: 35 minutes	
DRIVING DISTANCE: 39 miles from I-77/I-480 exchange	

someone wading in, pole in hand, angling for one of the river's many residents. Fishing is allowed, and it is good here in the Grand River. Steelhead Run Trail ends just a few feet beyond the bench.

As you walk beside and contemplate the relatively calm waters of the Grand River, you might wonder what's "wild" about it; certainly, there are no rapids here. In this case, *wild* refers to the Grand's inaccessibility (except by foot trail) and lack of development. Back in 1968, Ohio developed the Wild and Scenic River program to protect the natural beauty of rivers such as this one. Since then, portions of about a dozen other rivers have been designated scenic.

The Grand is one of three double designees (Conneaut and Little Beaver Creeks are Ohio's other State Wild and Scenic Rivers), due in part to being home to more than 70 species of fish and 60 rare plant species, as well as its rugged topography and limited human impacts. When bestowing the title in 1974, the state proclaimed, "The Grand River represents one of the finest examples of a natural stream to be found anywhere in Ohio."

As you make your way back along the bumpy path, tread lightly and enjoy deeply. When you return to the parking lot, walk down to the canoe launch on the northwestern side of the bridge. A plaque there relates the history of the Grand River and describes its wandering, 102-mile path, which begins in Geauga County. It also explains that this river is more than its wild and scenic designations—the river and its watershed drain about 456,000 acres of northeastern Ohio before emptying into Lake Erie.

Nearby Activities

If you have a canoe, bring it here. You can put in and paddle up the Grand River into Ashtabula County. If you prefer to stay on land, walk across the Vrooman Road Bridge and follow another footpath east to Indian Point Park, about a mile from Mason's Landing. Indian Point, also along the Grand River, is listed on the National Register of Historic Places. The park features two earthworks built by some of Ohio's earliest people, known as the Whittlesey culture, who lived here A D 900–1650. You can also see a totem pole here, carved by campers in the early 1900s.

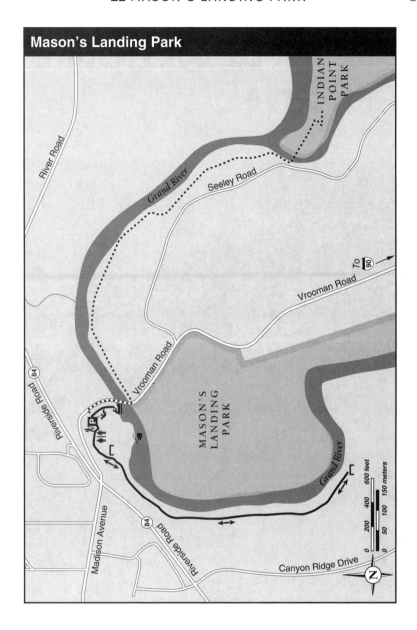

GPS TRAILHEAD COORDINATES

N41° 43.600' W81° 11.114'

Follow I-480 E to Exit 26 (I-271 N). Follow I-271 N for 13.8 miles, and exit onto I-90 E. Follow I-90 E for 14.8 miles. Take Exit 205, and turn left onto Vrooman Road. Follow Vrooman north about 1.5 miles. Mason's Landing Park is located on Vrooman Road, just south of OH 84, on the west side of the road.

22 Mentor Lagoons Nature Preserve

Keep it clean—pack out your trash.

In Brief

This great preserve protects the largest unbroken bluff forest in northeast Ohio and one of the finest coastal dune communities in the state. Rare plants and more than 150 species of birds can be found here—along with some solitude.

DISTANCE & CONFIGURATION: 3.4-mile loop	**MAPS:** USGS *Mentor;* also at trailhead, marina office, and **cityofmentor.com /wp-content/uploads/Mentor-Lagoons -brochure.pdf**
DIFFICULTY: Easy	
SCENERY: Lake Erie shore, riverine marshes, woodlands, wildflowers	**WHEELCHAIR TRAVERSABLE:** Woods, Lakefront, and Marina Overlook Trails are accessible via electric carts, available for those with mobility issues; call 440-205-3625 prior to visit to reserve a cart. Other trails not accessible.
EXPOSURE: Mostly exposed	
TRAFFIC: Moderate	
TRAIL SURFACE: Hard-packed lime-stone, dirt, soft sand	
HIKING TIME: 1.5 hours for all trails; allow more for a boat ride	**FACILITIES:** Pay phone and portable restrooms by marina office
DRIVING DISTANCE: 33 miles from I-77/I-480 exchange	**CONTACT:** Parks, Recreation & Public Facilities Department: 440-974-5720; **cityofmentor.com/visit/mlnp**
ACCESS: Daily, sunrise–sunset	

Description

Purchased by the city of Mentor in 1997, the 450-acre Mentor Lagoons Nature Preserve protects one of the few riverine marshes still surviving along Lake Erie's shore. (Even more land, more than 800 acres, is preserved next door, in Mentor Marsh State Nature Preserve, on the east side of Mentor Lagoons.) On the west side of this city preserve is Mentor's marina, dedicated to recreation, not preservation, which isn't necessarily a bad thing—after all, enjoying our natural resources makes us more likely to want to protect them.

With that in mind, head northeast from the trailhead parking lot and step onto Marsh Rim Trail. Follow the shady trail northeast about 0.5 mile to where it joins with Lakefront Loop heading north, skirting the border between this park and its neighbor, Mentor Marsh State Nature Preserve.

In the summer, you'll hear the roar of outboard motors even here, in the deep of the woods. (Think of it as audible proof of enjoyment.) Tangles of grapevines along the trail offer atmosphere for you, as well as shelter for many small animals. Speaking of animals, while leashed dogs are permitted on several trails, they're not allowed on Marsh Rim Trail or Lakefront Loop.

After traipsing about 1 mile through the woods, you'll emerge to find a bench perched high above the lake. You'll also find your feet on the limestone of Lakefront Trail. If you turn right, the trail continues northeast to a gated residential area immediately west of Mentor Marsh. Instead, head west–southwest for about a mile along this completely exposed section of Lakefront Trail, walking high enough above the water to enjoy a great view of wildflowers growing amid tall marsh grasses. This is a great place for bird-watching, and because you're not far from Lost Nation Airport, don't be surprised if a big bird (a small plane) buzzes by too.

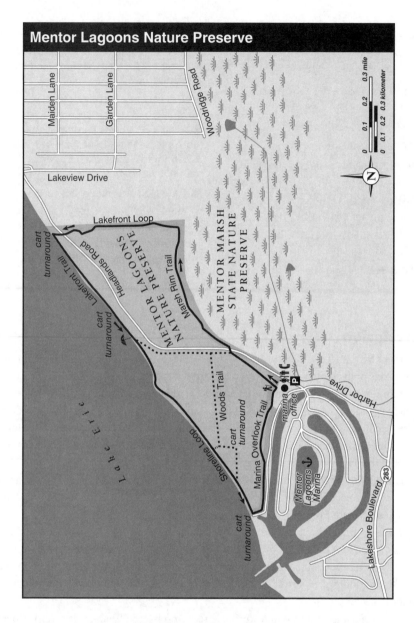

Mentor Lagoons Nature Preserve

About 2 miles into your hike, you'll reach a cart turnaround. Here, by a rocky out-crop, a narrow unmarked path leads down to a very narrow beach, which is not much wider than a hiking boot. If you're willing to take the narrow path, walk down to the shore and follow along the beach for the next 0.5 mile. Otherwise, you can continue along Lake-front Loop, which eventually turns into Woods Trail and intersects Shoreline Loop.

The shore of Lake Erie is interesting. You'll probably spot a working rig or two on the lake; when you look east, you can see the east pier light near the Port of Cleveland. On the coarse sand, driftwood as soft as a baby's skin rests among stones worn smooth and ringed with various pastel colors. Rather than the "sh-sssshh" of an ocean wave, these waves lap loudly, often with a bang and a crash. Rough-looking, rocky outcrops and ceaseless wind make the area seem especially wild; at times, you can imagine that it is too big to be tamed. At the same time, you cannot forget that you're surrounded by the civilization of a large industrial center, thanks to the eclectic collection of manufactured items also found here on the beach. The odd pieces of debris mingle on the beach next to the driftwood and sea oats. Gulls perch on antique machine parts; castaway tires embedded in the sand hold back erosion. On my first visit here I found a button that was threaded by a small vine. It's something of a compromise, this use and abuse of our unique landscape. (Note that swimming is prohibited here.)

As you continue south and west along the shore, about 2.5 miles from your starting point, you'll see two sets of wooden stairs leading up to the Woods Trail on your left. True to its name, the trail is entirely shaded. If you're looking for a cooler, greener trail, head in. It will take you east, and back to the inland portion of Lakeshore Trail, in about 0.6 mile. If you prefer to continue on the water's edge, you'll soon land on Shoreline Loop, which deposits you onto Marina Overlook Trail.

Bikes are allowed on both Woods and Marina Overlook Trails, but not elsewhere in the park.

Marina Overlook is a mix of sand and dirt with a bit of gravel here and there. It takes you east, along the docks, under the shade of tall maples and oaks. The trail leads you up a short hill and then flattens out into an S-curve before returning past the marina office and back to the parking lot.

Nearby Activities

There's plenty to do right here! During the spring and summer, you can rent kayaks, canoes, or bicycles to explore the preserve from both sides of the shore. (Contact the marina at 440-205-3625.)

For a look at a different sort of shoreline habitat, plan a visit to the lagoon's next-door neighbor, Mentor Marsh State Nature Preserve. The entrance is at 5185 Corduroy Road in Mentor. The nature center, managed by the Cleveland Museum of Natural History, is open April–October, Saturday–Sunday, and November–March, the first Sunday of each month. For more information and a schedule of events, see **cmnh.org/Mentor-Marsh.**

GPS TRAILHEAD COORDINATES
N41° 43.612' W81° 20.324'

Take I-77 N to Exit 163, and merge onto I-90 E, following signs to Erie, Pennsylvania. Go 10.9 miles to Exit 185, and merge onto OH 2. Continue on OH 2 E for 9.8 miles, and exit at OH 615/Center Street. Turn left (north) and follow Center Street as it becomes Hopkins Road. In 2.5 miles, turn right onto Lakeshore Boulevard and make an immediate left onto Harbor Drive. In 0.4 mile you will reach the trailhead parking, to the east of the docks and marina office.

23 Orchard Hills Park

No more scorecards—just enjoy the trails and scenery on the former fairways.

In Brief

Rolling over 237 acres, Orchard Hills Park is a unique park in Chester township. Operated as a golf course until 2007, the property situated immediately west of the Patterson Fruit Farm now invites nature lovers to enjoy its splendid rock outcrops, dramatic hills (one of which is lighted for nighttime sledding!), and a panoramic view of Lake Erie.

Description

Orchard Hills opened to the public as a golf course in 1962. The course saw its last tee time in 2007. Today, the hills offer visiting hikers both a challenge and a reward: You may feel a bit of a burn as you walk the "course," but you'll also enjoy a great view and wonderful perspective on many facets of this versatile land.

From the southeast end of the Orchard Hills Lodge parking lot, head south on a connector trail to the McIntosh Trail. You'll follow it north, then east, and then north again as the trail approaches a petite but pretty fishing pond. In the summer, noisy frogs and insects chatter here, and it's a good spot to watch butterflies and dragonflies along the

DISTANCE & CONFIGURATION: 1.6-mile loop	DRIVING DISTANCE: 30 miles from I-77/I-480 exchange
DIFFICULTY: Moderate	ACCESS: Daily, 6 a.m.–11 p.m.
SCENERY: Pine stands, pudding stones, orchard, meadows, wetlands, a glimpse of Lake Erie	MAPS: USGS *Chesterland;* also at trail-head and park website
EXPOSURE: Mostly exposed	WHEELCHAIR TRAVERSABLE: Yes, the paved trails are, though some are steep.
TRAFFIC: Moderately heavy on weekends and evenings, particularly in the fall	FACILITIES: None
TRAIL SURFACE: Mostly paved	CONTACT: 440-286-9516; **geauga parkdistrict.org/parks/orchard.shtml**
HIKING TIME: Allow 90 minutes or more	

exposed stretch. To make the most of your hiking distance here, when you reach a fork on the north side of the pond, veer left and continue on McIntosh Trail, the largest, outside loop of several interconnecting trails here.

The park district has encouraged native plants to return along the now-abandoned fairway. In order for this property to become the idyllic hiking destination that it is, the Patterson family worked closely with the Western Reserve Land Conservancy and Geauga Park District. They arranged to have a conservation easement placed on the former golf course property stating that the land would be used as a passive-use public park.

In this case, *passive* is a legal term; those who visit Orchard Hills Park can enjoy a variety of activities. Speaking of passive: Throughout the park, benches are strategically placed, making ideal spots to stop and consider the changes that this land has seen in a relatively short span of time. The natural rolling hills in this part of Geauga County lend themselves to cross-country skiing, and all of the trails are open for skiing when conditions are right. Though many of the trail sections, which were originally developed for golf cart traffic, are paved, some sections of the McIntosh Trail have been rerouted over natural surfaces.

The land is in the process of returning to a more natural state, but you may still notice some remnants of its former life as a golf course in both the trail layout and landscape. The wide clearings that were necessary for long drives have also made this piece of land a favorite haunt of hawks and other birds of prey; you'll probably see quite a few of them as you wander Orchard Hills's paths.

Inside the McIntosh Trail, the White Pine and Pine Warbler Trails offer chances to shorten the outer loop and see other features on the property, and you can take these in addition to the outer loop or use them to shorten your route. White Pine and Pine Warbler Trails slice through the midsection of the park to visit pine stands, native forest, and wetlands.

On the north side of the indoor-outdoor shelter, visitors can explore three short accessible trails. While hardly rustic, the paved Sedge, Cricket, and Harvest Trails make a

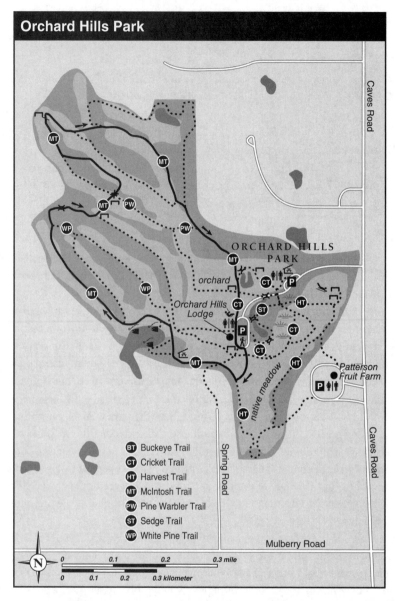

Orchard Hills Park

ORCHARD HILLS PARK

orchard

Orchard Hills Lodge

native meadow

Patterson Fruit Farm

Caves Road

Spring Road

Caves Road

Mulberry Road

BT Buckeye Trail
CT Cricket Trail
HT Harvest Trail
MT McIntosh Trail
PW Pine Warbler Trail
ST Sedge Trail
WP White Pine Trail

N

0   0.1   0.2   0.3 mile
0   0.1   0.2   0.3 kilometer

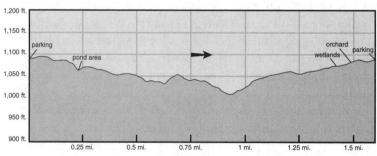

1,200 ft.
1,150 ft.
1,100 ft. parking
1,050 ft. pond area
1,000 ft.
950 ft.
900 ft.

orchard
wetlands parking

0.25 mi.   0.5 mi.   0.75 mi.   1 mi.   1.25 mi.   1.5 mi.

Even on a cloudy day, you can see Lake Erie from here.

great, easy introduction to hiking for toddlers. When the snow falls, the sledding hill just west of Caves Road is a popular destination with families.

After following the rolling landscape on McIntosh Trail in a long clockwise loop, follow Cricket Trail south and back toward the lodge parking area to complete your loop by walking along the edge of an apple orchard. The orchard is a sweet reminder of the annual treasure to be found here. But it won't be the first reminder you'll have—throughout the property, it's almost impossible to miss apples, as the fruit and their seeds have been scattered here for years by a variety of critters. (*Note:* Please don't pick the apples! The orchard here is still maintained by the Patterson family.)

If you'd like to explore a little more, use Sedge or Cricket Trail to connect with Harvest Trail, which will take you to the back (west) side of Patterson Fruit Farm.

Nearby Activities

Obviously, there's more to do right here. The supersmart design of the indoor-outdoor lodge gives visitors a nice place to warm up during the winter months or enjoy the sweet smell of the orchard during the warmer months. The park is popular year-round because the trails are groomed for cross-country skiing and the sledding hill is lighted for after-dark runs. Contact the Geauga Park District for sledding condition updates.

Don't pick the apples . . . but do pick up some from the fruit farm to take home.

Also worth a visit: Patterson Fruit Farm, accessible on foot via Harvest Trail or a very short drive to the parking lot on Caves Road. The market is open year-round, offering fresh produce and baked goods. A lunch concession (440-729-1964), open Saturday–Sunday, sits on a high point overlooking Orchard Hills Park. From there, visitors can enjoy a sweeping vista to the north, which includes a view of Lake Erie that's not available from most of Geauga County. Even on an overcast day, you can spot a layer of deep blue-gray on the horizon. (Admittedly, binoculars help.) That's the lake; the stacks to the far right belong to the Cleveland Electric Illuminating Company.

If it's more hiking that you're after, head east on Chardon Road/US 6 from here to find North Chagrin Reservation (see page 67).

GPS TRAILHEAD COORDINATES

N41° 33.672' W81° 22.030'

Take I-480 E to Exit 26 (I-271 N). Once on I-271 N, go 7.3 miles to Exit 34 (US 322 E/ Mayfield Road). Turn right (east) onto US 322 E/Mayfield Road, and go 4.6 miles. Turn left (north) onto Caves Road, and go 1.4 miles. The park entrance will be on your left.

24 The West Woods

You can find solitude within a few miles of the city limits.

In Brief

The West Woods, in Russell and Newbury townships, spans 902 acres and shelters several dwindling species. Learn how a small cave was shaped by the area's geology and how it played a role in the county's history.

Description

Start at Pioneer Bridle Trail, a wide dirt trail carpeted with pine needles that begins from the southwest end of the parking lot. As the trail dips and bends sharply to the right, it heads downhill, winding through the dense woods.

DISTANCE & CONFIGURATION:
4.5-mile connected loops

DIFFICULTY: Moderate

SCENERY: Forest, wildflowers, pristine Silver Creek, remarkable variety of bugs and butterflies

EXPOSURE: Mostly shaded

TRAFFIC: Light

TRAIL SURFACE: Hard-packed dirt, gravel

HIKING TIME: 1 hour and 40 minutes

DRIVING DISTANCE: 25 miles from I-77/I-480 exchange

ACCESS: Daily, 6 a.m.–11 p.m. Nature Center: Daily, 10 a.m.–4:30 p.m.

MAPS: USGS *South Russell*; also inside nature center

WHEELCHAIR TRAVERSABLE: No

FACILITIES: Emergency phone, restrooms, and water at nature center; two picnic shelters

CONTACT: Geauga County Park District: 440-286-9504; **geaugaparkdistrict.org /parks/westwoods.shtml**

Where the trail runs parallel to OH 87, you'll notice lots of chain ferns. The path narrows as it heads west. For a short time, you walk very close to the road, but then the shady path widens and drops down a short, steep hill, below the traffic, where it's a much quieter world. On your left is a small creek; during the summer, the surrounding joe-pye weed, tall thistles, ragweed, and Queen Anne's lace create a haven for birds, butterflies, and a crowd of dragonflies.

Before you've logged a mile, you'll cross the creek and turn left (south), leaving OH 87 traffic behind for good to enter a sweet-smelling pine forest. The path can be muddy here, but where it is at its stickiest, walk-arounds have been worn for you. Remember that this is a bridle trail, so yield to those on horseback.

You'll soon reach the Affelder Link trail heading right (west) off the trail—it leads to OH 306 and does not loop back. Stay on the main path, eventually crossing a wide, wooden footbridge where the creek is wider than before.

As the trail wiggles through the forest, traveling southeast, it continues to climb slowly. You move, gradually, from a thick stand of thin trees to an area of older growth. Under the taller trees, you'll find mulberry bushes, and in the summer you'll spot angel wings and jewelweed along the way. As you travel the southern edge of the park property, heading east to the nature center, ignore a connector trail (unless you want to visit the residential Music Street). Before you reach the back of the nature center, you'll cross a very shallow creek, roll up and then down a small hill, and pass two picnic shelters before arriving at The West Woods Nature Center via the Discovery Trail.

If you can, make time to visit inside the nature center for hands-on lessons about the geology, hydrology, and ecology of Geauga County.

From the nature center, follow Ansel's Cave Trail Link as it heads east to see some very different terrain and a unique man-made structure.

The hard-packed, dirt-and-gravel trail link eases up a gentle rise; several benches along the way offer rest. Continuing along the edge of a 15- to 20-foot-deep ravine, you'll

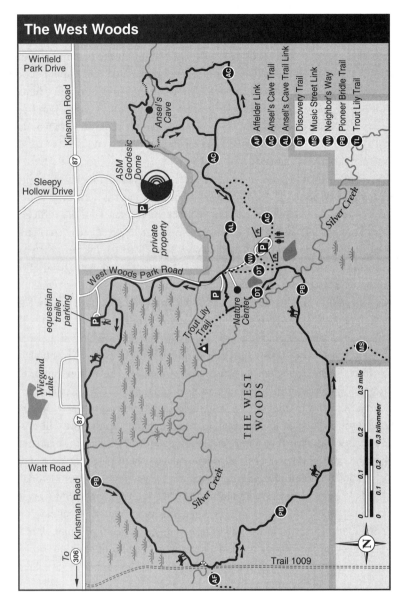

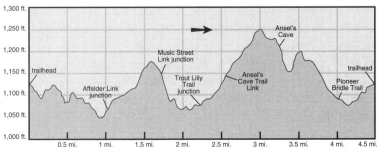

cross over a short wooden footbridge, passing increasingly larger outcrops of Sharon conglomerate sandstone infused with small, smooth pebbles.

The trail snakes a bit but heads generally east and up. At the beginning of the loop, head right to travel counterclockwise. After a few minutes of steady uphill action, you (and the path) will reach the top of a large shale formation. From here, you'll have a good look at the ravine, now 20–25 feet below. You're surrounded by maples and probably ready for a bit of a break. Ahead, you'll begin your descent with the aid of a wooden stairway, and then another. At the bottom of the second stairway, you'll see the rock formations for which the trail is named.

In the early 1800s, the cave—now more aptly described as a rock wall—might have been the temporary home of Ansel Savage. Whether he was a hermit, as some rather romantic accounts contend, is not certain. What hermit pursues political office? Savage served as a constable and trustee in Newbury township 1826–1828 and as clerk, treasurer, and justice of the peace in Russell township in 1830. Though he moved to Williams County in 1834, lore about the cave continues. It's also rumored that a band of counterfeiters both hid out and worked inside the cave.

But as you follow the boardwalk alongside a crooked creek bed, you may wonder, "What cave?" A waterfall and the feature popularly referred to as a cave stands about 75 feet off the trail to your right. Based on the best understanding we have of the area's geology now, there was no cave—regardless of its name, what we have here is actually an outcrop of Sharon conglomerate ledges, which form something like a three-sided structure. An assortment of graffiti remains here too, some of it dating to 1888. (Read it, but please, don't add to it. Also stay on the trail, for your safety and to protect the landscape.)

Once you've had a good look around, turn and continue up the dirt trail. A series of S-shaped curves will lead you in a semicircle, looping south and back to the main trail under tall black walnut and white pines. But as you near the top of the rise, just west of the cave, you can't help but notice another striking formation: the geodesic dome at Materials Park.

Materials Park is the world headquarters of ASM International. ASM (formerly the American Society for Metals) is an international society for materials engineers and scientists. ASM member Buckminster Fuller designed ASM's geodesic dome. It is 103 feet high and 274 feet in diameter at its base, containing 13 miles of aluminum tubing and rods; foundations for the dome pylons extend 77 feet belowground. It was added to the National Register of Historic Places in 2009.

While you're invited to gawk from here, Materials Park is private property. Visitors are welcomed from the main ASM entrance, just off Kinsman Road east of the entrance to The West Woods. The gardens and grounds are open to the public Monday–Friday, 7 a.m.–6 p.m. With development obviously chewing up large portions of the county, visitors can take comfort in the fact that, to complete The West Woods, the Geauga Park District purchased additional land from ASM, providing a land buffer to complete the park property that is home to barred owls, flycatchers, thrushes, vireos, and several threatened plant species.

Regarding the neighboring structure to the east of the park, it's worth noting that one of ASM's founders, William Hunt Eisenman, revered "big plans" and the magic they

What remains of Ansel's Cave

can contain. Obviously, The West Woods is a result of some big plans, and the park district has created some magic here, making wise use of donations of money, land, and volunteer hours. Follow the trail link as it rolls and bumps west and back to the nature center, where you can make your own "big plans" about where to go next. To return to your car, follow the Pioneer Bridle Trail right (north).

Nearby Activities

The West Woods hosts a variety of activities, from concerts to photography exhibits to children's nature programs. The Rookery, another Geauga Park District property just north of here, offers more trails, including the Interurban Trail for hikers and bicyclists. More hiking in Geauga County can also be found at Beartown Lakes Reservation (see page 87) to the south.

Special thanks to Geauga Park District volunteers who reviewed this hike description.

GPS TRAILHEAD COORDINATES

N41° 27.734' W81° 18.308'

Take I-480 E to Exit 26 (I-271 N). Once on I-271 N, take Exit 1 (Miles Road). Follow Miles Road east for 4 miles, and turn left (north) onto OH 91/SOM Center. Follow SOM Center 2.5 miles to OH 87/South Woodland Road and turn right (east). In 7.3 miles, The West Woods will be on the south side of OH 87, 2 miles east of OH 306. Park in the first lot on your right to begin the hike. The ASM Headquarters and geodesic dome are located at 9639 Kinsman Road in Russell.

SUMMIT (SOUTH), STARK, AND PORTAGE COUNTIES

Wingfoot Lake State Park (see page 198)

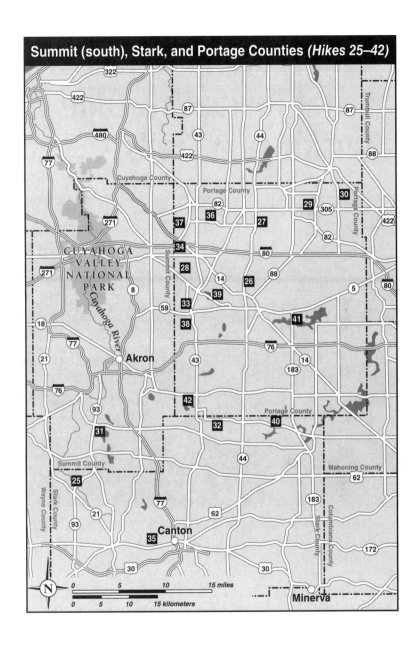

Summit (south), Stark, and Portage Counties *(Hikes 25–42)*

25 Canal Fulton: Ohio & Erie Canal Towpath & Olde Muskingum Trails

This section of the trail was created as a canal towpath in 1825–1827.

In Brief

Settled in the early 1800s, Canal Fulton has maintained and celebrated its rich canal history. Following the Ohio & Erie Canal Towpath Trail on the eastern side of the Tuscarawas River and the Olde Muskingum Trail on the west, hikers and bikers can enjoy historical landmarks and scenic views on both sides of the river.

Description

As you step up onto Ohio & Erie Canal Towpath Trail in Canal Fulton, you may plod alongside a couple of draft horses pulling the *St. Helena,* a restored canalboat. About 1 mile south of your starting point, you'll lose the horses and find a canal lock that still works. Stop at Lock 4 to read the interpretive sign.

DISTANCE & CONFIGURATION:
5.9-mile point-to-point (with shuttle) or
10.6-mile loop

DIFFICULTY: Moderate

SCENERY: Historical town Canal Fulton;
Tuscarawas riverbed, with wildflowers
and working canal lock

EXPOSURE: Mostly shaded; very
exposed when leaves have fallen

TRAFFIC: Busy, especially on warm
weekend afternoons

TRAIL SURFACE: Ohio & Erie Canal
Towpath Trail, crushed limestone; Olde
Muskingum Trail, grass and gravel

HIKING TIME: 2.5 hours with shuttle;
4.5–5 hours as loop

DRIVING DISTANCE: 41 miles from
I-77/I-480 exchange

ACCESS: April–September: Daily,
sunrise–9 p.m. October–March: Daily,
sunrise–7 p.m. Canal Fulton Canalway

Visitor Center: April–October: Saturday–
Sunday, 10 a.m.–4 p.m.; May–September:
Monday–Friday, 10 a.m.–4 p.m. and
Saturday–Sunday, 10 a.m.–6 p.m.

WHEELCHAIR TRAVERSABLE: Parts of
Ohio & Erie Canal Towpath Trail rough but
manageable; Olde Muskingum, some sections may not be suitable

MAPS: USGS *Canal Fulton* and USGS
Massillon; also at visitor center and trail
website

FACILITIES: Restrooms in visitor center
and along Ohio & Erie Canal Towpath Trail

CONTACT: Ohio & Erie Canal Towpath
Trail: 330-854-6835; **cityofcanalfulton-oh
.gov/departments/parks-and
-recreation-department** or **ohioand
eriecanalway.com/Main/Pages/The_
Towpath_Trail_56.aspx;** Olde Muskingum
Trail: 330-477-3552; **starkparks.com
/park.asp?park=16&view=9**

Continue south, enjoying the view as you stroll along about 10 feet above both the canal bed on your left and the river on your right. In many places from this point south, the canal bed is overgrown with cattails and duckweed, providing a haven for birds, but-terflies, and ducks. Pick a quiet evening for your trip and you're almost certain to see warblers, finches, robins, jays, and cardinals.

One mile south of the trailhead where you started, you'll come to the Butterbridge trailhead. Immediately west of the trail, a private farm with a majestic red barn paints a scene typical of Stark County's beautiful farmland.

A little more than 5 miles south of your start, you'll reach Crystal Springs Bridge, an obvious spot to rest and contemplate your next move. A couple of restaurants are open to visitors across the street to the northwest. If you'd like to extend your walk, continue on Towpath Trail less than a mile to Forty Corners Road. (There's a parking lot there, so if you'd prefer to complete this hike as a shuttle, you can.) Before going anywhere else, however, you'll probably want to learn more about the bridge.

Built in 1914, the bridge replaced one damaged in a flood. The slightly newer iron grid floor (added in the 1940s) has an almost lacy appearance. In 1996 the bridge was saved from demolition, and the area around it was designated Crystal Springs Bridge Park. This small park—no facilities are here other than a convenient spot for the canoe livery to collect tired paddlers—closes the gap between the Olde Muskingum Trail on the

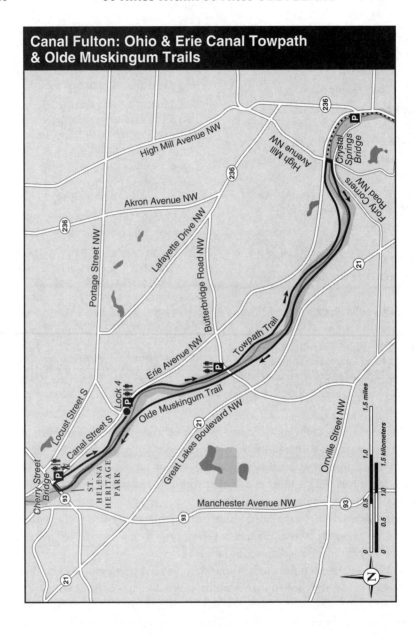

Canal Fulton: Ohio & Erie Canal Towpath & Olde Muskingum Trails

west and the Towpath Trail on the east bank of the river, creating an obvious loop for hikers who want to get two different perspectives of Canal Fulton's history. The route described here follows this loop, so turn right, crossing Crystal Springs Bridge, and then turn right again to travel north on the rail-trail.

(*Note:* Here you cross paths with the southern portion of the Little Loop of the Buckeye Trail, so you may notice blue blazes on nearby trees.)

If you've timed your hike correctly, you'll be able to watch the sun sink slowly in the sky as you head back to Canal Fulton. Stretches of farmland reach out to the west; the panorama is quite pretty. Toads, rabbits, and deer will join you, bumping along this old railroad right-of-way. You may also share the road with horses, as equestrian traffic is allowed all along the Olde Muskingum Trail, which is managed by Stark County Parks.

After crossing to the north side of Butterbridge Road, the trail winds slightly to the right before depositing you onto Cherry Street. Turn right and cross over the bridge, heading east. Pause to look upstream, and perhaps to wave at a canoe as it drifts under the bridge that has carried traffic through town for nearly 100 years.

Nearby Activities

Canal Fulton was incorporated in 1814, and visitors can relish a sort of time warp feeling here, walking along brick streets lined with historical-looking street lamps. May–September, the *St. Helena* offers an authentic canalboat ride experience; call 330-854-6835 for a schedule and rates. Those who prefer to paddle down the river can rent canoes from a livery on Cherry Street.

Budding botanists may want to visit Jackson Bog (**naturepreserves.ohiodnr.gov /jacksonbog**), just 2 miles east of Crystal Springs Bridge. The bog is managed as a state nature preserve; more than 20 rare plants, some considered threatened or endangered by the state, can be viewed from its 1.3-mile boardwalk trail.

GPS TRAILHEAD COORDINATES

N40° 53.267' W81° 35.819'

Follow I-77 S toward Akron, and take Exit 136 (OH 21 S toward Massillon). Continue onto OH 21 S for 17.4 miles. Turn left onto Arcadia Street Northwest, which becomes Cherry Street West. Follow Cherry Street for 1 mile to Tuscarawas Street Northwest. Turn right into the parking area for Canalway Visitor Center and the *St. Helena* boarding area.

26 Dix Park

Portage Park District

Dix Park is known for great wildflower displays.

In Brief

This small, unique Portage Park District property offers a short woodland trail set amid lovely farm fields. Depending on the time of year, you may get to watch planting, harvesting, or other farmwork in nearby fields. Go in the early spring for the best wildflower display.

Description

As you look east from the parking lot, you'll see farmland give way to rich woodland trails.

A trail system loops through approximately 60 of the park's 103 acres. Bluebird nesting boxes sit near the parking lot; the rest of the property has been left for cultivation.

From the parking lot, follow Farm Lane east. This lane is in use by the farm, and hikers will occasionally come across farm equipment here. This is the most exposed portion of the hike, and good birding opportunities exist along the hedgerow that parallels the gravel lane. The farm is on your left; maple and cherry trees line the fields of corn, soybeans, and hay.

DISTANCE & CONFIGURATION:
2.2-mile balloon

DIFFICULTY: Easy

SCENERY: Working farm, plus a variety
of trees and spring wildflowers

EXPOSURE: Mostly shaded

TRAFFIC: Moderate

TRAIL SURFACE: Trillium Trail and Fox
Loop, dirt; Farm Lane, gravel

HIKING TIME: 45–60 minutes

DRIVING DISTANCE: 35 miles from
I-77/I-480 exchange

ACCESS: Daily, sunrise–sunset; no
bikes or horses permitted; pets must be
leashed; farm fields not open for public
use. On occasion, agricultural activity may
temporarily close the Farm Lane and sub-
sequently the other trails.

WHEELCHAIR TRAVERSABLE: No

MAPS: USGS *Ravenna;* also at trailhead
and park website

FACILITIES: Picnic tables in parking lot;
portable restroom

CONTACT: 330-297-7728; **portagepark
district.org/parks-trails/dix-park**

About 0.6 mile east of the parking lot, a trail sign invites you to turn left (northeast) onto Trillium Trail. Follow the narrow dirt trail as it wanders by yellow birches and a few sassafras trees. You'll tramp across footbridges to save you from slogging through the wettest spots in the trail. What looks like a small creek in the early spring is actually an ephemeral (or seasonal) water flow. Usually dry in the summer months, the temporary drainage provides a perfect setting for buttonbush and a breeding ground for a number of winged insects.

Typical of Portage County, the woods here are rich in glacial history. You'll notice many small erratics strewn about as you skirt the higher ground around the drainage depression. As the trail bends to the right and returns to Farm Lane, look for sugar and red maples, black cherries, tulip poplars, white oaks, red oaks, bigtooth aspens, and dogwoods. Wildflower watchers may spot trilliums, Dutchman's-breeches, toothworts, anemones, marsh marigolds, blue cohoshes, violets, trout lilies, and bellworts. See if you can spot a spicebush. Its light-brown bark is coated with white specks, and when you rub the leaves, it smells like lemons and oranges.

When you reach Farm Lane, turn left (southeast) and follow it to pick up the short Fox Loop, the southernmost of the trails here. You'll turn right (southwest) off the lane, following the trail sign back into the woods. In the spring, this area is alive with wildflowers as well as the peculiar skunk cabbage. Its blooms usually appear in May, and while the plant is not as pretty as wildflowers, it has its own odd charm. In early spring, as early as February in a warm winter, the bulbous heads of new cabbage plants pop up through the soil. Inside, the flower of the new plant warms itself. The warmth is thought to appeal to pollinating insects that need the heat to move around. The temperature inside the flower may be as much as 36° warmer than the outside air.

As the path bumps along through the woods, wildflowers, and self-warming cabbage, you'll notice that this portion of the trail is generally higher than the northern loop.

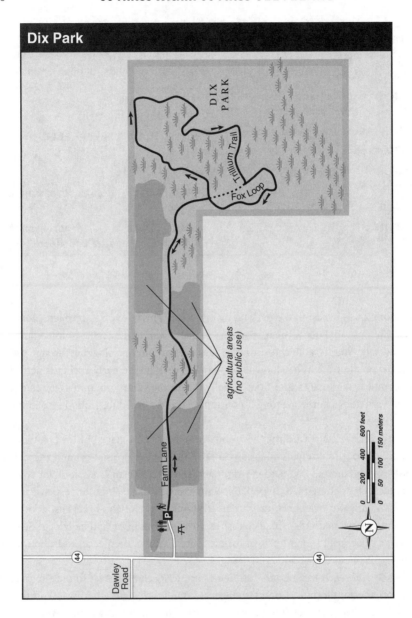

From here, you have a good view of the landscape in progress and the seasonal drainage that sustains a variety of plants and animals.

The southern loop quickly returns to the lane. Turn left (north) onto the gravel road to return to the parking lot. As you walk past the farm fields again, it's easy to draw comparisons between the water flow and the farm operations. Both are seasonal and supply the land—and the park—with a measure of diversity and richness.

Portage Park District

Trillium

Nearby Activities

To explore more woodland trails, visit nearby Towner's Woods (see page 186) or go northeast to Nelson-Kennedy Ledges State Park (see page 145) for a very different hiking experience.

    Thanks to the Dix family, who donated this land and the funds necessary to create this park; to former Portage Park District (PPD) staffer Brad Stemen for his work in creating the trails and identifying many of its natural attractions; and to PPD executive director Christine Craycroft for reviewing this hike description.

GPS TRAILHEAD COORDINATES
N41° 11.399' W81° 14.691'

Take I-77 S to Exit 146 (I-80 E). Follow I-80 E for 20.4 miles, and take Exit 193 to OH 44 S. Turn right (south) onto OH 44, and follow it about 4 miles. The park entrance will be on your left (east).

27 Headwaters Trail

Share the trail with equestrians.

In Brief

This rail-trail in Portage County makes for peaceful, easy walking (as well as jogging and biking). Running east and west between Mantua and Garrettsville, it abuts the Mantua Bog and Marsh Wetlands State Nature Preserves, making it a great trail for bird-watching.

Description

Starting at the High Street trailhead on the east side of the Cuyahoga River, near the historical brick town maintenance garage, you'll step onto the crushed limestone trail, walk up a short slope to meet the old railbed, and turn left to head east. (This section of the Headwaters Trail is also the off-road route of the Buckeye Trail, which continues until just past Asbury Road, where it leaves the hike and bike trail to head north, across Camp Asbury.)

To the south of the trail is the 152-acre Marsh Wetlands State Nature Preserve. On the west side of Peck Road, you'll walk alongside a different wetland: Mantua Bog (actually an alkaline fen). Both areas were designated as National Natural Landmarks in 1976 and as state nature preserves in 1990. Here in this wetland corridor, you can enjoy the migrating waterfowl as you stroll by the edge of these protected areas. You might also find

DISTANCE & CONFIGURATION: 6.3-mile point-to-point; 12.6-mile out-and-back	**ACCESS:** Daily, sunrise–sunset; pets must be leashed; horses (allowed only outside of village limits) and bikes frequent the trail.
DIFFICULTY: Easy	**WHEELCHAIR TRAVERSABLE:** No
SCENERY: Beech forests, creek ravine, lots of waterfowl; Western Reserve architecture in Mantua and Garrettsville	**MAPS:** USGS *Mantua* and USGS *Garrettsville;* also at park website
EXPOSURE: About half exposed	**FACILITIES:** Restrooms and water at trailheads at Gerald E. Buchert Memorial Park in Mantua and Garrettsville Village Park
TRAFFIC: Moderate	
TRAIL SURFACE: Crushed limestone	
HIKING TIME: 3 hours	**CONTACT:** 330-297-7728; **portageparkdistrict.org/parks-trails /headwaters-trail**
DRIVING DISTANCE: 32 miles from I-77/I-480 exchange	

a generously sized garter snake, or even a skunk that has wandered away from its protected habitat to gawk at the funny two-legged creatures plodding along the trail.

Along this stretch, you'll probably notice some sights indicative of the mixed-use nature of 21st-century trailways, such as a horse grazing on one side of the road and a mini-storage facility or a convenience store on the other. Keep going, and be happy that the trail managed to cut a swath through this interesting place and time.

About a mile into the hike, the trail offers some gradual changes of scenery: shallow but pretty ravines, cornfields, and a mix of both old and new homesites.

As you pass Vaughn Avenue heading east, you'll soon cross the Lake Erie–Ohio River Drainage Divide. While it hardly marks a cosmic shift, trivia fans should note that water east of here flows into the Ohio River, while waters west of here make their way to Lake Erie. Watershed fans will note that the trail more or less follows Eagle Creek, a tributary of the Mahoning River, but you won't see much of it from the trail. Most hikers will notice instead—depending on the season—cattails, thistles, and other delicious butterfly food growing on either side of the trail.

This portion of the trail east of Limeridge Road is nestled between banks of tall trees, which may make your trek feel extra dark and quiet. It's easy to forget that this trail came about largely thanks to the railroad that came through here long ago. A reminder is coming up: On the south side of the trail you'll soon see a large rock with a plaque describing a deadly train accident in 1949. After reading the somber story, you'll head up an ever-so-gentle slope to reach a clearing and greet Asbury Road. Stop and look north to enjoy a lovely vista.

Continuing east, you'll notice that the landscape changes on both sides of the trail rather quickly. Now, instead of being flanked by banks of trees, you can look into a ravine on either side of the trail. (It's steep in places, a good reminder to stay on the trail.)

Less than a mile farther down the trail, you'll reach OH 700, where additional parking is available. (This is a good place to park a shuttle vehicle if you're not sure that your

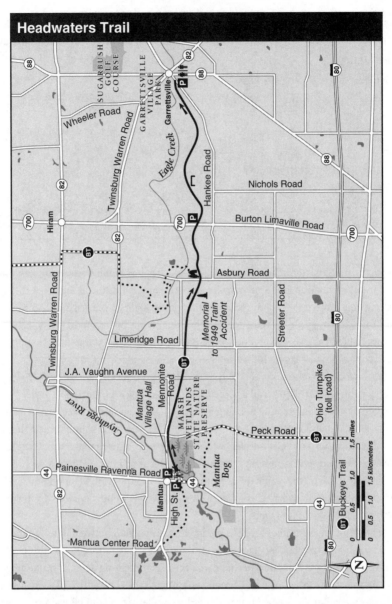

Headwaters Trail

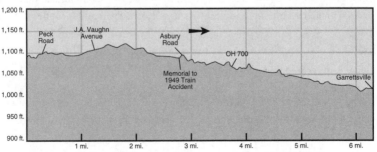

hiking group is up for the full 7 miles.) It's a pretty spot to end your hike, and there's no need to feel like a quitter because you've logged more than 4 miles since leaving Mantua at OH 44. If you continue on for about 3 miles east, you'll reach Garrettsville Village Park, another spot where you can park a shuttle vehicle. In the late summer, you'll find big milkweed pods at the end of the trail (more butterfly food!) and quite possibly get to watch a ballgame in progress.

Whether you walk, ride, or drive back to Mantua, you'll have great sunset views for company in the late afternoon or evening. Upon your return to Mantua, you can continue east on the path about 0.5 mile toward town to find a pretty footbridge. When you cross it and follow the path to the right, you'll see a wooden deck on the north side of the river that's perfect for fishing, reading, conversation, and contemplation.

You can also choose to continue on Headwaters Trail west for another mile, at least—the trail is young and still growing! Enjoy.

Nearby Activities

Interested in Western Reserve history? Have a look around Garrettsville, which, like Hiram and Mantua, was settled in the early 1800s, just as Ohio gained statehood. All three towns conjure up visions of New England—including central village squares with imposing churches surrounded by large frame-style houses.

Garrettsville came into being when John Garrett III of Christiana Hundred, Delaware, purchased 300 acres of land in Nelson, obtaining Silver Creek waterpower rights so he could build a gristmill. Unfortunately, Garrett soon died of pneumonia, but his widow, Eleanor, managed the mill, and it and the town thrived. A clock reminiscent of the gristmill era chimes at the corner of High and Maple Streets. And before you leave Garrettsville, you might want to pick up a pack of Life Savers. Clarence Crane invented the candy here in 1912.

More hiking can be found at Eagle Creek State Nature Preserve, heading east from the village by way of Center Street to Hopkins Road. The preserve is open 30 minutes before sunrise–30 minutes after sunset year-round; call 330-527-5118 or see **naturepreserves .ohiodnr.gov/eaglecreek** for more information. (Note that pets are not allowed in the nature preserve.) Also nearby: rocky Nelson-Kennedy Ledges State Park (see page 145).

Special thanks to Christine Craycroft, executive director of the Portage Park District, for reviewing this section.

GPS TRAILHEAD COORDINATES

N41° 17.013′ W81° 12.985′

From I-77, take Exit 156 and merge onto I-480, heading east. In 6.6 miles, take Exit 26 (US 422 E), following signs to Warren, and in 2 miles, continue to follow US 422 E. In 15.4 miles, exit and turn right (south) onto OH 44 toward Ravenna. Follow OH 44 approximately 7 miles, and then turn left (east) onto East High Street in Mantua, where trailhead parking is available on the south side of the road. Additional parking is available behind the McDonald's on OH 44 at Mill Street.

28 Herrick Fen State Nature Preserve

Native and alien species vie for space at Herrick Fen.

In Brief

Who knew that carnivorous plants could be so cute? Who knew that beavers could cause such trouble? As pretty and peaceful as this place is, you may not notice the battles raging all around you. This fen harbors the tiny insect-eating sundew plants, state endangered bayberries, and rare sedges. While only careful observers will notice many of the rare and endangered species here, the tamarack trees are easier to spot. Tamaracks,

DISTANCE & CONFIGURATION: 1.6-mile balloon	**WHEELCHAIR TRAVERSABLE:** The northernmost portion allows handi-capped-equipped vans to access the boardwalk, but the gate to the road is locked. To arrange access, contact The Nature Conservancy through **nature.org** or call 614-717-2770. Please allow two days advance notice when requesting gate access. The ADA-compliant boardwalk has turnaround points.
DIFFICULTY: Easy	
SCENERY: Rare plants, herons, beavers, muskrats; good bird-watching	
EXPOSURE: Mostly shaded	
TRAFFIC: Moderate	
TRAIL SURFACE: Wooden boardwalks, dirt trail	**MAPS:** USGS *Kent*
HIKING TIME: 45 minutes	**FACILITIES:** None
DRIVING DISTANCE: 28 miles from I-77/I-480 exchange	**CONTACT:** Nature Conservancy: 614-717-2770; **tinyurl.com/herrickfen**
ACCESS: Daily, sunrise–sunset; pets and bicycles prohibited.	

Ohio's only native deciduous conifer, are not evergreen. They have needles that turn bright yellow in autumn and then fall off. Visit in autumn to see the tamaracks' remarkable display; visit anytime to watch for birds, and stay, perhaps, for a sunset.

Description

If you know the difference between a fen and a bog, you probably paid very close attention in biology class. (Unfortunately, I didn't.) While bogs, swamps, fens, and other wetlands have some commonalities, they're not the same.

So what is the difference between a bog and a fen? An overly simplified explanation: A fen is alkaline and a bog is acidic. Both areas are ecologically important, too scarce these days, and generally damp. Bogs receive their water from aboveground sources (mostly rain and snow). Groundwater seeps and springs, usually coming out of glacial deposits, feed fens. Bogs are often isolated from groundwater—sometimes from impermeable soil conditions but frequently from an impermeable layer of compressed, humified peat. Peat is what really sets bogs and fens apart from other wetlands. Peat, combined with the continual wetness, causes and perpetuates extreme soil conditions. You don't have to be a science whiz to realize that different types of plants live in alkaline and acidic soils. But shades of gray exist in nature—and in the relative acidity of bogs and fens. Because bogs and fens are both generally wet, some plants exist in both, and some of those species cannot exist anywhere else. This concludes the science lesson; now it's time for a field trip. Well, make that fen trip.

While the fen isn't well marked from the road, the drive can be found just east of a (privately owned) red barn. The barn sits on a small hill on the eastern end of the preserve and trailhead. Follow the wide gravel path past tall marsh grass and seasonal wildflowers. When the goldenrods explode under a sunny fall sky, the scene is as colorful and

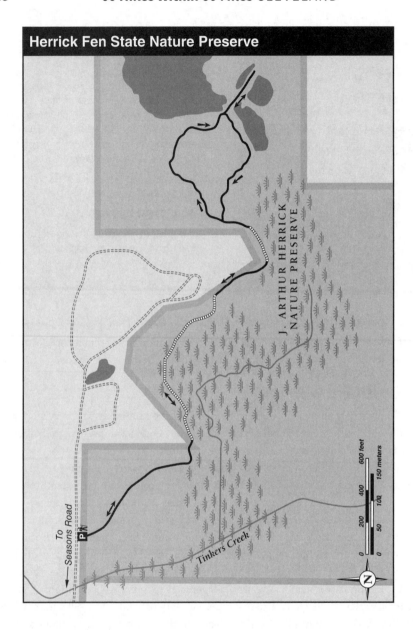

Herrick Fen State Nature Preserve

J. ARTHUR HERRICK
NATURE PRESERVE

To
Seasons Road

Tinker's Creek

600 feet
400
200
0

150 meters
100
50
0

glossy as a still-wet painting. But behind the pretty picture, there is turmoil. Battles rage, quietly but constantly, among the fen's inhabitants.

About 0.2 mile from the trailhead, you'll come to a large stone recognizing the work of The Nature Conservancy and the Akron Garden Club in preserving this land. Step onto the boardwalk, where you'll have a chance to stop at three inviting benches. These are good seats for watching the herons and marsh wrens that commonly appear here. Believe it or not, these seats are in the middle of the battlefield.

A few cattails appear here and there, almost like sentries on guard along the boardwalk. But are they here to protect or invade? The answer depends on whom you ask. Cattails provide high-energy food for migratory birds and butterflies; so birds and butterflies, and people who watch them, may root for the cattails. But the answer also depends on the type of cattails. Some are native and nonaggressive, content to enjoy their view of the fen without overtaking it. Other cattail species are invasive and quite aggressive, threatening some of the fen's indigenous plants. What needs protection here? Bayberries, for one, are on the state's list of endangered plants. This fen is one of just three spots in Ohio where it grows. Unfortunately, the cattails and bayberries aren't the only species at odds in this preserve. The invasive cattails and reed canary grass threaten the open fen as a whole, driving out the sedge meadow and shrubby cinquefoils. Glossy buckthorns, small trees or large shrubs (distinguished by their shiny oval leaves and speckled bark), threaten the tamarack population as well as the bayberries. The skirmishes among the plants and animals here started long ago; along the way, people have stepped in—for better or for worse.

The lakes and dam on this property—though on portions not open to the public—date to the 1950s, when the Frame family raised mink and muskrats here. J. Arthur Herrick bought the initial tract of land that would form the preserve in 1969; for some time after that, the area was known as Frame Lake Bog. The muskrats (who didn't care what the place was called) stayed, and beavers joined them. But beavers, like cattails, can be troublemakers. Beaver dams cause the water levels to rise, threatening the tamarack population. The tamaracks in this fen comprise one of the few reproducing populations of this tree in the state.

What can—and what should—be done to tip the balance in favor of the bayberries and the tamaracks? Again, the answers vary depending on whom you ask, and a resolution is not expected in the near future. The good news is that the fen has been preserved, so the battles may continue. The Nature Conservancy sends aid in the form of volunteers. They diligently thin the ranks of invaders in hopes that the natives can continue to fight for themselves. While some of the natives are under duress, the volunteers who visit typically report finding the battlegrounds overwhelmingly beautiful. So march on . . .

As you continue south on the boardwalk, tamarack trees line the trail; you're likely to see or hear a catbird at this point. It's easy to spot the mayapples and skunk cabbages growing along the boardwalk. Skunk cabbage is probably most noticeable in the spring, thanks to its white flower that resembles a lily. In the fall, however, its fruit is worth a look. Waxy and dark brown, with a hint of purple, its shape might be described as oblong, somewhat reminiscent of a hand grenade (in keeping with the battlefield imagery).

Notice, too, the fen-loving shrubby cinquefoils, whose bright-yellow flowers bloom May–September. You'll have to look hard for the less common sundews, small but mighty carnivorous plants resembling a sunburst. When an insect lands on the plant's hairy, sticky leaves, it triggers an enzyme reaction that makes a leaf grow very quickly—so quickly that it wraps up the insect like a burrito before absorbing the bug's nutrients. Another unusual plant to look for is turtlehead. It has waxy, dark-green stems and white flowers. Each bloom is about a half-inch long. When viewed from the side, with just a bit of imagination, the bloom indeed forms the outline of a turtle's head. Also look for poison sumac, cousin to the more common sumacs that occur only in fens. (Admire, but don't touch it if you are remotely sensitive to poison ivy!)

Just 0.4 mile into the trail, the boardwalk ends, and you'll step down onto a narrow, rooty dirt trail that winds between the base of a wooded hill and the shrub swamp. Soon, the boardwalk begins again, curves to the left, and then redeposits you on the dirt trail.

The hard-packed dirt path bends left, leading you up a small hill into a beech-maple wood that offers color-charged spring wildflower displays. Circling back down the hill, you'll find two shallow lakes separated by a narrow dam. The water levels are dropping here, by design. Releasing the dams that created the man-made lakes allows more native wet meadow plants to return.

The trail loop rejoins the original path at this point; you will retrace your steps back to the boardwalk and return home from here. You probably won't have any war stories to tell when you return, but you should bring home some lovely pictures.

Nearby Activities

This nature preserve sits about 5 miles northwest of Towner's Woods (see page 186) and about 5 miles south of Tinkers Creek State Nature Preserve in Aurora (see page 178). If you're stuck on wetlands, though, two bogs nearby are open to the public. The Tom S. Cooperrider–Kent Bog on the south end of Kent preserves what is thought to be the southernmost stand of tamarack trees in the country (see page 182). Triangle Lake Bog State Nature Preserve in Ravenna, while short on trails, is long on rare and beautiful bog-loving species, including a healthy population of pitcher plants. For more information about Triangle Lake Bog, see **naturepreserves.ohiodnr.gov/trianglelakebog.**

Interested in volunteering to protect Ohio's natives? Contact the Nature Conservancy at **nature.org.**

GPS TRAILHEAD COORDINATES
N41° 12.839' W81° 22.268'

From I-77, take Exit 156 and merge onto I-480, heading east. In 6.6 miles, keep right to stay on I-480 E, and in another 5.5 miles, keep right again to stay on I-480. Continue to follow I-480 E another 10.6 miles to OH 14 in Streetsboro. Follow OH 14 E 1.7 miles, and turn right onto OH 43, following it 0.2 mile to Seasons Road. Turn right. Approximately 2 miles west of OH 43, Seasons Road curves sharply to the left and crosses a railroad track. Turn left into the gravel drive providing preserve access on the eastern side of Seasons. Follow the drive past a stream crossing to the small parking lot on the right.

29 Hiram College: James H. Barrow Field Station

Wear boots here; you'll need them to splash through the creek.

In Brief

Wandering through these woods, you can breathe easy. With one of the largest mature beech-maple forests in Ohio, the James H. Barrow Field Station is quiet and beautiful, teeming with diverse plant and animal life. Watch for barred owls and pileated woodpeckers in the trees.

Description

If urban sprawl is getting to you, this is the place to come. The woods are thick and tranquil, and the trail is not well worn. Established in 1967 by Hiram College, the James H. Barrow Field Station features 250 acres of woods that are essentially an oxygen factory—where you can get a lungful of scents, including pine, sassafras, and other truly organic smells—situated between Cleveland's and Youngstown's industrial development.

DISTANCE & CONFIGURATION: 5-mile loop	**WHEELCHAIR TRAVERSABLE:** No
DIFFICULTY: Moderate	**MAPS:** USGS *Garrettsville;* also at trailhead, inside Frohring Laboratory Building, and on station website
SCENERY: Wide variety of trees, ferns, wildflowers, wildlife	
EXPOSURE: Mostly shaded	**FACILITIES:** Public restrooms in Frohring Laboratory Building near trail entrance (Monday–Friday, 10 a.m.–3 p.m.); emergency phones available on the Hiram College campus
TRAFFIC: Light	
TRAIL SURFACE: Dirt and leaves	
HIKING TIME: 2 hours	**CONTACT:** James H. Barrow Field Station: 330-527-2141; **hiram.edu /field-station;** educational visits for students and community programs: 330-569-6003
DRIVING DISTANCE: 36 miles from I-77/I-480 exchange	
ACCESS: Daily, sunrise–sunset; dogs on leash are permitted, but bikes and horses are not.	

Start your hike in the small gravel parking lot by the green building known as Frohring Laboratory. Inside, you'll learn about some of the animals you're likely to find on the trail, such as American toads, black rat snakes, various frogs and salamanders, and painted turtles.

From the lab, stop at the pavilion to view the educational displays. Then take the gravel road west to the Kennedy Observation Building. There, on the edge of a pond, you can enjoy watching waterfowl, such as wood ducks, great blue herons, and kingfishers. Among the wild birds you'll encounter, a pair of trumpeter swans lives here year-round.

The official trail sign for the Ruth E. Kennedy Memorial Nature Trail stands to the left of the Kennedy Observation Building. Follow the trail west. Going through young but dense growth, the trail splits before entering a meadow. In 1967 when Hiram College acquired this land, few of the trees around you existed; this land had been part of a local dairy farm. Turn left (south) at signpost 2 for a longer hike on the main loop. The trail meanders through young forest and eventually into an extensive meadow, providing a spectacular vista of the rolling landscape so typical of Portage County and northeast Ohio.

At the far end of the meadow, the trail enters the forest. Look for tulip, red maple, and black cherry trees, as well as the occasional white pine. Hike down a steep hill and onto what remains of a spur of the interurban railroad that connected Garrettsville and Hiram to Chagrin Falls and eventually Cleveland. The electric trolley that traveled the tracks was functional only for about 11 years, 1903–1914. This part of the trail cuts through the Silver Creek valley. Note the sycamore trees and abundant skunk cabbage off to the sides of the trail. Silver Creek, a high-quality tributary of Eagle Creek and the West Branch Mahoning River, owes its name to the first white settlers of Hiram, who arrived in 1802.

The path descends off of the old railroad bed. Climb a steep hill and rest on the bench at signpost 5, where a trail map is posted. From this vantage, you are overlooking

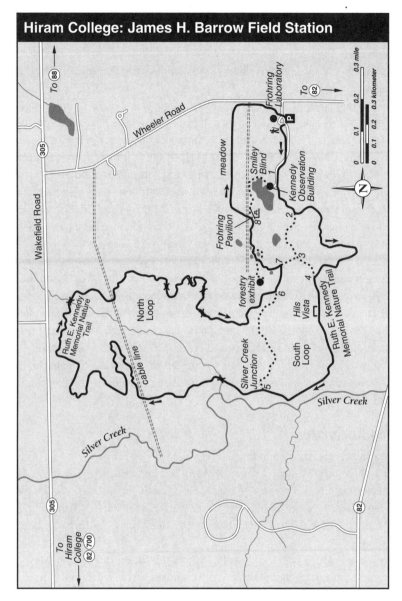

Hiram College: James H. Barrow Field Station

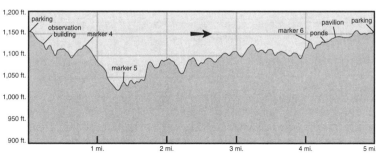

the beautiful Silver Creek valley. For a shorter hike, take the trail east, away from the creek. This path cuts through part of the mature beech-maple forest before returning to the trailhead.

Continue northward on the main loop to complete the 5-mile hike. The path takes you along the rim of the Silver Creek valley and down two steep hills to cross small creeks. The trail winds its way through middle-stage forest and crosses a bridge and several boardwalks. Shortly after the long boardwalk, you will be able to hear cars passing along OH 305 to the north. That's about the only time that civilization will encroach on your thoughts on this trail. At this point, the land levels off. A little farther ahead is another posted trail map. Beyond, the path cuts through a spectacular section of the mature forest. Rest on one of several wooden benches, or sit quietly on the large glacial boulder and marvel at the enormous beeches and maples, some 300-plus years old. From this vantage, it doesn't take much to imagine that nearly all of Ohio and the eastern part of the United States were at one time blanketed by primeval forests such as this.

The trail curves through mature forest and then younger forest before entering a small grove of white pines at signpost 6. At this point, you've logged about 4 miles. From here, you'll follow the trail east, back toward the trailhead. There are several options for the return hike. If you stay on the main loop, the trail opens onto an old farm field, now an old meadow. Stop by the small educational ponds to catch a glimpse of frogs, tadpoles, and possibly salamanders. Once you reach the Frohring Pavilion, you can return to the Kennedy Observation Building by going south, or choose to walk the trail east through the meadow, which returns you to the parking area next to the Frohring Laboratory Building.

Nearby Activities

Before leaving Hiram, you may enjoy touring Hiram College and the town of Hiram, both of which reflect their Western Reserve heritage. You may also want to visit the Headwaters Trail (see page 132), about a 5-minute drive from the field station. To get there, follow Wheeler Road 0.7 mile south to Twinsburg Warren Road/OH 82. Turn right, heading west 1.9 miles to OH 700. Turn left and follow OH 700 south 1.3 miles to the Headwaters Trail parking lot.

Special thanks to James H. Barrow Field Station associate director Jim Metzinger for supplying additional information on the station and for reviewing this hike description.

GPS TRAILHEAD COORDINATES
N41° 17.927' W81° 6.533'

From I-77, take Exit 156 and merge onto I-480, heading east. In 6.6 miles, take Exit 26 (US 422 E), following signs to Warren, and in 2 miles, continue to follow US 422 E. In 19.5 miles, turn right (south) onto OH 700. Follow OH 700 for 5.3 miles, and then turn left (east) onto OH 305/Wakefield Road. In 1.7 miles, turn right (south) onto Wheeler Road. The entrance to the James H. Barrow Field Station will be on your right in about a mile.

30 Nelson-Kennedy Ledges State Park

Looking up at Shipwreck Rock

In Brief

Nelson-Kennedy Ledges State Park offers what may be the wildest 2-mile walk in the eastern United States. Don't let the short distance fool you; you could easily spend several hours here. Dramatic ledges and tight crevasses team up with a waterfall and several small caves, creating striking beauty. Bring a flashlight to peer into some of the narrower passages in this small, surprising state park. Beginners longing for a rocky hike should start with Gorge Metro Park (see page 243) or Whipp's Ledges (see page 248) and work their way up to this one.

Description

With formation names such as Devil's Hole and Fat Man's Peril, these trails sound a little scary. Dire warnings posted on park bulletin boards don't offer any warm fuzzies either.

DISTANCE & CONFIGURATION:
2-mile balloon

DIFFICULTY: Difficult

SCENERY: 60-foot cliffs, creek, caves, crevasses; tall, skinny waterfall

EXPOSURE: Mostly shaded

TRAFFIC: Moderately heavy

TRAIL SURFACE: Rock surfaces, dirt, peat

HIKING TIME: 2 hours

DRIVING DISTANCE: 37 miles from I-77/I-480 exchange

ACCESS: Daily, 30 minutes before sunrise–30 minutes after sunset; cars in the lot 30 minutes after sunset are subject to towing. Do not attempt hiking here when icy conditions exist. Pets are allowed on leashes; however, I don't recommend bringing them or young children here.

WHEELCHAIR TRAVERSABLE: No

MAPS: USGS *Garrettsville;* also at park website

FACILITIES: Restrooms at parking lot; picnic tables on both sides of OH 282

CONTACT: 440-564-2279; **parks.ohiodnr .gov/nelsonkennedyledges**

The park service strongly (and effectively) discourages horseplay here by posting recent accident information at the trailhead. Unfortunately, life-flight rescue has been called to the park several times for serious injuries. In short, the rock formations that give this park its amazing beauty also make it dangerous. By heeding the posted warnings and proceeding with respect and caution, you will certainly enjoy the cliffs, caves, and crooked trails here on this little plot of land in Portage County.

Four trails run through the park; their combined length is about 2 miles. While the park's direction is STAY ON MARKED TRAILS ONLY, you may be hard-pressed to do so. The trails dart in and out of huge rock formations, and it's easy to lose the trail. Study the map and take care in your exploration. With warnings duly noted, start with the easy, relatively speaking, White Trail.

Head west a few strides from the trailhead sign, passing the Blue, the Red, and then the Yellow Trails, before turning left (south) onto the White Trail. Though the White Trail is rated the easiest to walk, part of it follows along the top ridge of 65-foot cliffs—highlighting the need to use caution on all of the trails, regardless of their individual ratings.

The White Trail gives you a good overview of the south end of the park and a glimpse of what to expect on the trails below. About 0.4 mile south, the path loops to the left (east), where you'll see the trickle of Minnehaha Falls tumbling into Sylvan Creek below. A chain-link fence here marks the southern boundary of the park. Follow the trail as it loops back to its beginnings, and turn right (east), going downhill a few steps to find the Red Trail on the right, heading south.

You'll enter the Red Trail through a "tunnel" of 20- to 25-foot-tall boulders. The Red Trail is rated difficult. No kidding. It leads through a 20-foot-long corridor that will not accommodate much larger than a size 44 belt. If you make it through Fat Man's Peril, two more tricky maneuvers await: The Squeeze and Devil's Icebox.

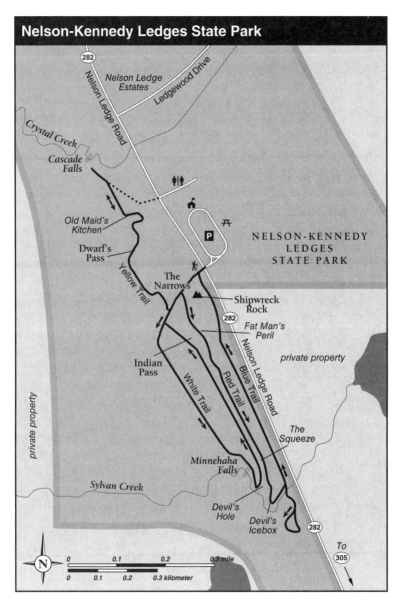

Nelson-Kennedy Ledges State Park

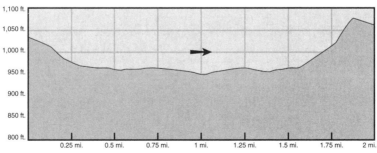

Cascade Falls

Once through Devil's Icebox (where you and an assortment of moss and ferns emerge by Sylvan Creek), you'll find a short set of steps leading down to the Blue Trail. At the bottom of the steps, turn right, heading south among some relatively small rocks (still taller than you) and loop around to head north, back to the trailhead. While the Blue Trail is rated moderate, it has much in common with the Red Trail: Both give you a squeeze, challenge your knees, and cause you to wonder at the trees, with their roots hanging onto the rocks for dear life. The blue line on the park map is a straight line, but don't be fooled.

Stunning ledges beg to be explored, but heed the warnings.

The actual trail wiggles through the woods and rolls over lots of small rocky bumps—all the way, however, it is well marked.

When the Blue Trail returns you to the trailhead sign, turn left and head uphill again. This time you'll pass the Red Trail. Beyond it, turn right to follow the Yellow Trail (also rated moderate). Yellow metal signs point you north; you'll also find yellow markers painted on rocks and trees. Even with these clues, you'll find that it's easy to lose the trail.

Like the White Trail, Yellow leads you along the top edge of the cliffs. From there, it takes you downhill fast—first on a dirt path and then along makeshift stone steps. It bottoms out, cools off, and lurches to the right. The Yellow Trail heads into a closet of sorts, created by two massive boulders. Moving north from there, you'll jog right then left again to pad along a sturdy wooden bridge into Old Maid's Kitchen. The "kitchen" is about as big as a New York City loft apartment. When you exit the dark and drafty "room," it's nice to see the sky again! You can also see the parking lot across the road—but don't leave yet. Follow the trail abruptly west, turning left and heading along a wooden boardwalk to the bottom of Cascade Falls. The small stream that tumbles over a 40-foot drop enters the Grand River, eventually making its way to the St. Lawrence River. (For trivia buffs: This park sits on a watershed divide. This stream, and water north of here, ultimately lands in the St. Lawrence River; Sylvan Creek, on the park's south side, finds its way to the Mississippi River via the Mahoning and Ohio Rivers.)

At the bottom of the falls, you can peer into Gold Hunter's Cave. Though the cave is not open to explorers, you can see inside from the wooden platform at the bottom of the falls. Retrace your steps back to the trailhead, or simply cross OH 282 to the east to return to the parking lot.

Nearby Activities

You probably passed through Hiram to get here. Why not visit the field station (see page 141) on your way back?

Thanks to naturalists Laurie Wilson and Megan Acord for reviewing this description.

GPS TRAILHEAD COORDINATES
N41° 19.706' W81° 2.338'

From I-77, take Exit 156 and merge onto I-480, heading east. In 6.6 miles, take Exit 26 (US 422 E), following signs to Warren, and in 2 miles, continue to follow US 422 E. In 19.5 miles, turn right (south) onto OH 700. Follow OH 700 for 5.3 miles into Hiram. Turn left (east) onto OH 305/Wakefield Road, and go 5.7 miles to OH 282/Nelson Ledge Road. Turn left (north). The park entrance is 1.3 miles north of OH 305. Parking is on the eastern side of the road; the trails are on the western side of OH 282.

31 Portage Lakes State Park

Swimmers can enjoy watching small boats on Turkeyfoot Lake.

In Brief

Portage Lakes State Park extends from Akron's southwest side well into the heart of Summit County. These short hikes showcase just two of the park's many assets: its popular swim beach and little-known observatory.

Description

The Portage Lakes area south of Akron boasts eight or more lakes (depending on how you classify reservoirs), and none are named Portage. Most are kettle lakes formed by glacial activity long ago, which created the habitats that allow unique plant communities to thrive here. The fact that most of the Portage Lakes are natural, and not man-made, is very important to the biology of the lakes and shoreline. While the water levels in man-made lakes fluctuate (especially in those created for flood control or as canal feeders), the levels in natural lakes remain more constant, which allows for a more stable environment for native plants and animals.

One of the species you'll see here is *Larix laricina,* commonly known as tamarack trees, which are rarely found this far south. Members of the pine family, tamaracks are deciduous conifers. Every autumn, their needles turn yellow and then fall off, to be replaced in the spring. More tamarack trees and other unusual plants abound in several bogs and fens north of here, in Portage County. (See pages 136 and 182.)

Interspersed among the lakes are dams and canals created by people to serve their own needs—first industrial, then recreational. Today, Portage Lakes State Park

DISTANCE & CONFIGURATION: 1.5-mile loop and 1.0-mile out-and-back	**ACCESS:** Daily, sunrise–sunset
DIFFICULTY: Easy	**WHEELCHAIR TRAVERSABLE:** No
SCENERY: Thick deciduous forest, pines, wetlands, sandy lakefront	**MAPS:** USGS *Canal Fulton;* also at camp office (5031 Manchester Rd.) and park website
EXPOSURE: Mostly shaded	**FACILITIES:** 900-foot sand beach swim area, boat launch ramps, restrooms, volleyball and basketball courts, disc golf course, skate park, playgrounds, and picnic shelters throughout park
TRAFFIC: Light	
TRAIL SURFACE: Dirt with some gravel; beachfront is sand	
HIKING TIME: 45 minutes per trail	**CONTACT:** 330-644-2220; **parks.ohiodnr .gov/portagelakes**
DRIVING DISTANCE: 35 miles from I-77/I-480 exchange	

encompasses more than 400 acres of land and 2,000 acres of water, ensuring that the habitat for wetland-loving birds and animals remains more or less undeveloped and creating a popular destination for outdoors enthusiasts.

The park attracts picnickers, hikers, sunbathers, and stargazers. The Shoreline Trail described here makes a good starter hike, which could be easily included in a family swim outing. The Planet Walk Trail, while it may appeal to budding astronomers, is a great trail that has not been well maintained. If you choose to follow it, keep your sense of direction handy, as the trail is difficult to follow in places. And if it's mosquito season, take repellent.

Starting from the eastern end of the Turkeyfoot Beach parking area, follow signs to the Tudor House and join the Shoreline Trail. After surveying the outside of the Tudor House (see details at the end of this section), turn left and follow the shady dirt trail northeast as it rambles toward the beach. The narrow path isn't all shoreline as its name suggests. Poison ivy, mayapples, and Virginia creeper all crowd the path, but there's room for you too. You'll likely enjoy solitude along this stretch of trail and all the way to the end of Turkeyfoot Lake, where the path bends sharply to head for the swim beach. And though trees will obscure your view of the swim beach for several yards, your ears will tell you that you're getting close.

During the warmer months, the beach is well used by people of all ages, but even in the cooler months, gulls and other shorebirds are on the scene, and their cries will remind you that you're not alone here. Up a slight hill to your left, under the shade of magnificent maples and other hardwoods, picnic tables, grills, a small changing/restroom area, a volleyball court, and a children's playground dot the landscape. Once your feet hit the sandy beach, to your right you may see windsurfers and other small crafts out on Turkeyfoot Lake.

Take off your shoes or boots if you like to feel the sand beneath your feet, and walk across the beach and then past a restroom and assorted picnic tables, leaving the swimming area as you amble toward the edge of Turkeyfoot Lake under the shade of big trees once again. No swimming is allowed at this point of land, but you won't stay long, as the

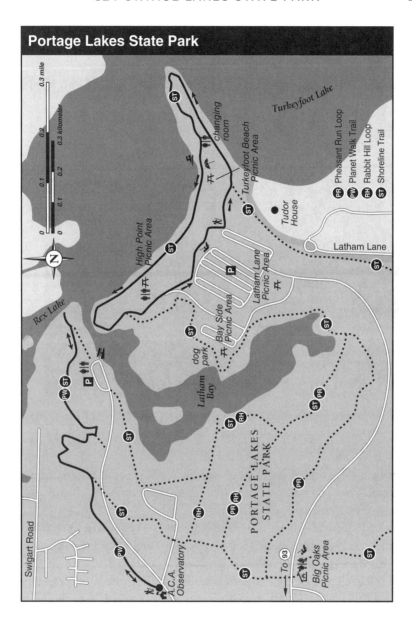

Portage Lakes State Park

0.3 mile

0.3 kilometer

Turkeyfoot Lake

Changing room

Turkeyfoot Beach Picnic Area

PR Pheasant Run Loop
PW Planet Walk Trail
RH Rabbit Hill Loop
ST Shoreline Trail

Tudor House

Latham Lane

High Point Picnic Area

Rex Lake

Latham Lane Picnic Area

Bay Side Picnic Area

dog park

Latham Bay

PORTAGE LAKES STATE PARK

Swigart Road

A.C.A. Observatory

To 93

Big Oaks Picnic Area

trail bends sharply and heads away from the water, leading you to High Point Picnic Area and the small playground. Now back to the parking lot, you've had a taste of what this park has to offer. Ready for more? Head for the "otherworldly" experience of the Planet Walk Trail.

From the swimming beach parking area to the Astronomy Club of Akron's Planet Walk Trail, the distance is just about 1.3 miles along lightly traveled park roads, an easy walk or drive. If you choose to walk it, you'd be smart to reapply sunscreen, as it's entirely exposed.

Some park visitors fly in for lunch.

To reach the trailhead, follow the park road on which you entered, turning right (north) before you reach Manchester Road. (A sign indicates that the road leads to the ACA's observatory and park offices.)

The trailhead sits behind the ACA building, marked by a sign that describes Mercury's hot spot in the solar system, located *only* 36 million miles from the sun. Not far behind, you'll find Venus, 67.2 million miles from the sun and 872°F on the surface. You'll veer left and into the woods to find Earth a much more inviting place, at 93 million miles from the sun and with a surface made mostly of water. The path is overgrown in spots, but the signs indicating you've reached another planet will keep you in the proper orbit.

As you continue along the narrow path, you'll encounter Mars and its moons, as well as an asteroid belt. The trail is a little bumpy and the woods can be buggy, but we all know that space travel has yet to be perfected. There's good news for Earth hikers, though. The thick, young growth creates terrific birding opportunities along Planet Walk Trail, and many different butterflies enjoy this wetland woods. Have a camera at the ready; they don't sit still very long.

The path rolls downhill to visit Jupiter and eventually bumps along to find Neptune (2.8 *billion* miles from the sun) and the end of this odyssey. When you've landed here, it's time to turn around and retrace your steps back through the solar system—or cheat a little, and walk back along the edge of the road. Or, if you're ready for a longer hike, you can continue past Neptune to join the northwest edge of Shoreline Trail and finish out its 5-mile loop, here in our watery, habitable world.

Nearby Activities

If it's a longer hike you want, stay here and hike the whole Shoreline Trail, which covers 5 miles of the park, passing by such attractions as the dog park and Big Oaks Kids Zone, a gated, paved playground that appeals to kids and their parents alike. If you have a special event coming up, you might want to revisit the historical, 20-room Tudor House and its lavish grounds (accessible from the Turkeyfoot Beach parking area), which can be rented for parties, reunions, and other events. For information, contact the city of New Franklin at 330-644-1728 or **newfranklin.org/index.php/tudor-house.** Also worth considering: more hiking at nearby Quail Hollow State Park (see the next page), which also features a beautiful manor house, open Saturday–Sunday, May–October, and by appointment.

GPS TRAILHEAD COORDINATES

N40° 58.079' W81° 32.744'

From Akron, take I-77 S to Exit 122B, following I-277 W. In 2.2 miles, take Exit 2 (OH 93/Manchester Road toward Waterloo Road), and turn left onto OH 93/Manchester Road. In 4.5 miles, turn left into Portage Lakes State Park. Follow the park road 1.1 miles to Turkeyfoot Beach and Picnic Area.

32 Quail Hollow State Park

Enter to find Quail Hollow's extensive gardens.

In Brief

From an herb garden with a sundial to rough-and-tumble mountain bike trails, Quail Hollow State Park will satisfy a wide range of interests—even if you want to stay indoors. A unique, glass-enclosed nature viewing area in the visitor center allows you to watch birds and small critters up close.

Description

From the manor house parking lot, head south through stone gates to the herb garden. Established in 1986 by the Quail Hollow Herbal Society, the garden includes a rose arbor and features a traditional sundial. The beds highlight plantings of irises, lamb's ears, and Oriental poppies that bloom late May–early June. Thankfully, almost all of the plantings are labeled, so you don't have to wonder what's blooming. You'll have to identify the buzzing on your own; the butterflies and other insects that frequent the garden in late

DISTANCE & CONFIGURATION: 2.2-mile loop	**ACCESS:** Daily, 6 a.m.–11 p.m.
DIFFICULTY: Easy	**WHEELCHAIR TRAVERSABLE:** No
SCENERY: Marsh and prairie, pine and deciduous forest, herb garden, evidence of beavers	**MAPS:** USGS *Hartville*; also inside visitor center and at park website
EXPOSURE: Woodland trail, shaded; herb garden and marsh, exposed	**FACILITIES:** Restrooms, water, phone, and drink vending machine by manor house/visitor center parking lot; restrooms, playground, and volleyball and basketball courts at Shady Lane Picnic Area; picnic tables and grills throughout park
TRAFFIC: Moderate	
TRAIL SURFACE: Dirt and grass	
HIKING TIME: 1 hour	
DRIVING DISTANCE: 46 miles from I-77/I-480 exchange	**CONTACT:** 330-877-6652; **parks.ohiodnr .gov/quailhollow** or **quailhollowpark .net**

summer are so colorful that they compete with the flowers. Several benches in the herb garden provide rest in the shade of tall trees and offer a view of the manor house.

Wander just a few hundred feet west of the herb garden to a waiting picnic table and quiet fountain for a picturesque stop. Returning to the herb garden, have another look at the manor house from below, and then turn left (northeast) and step onto the short Tall-Grass Prairie Trail. As you might expect, it follows a mown grass trail amid taller prairie grasses. Soon you'll turn right (southwest), and then left, stepping onto Sedge Marsh, a 0.5-mile trail that bends south and then west. Along the trail, you'll find sweet flag and cattails and perhaps see some of the many frogs (spring peepers, chorus frogs, and American toads) or birds that frequent this marsh. In the summer, watch and listen for yellow warblers.

A small, quiet creek runs along the eastern side of Sedge Marsh Trail. On wet spring days, Sedge Marsh can be impassable unless you're wearing high, dry boots. That's OK because the natives can still get around—the marsh teems with animal life, though much of it is microscopic. Squishy marshes, not surprisingly, are important foundations in food webs. As you move south on a long stretch of boardwalk, you approach a meadow where larger links in the food chain live.

At the southern end of the marsh, you'll connect with the 1.5-mile Meadowlands Trail loop and turn left to follow the trail clockwise. About 0.3 mile from the marsh, the wide, grassy trail turns into a sea of pine needles. You'll rise and fall over several 10- and 20-foot hills as the trail turns along a pine stand. Now you're heading west, and deciduous trees, 30 and 40 feet tall, line the trail. Among them are crab apples, beautiful in bloom in the late spring.

It's important to note that the thick grass here camouflages some deep holes in the trail; folks with weak ankles should watch their steps through here. If you stop and look into the woods, you may see a red fox, white-tailed deer, or a wild turkey on this trail. If you miss them, don't despair. Look carefully and you'll surely see some smaller life-forms.

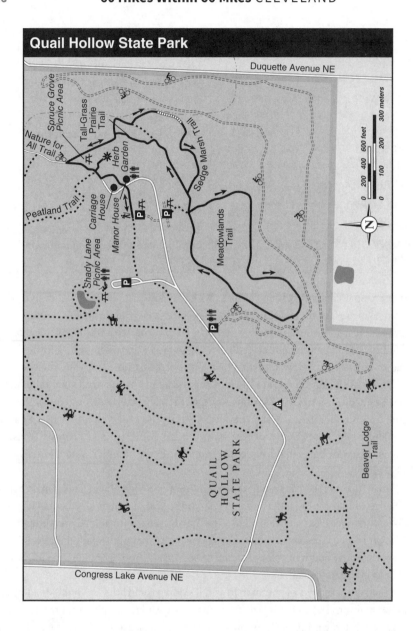

Quail Hollow State Park

Signs along the Sedge Marsh and Meadowlands Trails encourage you to get down on your hands and knees to look for caterpillars and other small insects and unusual plants. (Unfortunately, the signs don't tell you how to explain yourself to other hikers when they stumble upon you, crawling about. Not that I've ever been in that position, mind you. . . .)

As the path bends and rolls along, you'll pass a sign pointing the way to mountain bike trails and to the Beaver Lodge Trail. Stay on the Meadowlands Trail and, as you turn right, you'll come to a clearing where you'll have a view of the entire meadow. It's one of

You can use the sundial to check your hiking time.

those wide-open spaces where—just for an instant—you'll wish that this were your own backyard. The view is fantastic.

Looping eastward, the Meadowlands Trail leads you back to the manor house; it sits north and to the left of the end of the trail. From here, you can go up a dozen wide stone steps into the manor house. The building started life as a humble farmhouse back in 1838. Harry Bartlett Stewart, chief executive officer of the Akron Canton & Youngstown Railroad, began acquiring adjacent land in the early 1900s, and he passed it down to his son,

Harry Jr. The Stewart family lived here and enlarged the home several times until 1975, when they offered the property to the state for half its appraised value.

Today, the 40-room manor house hosts a variety of nature-oriented educational programs and workshops throughout the year. Part of the home's lower level serves as a visitor center and is open May–October, Saturday–Sunday, 1–5 p.m. A glass-enclosed room looks out onto a stone landscape featuring a small fountain and bird feeders. Inside, visitors enjoy watching chipmunks, squirrels, bright cardinals, and jays year-round, from the warmth of an old farmhouse.

Nearby Activities

Tours of the manor house are offered throughout the year—call 330-877-6652 for available dates. Educational programs are also offered regularly, both inside the visitor center and on the trail. While you're here, you may want to do a lot more hiking. The extensive bridle trails are open to hikers (be smart about sharing the trail, please) and offer some delightful hills to give your legs a good workout. As a bonus, a beaver lodge can be seen from the bridle trail on the park's southern edge.

Quail Hollow's 701 acres also include mountain bike trails, ice-skating, and cross-country skiing (equipment rentals are even available from the park). Once you've worked up an appetite here, you won't have to go far to satisfy it. Several restaurants in Hartville, near the junction of OH 43 and OH 619, serve hearty meals in the Mennonite tradition. Two wineries in or near Hartville are also popular stops—if you don't have a designated driver, though, buy a bottle to open at home.

GPS TRAILHEAD COORDINATES

N40° 58.786' W81° 18.274'

From Cleveland, follow I-77 S through Akron, and take Exit 129 (I-76 W). Follow I-76 W 1.7 miles to Exit 18 (I-277). In 3.9 miles, continue straight onto US 224, and go 9.5 miles, heading east. past I-76 and Turn right (south) onto Congress Lake Road. In 2.6 miles, the road turns left (east) and becomes Pontius Road. In 0.5 mile, turn right (south) onto Congress Lake Avenue Northeast. The park entrance will be on your left (east) in 0.7 mile at 13480 Congress Lake Avenue. Follow the long park driveway approximately 1 mile, following signs to the manor house on the park's eastern side.

33 Riveredge Trail & City of Kent

Riveredge Trail offers several vantage points to view the Cuyahoga River.

In Brief

This stroll along the Cuyahoga River and through the city of Kent highlights the town's history since the 1800s. It will lead you through a pioneer cemetery, by Ohio's oldest masonry dam, and by some of Kent's historical buildings, many of which are still in use. You'll also visit a large city park, filled with tall shade trees and fun playground areas.

Description

Legend has it that Captain Samuel Brady leapt across the Cuyahoga River to escape from American Indians in 1780. The river is narrow as it runs through Kent; still, it must have been a mighty leap. We'll never know just how far he jumped or how much credence to give the story. Nevertheless, Riveredge Trail in Kent is the setting for this and many other interesting tales in American history.

DISTANCE & CONFIGURATION: 2.5-mile figure eight	**DRIVING DISTANCE:** 31 miles from I-77/I-480 exchange
DIFFICULTY: Easy	**ACCESS:** Daily, sunrise–sunset
SCENERY: Great variety—from river fowl and ravine views to a rail station from the 1870s	**WHEELCHAIR TRAVERSABLE:** No
	MAPS: USGS *Kent;* also inside the park office at Fred Fuller Park
EXPOSURE: Mostly shaded, with a few short exposed stretches	**FACILITIES:** Restrooms at east end of Fred Fuller Park and at the Kramer ball fields; water fountain in the parking lot by the ball field
TRAFFIC: Moderate	
TRAIL SURFACE: Dirt and wooden boardwalks, sidewalks	
HIKING TIME: 50 minutes	**CONTACT:** 330-673-8897; **kentparks andrec.com/parks**

Start your hike at John Brown Tannery Park, where a paved path leads from the parking lot down a slight slope toward the river. A seasonal canoe livery operates here in the warmer months; in addition to paddlers, you're likely to see ducks and Canada geese at this spot. Veer right and pick your way along the river's edge a few hundred feet, where you'll find a wide, paved, shared trail.

Riveredge Trail is true to its name; it doesn't stray far from the Cuyahoga River. The river was the primary reason that Kent was a popular settlement in the early 1800s. At first, the town was named Franklin, for the son of the original landowner. In 1805 the Haymaker family moved to Kent and built a dam to power a gristmill. As other mills popped up, the town came to be known as Franklin Mills.

What was then Franklin Mills is now a busy university town, full of folks with flexible schedules, so the trail sees a fair share of traffic all week long.

But as you continue south, you'll find yourself feeling comfortably far away from the busy streets of the college town and enjoying the river's company.

You'll soon pass the Harvey Redmond Bridge on your left, which leads to the Kramer ball fields. A small fenced-in playground and portable restrooms are situated near the ball fields.

Cross the street and continue on the trail. To your right, a set of wooden stairs climbs up a steep hill to one of Fred Fuller Park's many swing sets and picnic areas, but you'll continue straight on the trail to enjoy the thick of the woods along the river.

The path forks again about 0.2 mile later. The rocky path to the right leads to Fred Fuller Park's main shelter and picnic area. Veer left instead, following the wide path as it winds along the riverbed. With a screen of mature trees between you and the river, it's a good place to do some bird-watching. Herons, among others, frequent this quieter portion of the river.

Continue another 0.3 mile or so to the edge of the park property. (You'll know you're there when shade trees are replaced with a view of the city's water treatment plant.) From here, you may decide to continue on the paved trail, across an old bridge truss. If you

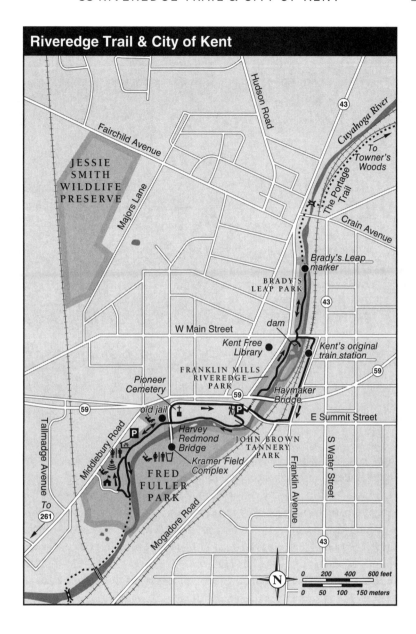

choose to, you can follow the trail south to the edge of Kent, where a Summit County hike/bike trail continues to Akron.

To complete the shorter figure eight hike, turn around and take a walk in the park.

Follow the gravel trail leading up a steep, shady hill, and you'll emerge at the southern end of Kent's largest city park. Restrooms and a playground are located here to the left; you'll spot a small amphitheater to the right.

Fishing here can be interrupted by the occasional canoe or kayak launch.

Follow the dirt road to the right. Cars are permitted here, but traffic is light. Walk 0.2 mile past the shelter house and park office to see the historical Kent Jail.

The jail was built in 1869 by the order of Mayor John Thompson, though it might easily have not existed, as Mayor Thompson won the office by just two votes. (Votes for Thompson totaled 145; runner-up Luther Parmelee had 143.) The jail was moved to the park in 1999 and completely renovated, and while it's now used for meetings and other events, elements of the original building remain.

From the jail, you'll head north down a steep, grassy hill. Swings, grills, and another picnic shelter sit at the bottom of the hill. Cross Stow Street, now heading west, and follow the sidewalk to the left to find Kent's Pioneer Cemetery, dating to 1810. Headstones here represent the families who figured prominently in Kent's history, including Haymaker and DePeyster. The cemetery gate is open sunrise–sunset.

Back on Stow Street, follow the sidewalk down to the John Brown Tannery Park parking lot. Cross Stow to the north to continue along the river trail. A sign here marks the entrance to Franklin Mills Riveredge Park. Head down about 20 wooden steps, under the Haymaker Bridge. At the bottom of the stairs, the path bends left; shallow river rapids gurgle to your right. This part of the trail is the least improved, but thanks to the sandy soil, it's rarely muddy enough to dissuade hikers.

The elevated boardwalk offers great views of the river.

From wooden stairways and elevated boardwalks, you'll see some of Kent's historical industrial buildings on the left; the old downtown is on your right. From the top of a set of stairs, you'll get a good look at the Kent Dam, the oldest masonry dam in the state of Ohio. This area, including the Kent Dam (constructed circa 1836) and canal basin from the Main Street Bridge to the Stow Street Bridge, comprises the old industrial district that is listed on the National Register of Historic Places. The dam was modified in the first few years of the 21st century to allow the river to flow freely again. Spared demolition because of its historical significance, the structure was retrofitted to become the center-piece of a small park. Climb the steps to the top of the dam and enjoy a unique view of the town. To the west, at the corner of River (OH 43) and Main Streets, is Kent Free Library. At first glance, it doesn't hint at its age. In fact, the library has been there for well over 100 years. The original building, built in 1903 with Andrew Carnegie's money on land donated by Marvin Kent, was incorporated into a much larger building that opened in 2006.

Looking east, you'll see the iconic two-story redbrick structure that was the city's original train station, built in 1875. The railroad's arrival here meant that the town would continue to grow, even as canal transportation declined. The man most responsible for bringing the new Atlantic and Great Western line to town was Marvin Kent. In 1864 the grateful residents of Franklin Mills changed the town's name to honor him, and the name stuck.

After descending from your observation point atop the old dam, continue north on Riveredge Trail, crossing under the bridge, where the path is again a wide brick walkway. Follow it about 0.3 mile, and you'll find a large rock and plaque marking the spot of Captain Brady's famous leap and describing how he managed to outsmart his would-be captors. (Believe it or not.)

From here, you can simply turn around and retrace your steps on Riveredge Trail, returning to Tannery Park along the river. If you'd like to keep going, the trail will take you east (following The Portage) to Towner's Woods (see page 186) and beyond. Or you can take one of several exits from Riveredge Trail to explore the city of Kent. Now that you know its history, its modern style might surprise you. Main Street is a center of activity, lined with art galleries, unique shops, and restaurants for every taste. If you decide to explore the city, cross the river at Main Street. Travel south along Franklin Avenue, and turn right (west) where Summit Street intersects Franklin to return to Tannery Park.

Nearby Activities

While children probably won't want to leave Fred Fuller Park's playground equipment, Kent's downtown and the university offer much more to see and do. Local merchants host numerous festivals and activities all year long. (For a schedule, see **mainstreetkent .org**.) An adventure outfitter managed by the university offers daily pedal-and-paddle trips along the Cuyahoga River throughout the spring and summer. (See **kent.edu /recservices/crooked-river-adventures.**)

Kent State University is located 1 mile east of the John Brown Tannery Park parking lot. There, you can visit the May 4 Site and Memorial—a somber spot recalling the day in 1970 when four students were killed during an antiwar protest. Or visit the university's nationally known fashion museum (330-672-3450; **kent.edu/museum**).

GPS TRAILHEAD COORDINATES

N41° 9.033' W81° 21.795'

From Cleveland, take I-77 S to Exit 156, and merge onto I-480 E. In 6.6 miles, keep right to stay on I-480 E. In another 5.5 miles, keep right again to stay on I-480 E/OH 14. Go 10.6 miles, and continue straight on OH 14 for another 1.7 miles. Turn right onto OH 43/Cleveland Canton Road, heading south into Kent. In 6.3 miles, turn left (east) onto Main Street and then, in 0.3 mile, right (south) onto Water Street. Follow Water Street 0.3 mile south to Summit Street and turn right (west). Tannery Park is about 0.3 mile west on your left.

34 Seneca Ponds

This park is popular with both anglers and hikers.

In Brief

Surrounded by corporate offices and light industry, a small parcel of land protects wetlands, breeding pairs of swans, and possibly our sanity.

Description

As has happened in countless outlying suburbs, Streetsboro's commercial district developed quickly. The urban sprawl steamroller of big-box retailers, manufacturers, and other employers threatened to engulf the entire city. Fortunately, Western Reserve Land Conservancy and Portage Park District were able to create a small preserve in the middle of an office park. The trail loops around two of the three ponds on this rustic 48-acre preserve.

While visitors can see neighboring businesses from at least two spots on the trail and will never completely escape the droning sounds of traffic coming from the Ohio Turnpike, the unassuming little path through wetlands and forest is a welcome addition to the neighborhood, drawing walkers from nearby businesses at lunchtime and evenings throughout the workweek. Seneca Ponds is also a popular fishing destination; bass and sunfish can be hooked here. (See tips for successful catch-and-release techniques at **wildlife.ohiodnr.gov/fishing/fishing-basics.**)

Enter the trail from the northern edge of the small parking lot, heading up a gentle slope to the first of many trail markers. Follow the trail as it curves to the left and you'll

DISTANCE & CONFIGURATION: 1.1-mile loop	HIKING TIME: 35 minutes
DIFFICULTY: Easy	DRIVING DISTANCE: 23 miles from I-77/I-480 exchange
SCENERY: Deciduous forest, wetlands, three ponds, swans, beavers, wildflowers	ACCESS: Daily, sunrise–sunset
	WHEELCHAIR TRAVERSABLE: No
EXPOSURE: Shaded in spring and summer, when trees are full	MAPS: USGS *Hudson* and USGS *Twinsburg;* also at trailhead and park website
TRAFFIC: Moderately heavy on weekends, evenings, and weekday lunchtimes	FACILITIES: None
TRAIL SURFACE: Dirt, mulch, grass, and gravel	CONTACT: 330-297-7728; **portagepark district.org/parks-trails/seneca-ponds**

soon be on the edge of the largest of the three ponds. A bench is perched on the water's edge. Be quiet and look closely and you may see beavers at work—and even if you don't, you're almost certain to see anglers at work. Proceed clockwise and note the different types of rocks you find along the trail. These erratics, typical of the area, were deposited by glacial activity 10,000 years ago, give or take a few years. As you cross over a couple of footbridges to avoid some very squishy sections of the trail, Beaver Trail meanders slightly west, and you can peer through the trees at a still-active railroad track. (Trains chug through infrequently, however.)

Much of the trail and its boardwalks were built by local Boy Scouts from the Seneca District; the park's name is a nod of appreciation to their hard work that made this property more accessible without damaging its natural assets.

Soon you'll leave the woods to cross over a narrow strip of earth between two ponds, and you'll then return to the shaded path where another wooden park bench greets you. A sign alerts you to another trail, marked by a swan. It's essentially a shortcut through the middle of the property. Ignore it and continue venturing left, where you may have a chance to see a swan family that sometimes resides here.

Curving east around the northern edge of the large pond, you'll walk over a variety of different surfaces, including gravel, grass, and mulch, each doing a good job of keeping the trail dry in this wetland habitat. Numerous marsh-loving wildflowers can be found on this short stretch of exposed trail. Naturally, during most of the spring and summer, this is also a good spot to spy dragonflies and damselflies.

Before the path returns to the shade of young oaks, you might see a bear—a statue of one, that is—gracing the picnic/patio area of one of the neighboring businesses. (Though it's not marked as such, the statue stands on private property and visitors are discouraged from getting too close.)

Back in the woods, heading south, you'll find another park bench, this one ideally situated for enjoying a sunset. (Insect repellent will make the watching that much more enjoyable, as the mosquito population comes out in force on summer evenings.) The

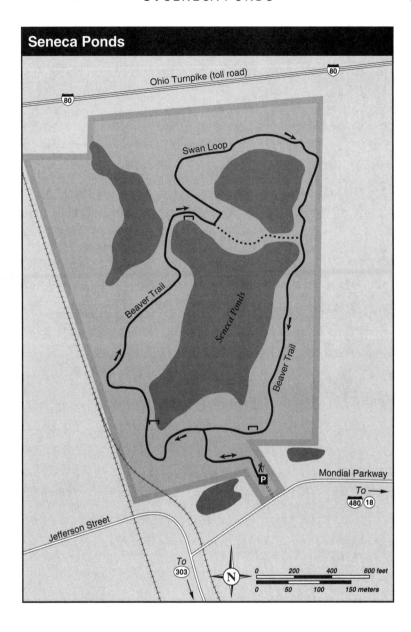

path rolls up a slight incline before veering east and returning you to your starting point, a stark reminder that you just might have to go to work tomorrow.

Nearby Activities

Don't get sucked into shopping while in Streetsboro; instead, visit another natural area nearby. Herrick Fen (see page 136) is about 5 miles away, Towner's Woods (see page 186) about 8.5, and Sunny Lake Park (see page 174)—a park with a completely different

Hummingbird moths and other winged marvels delight hikers at Seneca Ponds.

personality—is about 7 miles northeast of here. A highly rated KOA campground is also nearby, about 1 mile west on OH 303.

GPS TRAILHEAD COORDINATES

N41° 14.993' W81° 22.927'

From Cleveland, take I-77 S to Exit 156, and merge onto I-480 E. In 6.6 miles, keep right to stay on I-480 E. In another 5.5 miles, keep right again to stay on I-480 E/OH 14. Go 10.6 miles, and continue straight on OH 14 for another 0.5 mile. Turn right onto Mondial Parkway, following it about 1 mile to the park entrance on the north side of Mondial.

35 Sippo Lake Park

Rent a boat from Sippo Lake Marina, and view the lake from another perspective.

In Brief

Taking recreational land to a new intellectual high, this park features a built-in library! The 100-acre lake vies with the library as the main attraction. The marina rents small boats, and Sippo Lake is a favorite stop for many migrating birds.

Description

Combining the Sippo Lake Trail out-and-back with the shorter Marina Trail loop gives you a good look at both sides of this Stark County property, as well as some gentle hills on the Marina loop to offer your legs a bit of a workout. Several rustic trails on the north side of the park are slightly less trafficked than the lakeside trail, so if you're looking for more solitude, you can find it there.

From the parking lot trailhead, follow the crushed limestone trail around the back of the library building, where you'll find a wide wooden bridge ideally situated for watching the many birds that enjoy the lake. Continue northeast on the trail when you're ready. You'll soon lose sight of the lake, at least until you reach the Marina Trail.

The limestone trail is popular with locals, as it provides a path from a nearby neighborhood. Anytime the library is open, and often when it's not, you'll find families on foot and various wheels (bikes and strollers) making their way through here. As soon as the trail skirts the neighborhood, it starts to roll uphill ever so slightly, and then it's one steady climb to the marina parking area, which can be accessed from Perry Drive.

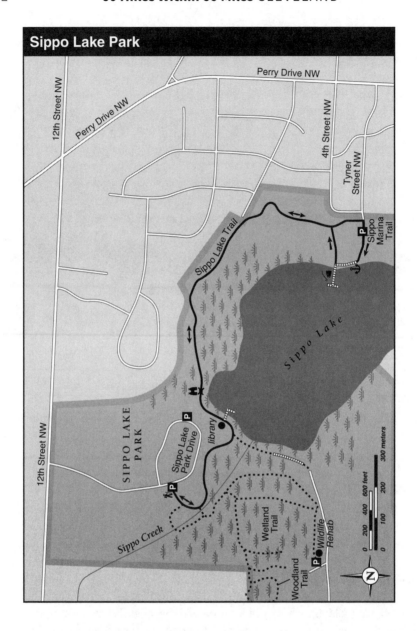

Walk around the front of the marina and go inside if you like. Concession and fishing items are available here. During the warmer months, you can also rent canoes, kayaks, and pedal boats. (Bring cash and a state-issued ID to complete the transaction.) The clubhouse and boat shelter are popular sites for family reunions and other friendly gatherings, as both can be reserved in advance through the park system.

Walk from the marina to a boardwalk leading to a long pier where fishing is permitted. From there, you can pick your way through the woods just a few hundred yards to

DISTANCE & CONFIGURATION: 2-mile balloon	**ACCESS:** Daily, 6 a.m.–11 p.m.
DIFFICULTY: Easy	**WHEELCHAIR TRAVERSABLE:** No
SCENERY: Lake, mature shade trees, good birding opportunities	**MAPS:** USGS *Canton West;* also on trailhead bulletin boards, inside library, and on park website
EXPOSURE: Almost completely shaded when trees have leaves	**FACILITIES:** Restrooms, water, concession stand (open June–August), and pay phone in main parking lot; picnic shelters, playgrounds, fishing pier, and marina (open May–October)
TRAFFIC: Moderately busy	
TRAIL SURFACE: Dirt and crushed limestone	
HIKING TIME: Allow an hour or more to visit the marina or library	**CONTACT:** 330-477-3552; **starkparks .com/park.asp?park=1**
DRIVING DISTANCE: 48 miles from I-77/I-480 exchange	

find yourself again on the limestone trail. Turn left, and you'll be on your way back to where you began.

If the library is open, you may want to stop in and learn more about the white oak, wild black cherry, and wetland dogwood trees you probably saw in the woods, or the herons and other birds you may have spotted near the lake.

Nearby Activities

If you haven't had enough of a hike, venture onto the Conservation and Lonesome Pine, Woodland, Cottonwood, and Wetland Trails just northwest of the trailhead where you began. Be aware that the trails are aptly named for the wetlands and species that live here—you're likely to have some squishy footing, and you may wish for some mosquito repellent there.

GPS TRAILHEAD COORDINATES

N40° 48.514' W81° 27.588'

From Cleveland, take I-71 S to Exit 218 (OH 18). Turn left (east) onto OH 18/Medina Road, and go 7.3 miles. Turn right onto I-77 S, and in less than a mile, take Exit 136 (OH 21 S). Follow OH 21 S for 24.4 miles, and turn left (east) onto Lake Avenue. In 1 mile, turn right (south) onto Wales Road, and go 0.3 mile. Turn left (east) onto Hankins Road, and go 1.4 miles. Continue straight onto 12th Street for another 1.3 miles. The park entrance will be on your right.

36 Sunny Lake Park

The city of Aurora operates a seasonal boat rental concession here.

In Brief

Sunny Lake Park serves many different interests. Want to soak up lazy lake views or watch great blue herons come in for long-legged landings? There are plenty of birds (and benches) to keep bird-watchers happy. Green thumbs will admire the Memorial Tree Garden on the park's south side. A dog park on the west side of the park keeps tails wagging. And active visitors of all ages can enjoy volleyball courts, boat rentals, an exercise circuit, and two playgrounds.

Description

From the shelter/office, follow the paved path east across a short wooden bridge; then begin your tour of the Memorial Tree Garden. It features a wide variety of trees, including flowering crabs, 'Ivory Silk' Japanese tree lilac, dawn redwoods, Kentucky coffeetrees, red buckeyes, and several varieties of oaks and ash. In 1999 the Aurora Garden Club planted a garden celebrating Aurora's 200th birthday. Daylilies, 'Overdam' feather reed grass, 'Autumn Joy' sedum, and flame grass grow there, amid other decorative trees and bushes.

The paved trail curves to the left, hugging the lake's eastern shore. In places, cattails grow so thick and tall that they obscure views of the lake. Sunny Lake is indeed sunny; most of the trail around it is exposed. That's not unusual for a lake trail.

DISTANCE & CONFIGURATION: 2-mile loop	main parking is closed, park at Memorial Tree Garden, east of main entrance, off Mennonite Road.
DIFFICULTY: Easy	
SCENERY: Arboretum, natural forest, birds, lake	**WHEELCHAIR TRAVERSABLE:** Yes; lake loop is paved, but nature trails are not.
EXPOSURE: Mostly exposed	**MAPS:** USGS *Aurora;* also from City of Aurora Parks & Recreation Department (330-562-4333)
TRAFFIC: Moderate–heavy, especially during warm weather	
TRAIL SURFACE: Main loop, paved; optional footpaths, dirt and wood chips	**FACILITIES:** Restrooms and water by main parking lot; picnic tables, shelters, grills, and playgrounds throughout park; dog park, volleyball court, and boathouse with boat rentals
HIKING TIME: 50 minutes	
DRIVING DISTANCE: 19 miles from I-77/I-480 exchange	
ACCESS: Daily, sunrise–sunset. If gate at	**CONTACT:** 330-562-4333; **auroraoh .com/599/Sunny-Lake-Park**

At 0.5 mile into the trail, you can't see the lake for the trees. A couple of well-traveled but unmarked dirt trails on the left head through the woods toward the lake. (They're very short and loop back to the main trail quickly, so follow them if you want.) As the woods thin out, you'll be able to see most of the lake again from its midpoint. There's a lot to see.

Great blue heron sightings are almost guaranteed here. Birds often travel between here and Tinkers Creek State Nature Preserve, about 2.5 miles from here as the crow—or heron—flies. Gulls and goldfinches gather here as well. At 0.8 mile into the trail, you'll come to a small clearing and several birdhouses. A mown but unmarked utility path leads east, to your right. The paved path veers left, curling down to the lakeshore.

You may choose to leave the pavement here and dive into the woods via a hard-packed dirt trail that winds through the oak and maple trees and over a couple of small hills, before leaving the woods, depositing you back on the paved path. Or, while on that dirt path, you can pick your way onto the unmarked (but fairly well-used) trails that lead to Moebius Nature Center. While the volunteer-run center is open only during scheduled programs and events, the grounds are open to hikers, and the pond provides a great place to listen to frogs and watch a surprisingly thick population of birds and butterflies.

Back on the paved loop trail, where the path curves left as you continue counterclockwise, you'll near a small picnic shelter. Just south from here, you can see the whole lake. Lily pads cover the water in places; this is an ideal spot to listen as frogs, birds, and bugs sing to you. The woods are thick again as you round the lake's western edge; several park benches are placed to take advantage of the resulting shade and birding opportunities.

Other than some basic grounds and trail maintenance, and the obvious care put into the Memorial Tree Garden, Sunny Lake's trees and vegetation have been left to their own devices. The snarled brush shelters a large population of rabbits, black and gray squirrels, fat robins, noisy jays, singing spring peepers, and a few harmless snakes.

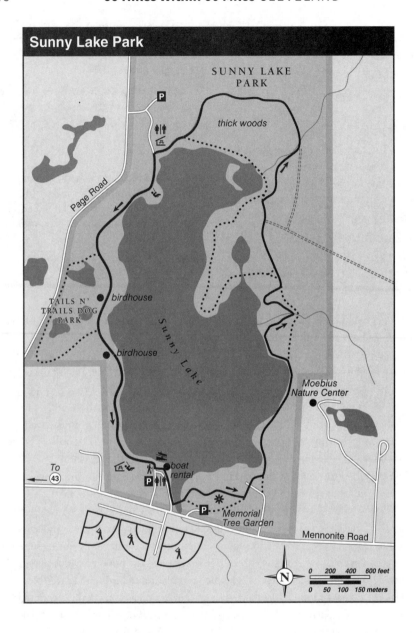

Sunny Lake Park

Returning to the main parking lot, you've logged at least 2 miles; perhaps 0.5 mile more if you explored the short nature trails. Over that distance, you've probably met up with a number of dog walkers, stroller pushers, and maybe a bike or two. Sunny Lake's loop is also a popular spot at lunchtime, as workers escape the nearby industrial parks, if only for an hour.

Nearby Activities

Sunny Lake Park's 463 acres offer plenty of activities. On the western side of the main parking lot, there are swings, volleyball courts, and horseshoe pits, plus a sledding hill that's popular in the winter. Pedal boats and rowboats can be rented at the park office. Catch-and-release fishing is allowed with a permit from the city. Aurora residents can launch their own nonmotorized crafts here for free; nonresidents pay a nominal fee for the privilege. Details are available at the website, **auroraoh.com/599/Sunny-Lake-Park,** or by calling 330-562-4333. Just east of the park and accessible by car off Mennonite Road, Moebius Nature Center hosts a variety of educational programs for folks of all ages. See the events schedule at the website, **mymnc.org,** or call 216-402-4361. For more hiking options, you can visit Tinkers Creek State Nature Preserve (see page 178), about 2.5 miles southwest of Sunny Lake.

GPS TRAILHEAD COORDINATES

N41° 17.473' W81° 19.096'

From the I-77/I-480 exchange, follow I-480 E 8.9 miles; keep right at the fork to continue on I-480 E for another 5.5 miles. Keep right at another fork to stay on I-480 E/ OH 14 for another 9.7 miles, and take Exit 41 (Frost Road). Turn left (east) onto Frost Road, and go 1.8 miles; turn left (north) onto OH 43/South Chillicothe Road. In 2.1 miles, turn right (east) onto Mennonite Road. Follow Mennonite about 1.5 miles east to the park's main entrance on the left at 885 E. Mennonite Rd.

37 Tinkers Creek State Nature Preserve

Eagle nests are so heavy that they sometimes fall down, like this one did.

In Brief

This 786-acre nature preserve offers great waterfowl and other wildlife viewing opportunities, as well as a peaceful, quiet marshland in which to be still and enjoy a bit of solitude.

Description

Though the parking area is on the north side of Old Mill Road, the main entrance to the preserve is across the street. But before you head south, make your way to the northeast end of the parking lot and follow the short Eagle Point Trail through the woods. The dirt trail through young deciduous trees may not impress you at first, but once you reach the raised observation platform, you'll be glad you made the trip. The vista that greets you—a wide expanse of marshy wetlands—is outlined by tall trees that eagles like to call home.

DISTANCE & CONFIGURATION: 2.8-mile balloon/figure eight	**ACCESS:** Daily, 30 minutes before sunrise–30 minutes after sunset; pets not allowed
DIFFICULTY: Easy	
SCENERY: Seven ponds, marshlands, herons, nesting Canada geese and wood ducks, beavers, raccoons, deer, snapping turtles	**WHEELCHAIR TRAVERSABLE:** No
	MAPS: USGS *Twinsburg;* also at trailhead and preserve website
EXPOSURE: Mostly shaded	**FACILITIES:** None
TRAFFIC: Light	**CONTACT:** Ohio Department of Natural Resources: 330-527-5118; **nature preserves.ohiodnr.gov/tinkerscreek;** Summit Metro Parks: 330-867-5511; **summitmetroparks.org**
TRAIL SURFACE: Dirt trail with some boardwalk	
HIKING TIME: 1 hour for three trails and observation time at the overlook	
DRIVING DISTANCE: 22 miles from I-77/I-480 exchange	

State naturalists found a nest that had fallen out of a tree (it happens; the nests are quite heavy!) and rehabbed the fallen home, so visitors could appreciate it here. It sits on the wet ground just out of reach, but close enough to get a good look at the amazing construction techniques of our national bird. An active nest across the marsh area may provide you with an eagle sighting while you're here. Once you've had plenty of time to admire the marvels of avian engineering, and maybe even an aerial display, retrace your steps back to the parking lot to begin the real hike.

When you cross Old Mill, you'll enter the preserve on a path that runs parallel to, and just a few hundred feet from, active railroad tracks, but they don't detract from what you're about to see.

The path narrows as it heads south. Not long after it narrows, about 0.3 mile south of the trailhead sign, the path forks—turn left (east). You'll soon step up on another portion of wooden boardwalk. About half of this 0.5-mile loop is boardwalk, necessary because it travels over marsh. Ohio's early pioneers liked to hunt here, but they were also wary of the squishy ground. Some referred to it as a "perilous" place, full of sinkholes and quicksand. Though the thick peat is messy, deerflies and mosquitoes are really all that hikers in this area have to fear today. You're likely to come upon deer or hear the slap of a beaver's tail as you near the pond. The boardwalk ends just about the time the pond comes into sight. The marsh, full of cattails, is on your right; the pond is on your left. The path can be quite muddy (this is a wetland, after all), and if your insect repellent fails here, you'll be sorry. Continue across the trail intersection and begin to circle the pond counterclockwise. Old-growth pines and young oak trees almost completely shade the trail. In the spring and summer, an abundance of ferns and wild purple violets line the path. Water in the pond itself is clean enough to watch crappie and turtles swimming around below the surface.

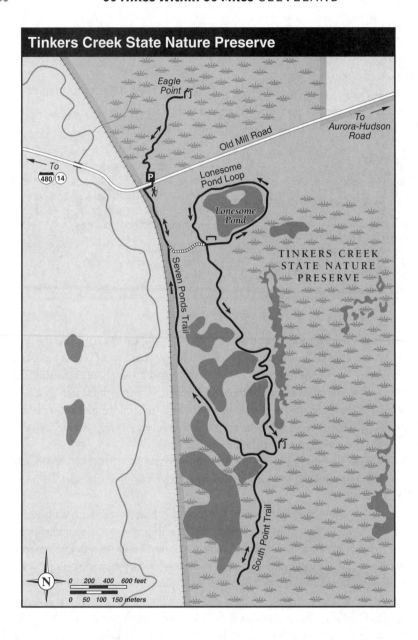

Several types of ferns dot the trail; in spring, a thick covering of mayapples appears. Their umbrella-like leaves shade the pretty white flowers. On the north side of Lonesome Pond, grass and roots have overtaken much of the trail, making for less sloppy footing, even on wet days. After circling the pond, leave it lonesome once more and head south. A bench at the intersection of Lonesome Pond Loop and Seven Ponds Trail is a good place to contemplate what you've seen and consider your next steps.

Seven Ponds Trail heads south from here. Follow it as it weaves around the small ponds (which total seven, as advertised) and leads to a wooden observation deck. The deck faces east, and from here you can see almost all of the marsh. Herons like to fly between here and nearby Sunny Lake Park (see page 174). It's a rare visit to either park that doesn't include a heron sighting. While this trail (and the whole preserve) sees little traffic, you may meet an avid birder or photographer here on the deck; it's popular with both.

When you can tear yourself away from the view, follow the path around a gentle bend to the right. Soon after, the path splits. Follow the left fork south to the tip of the "peninsula" surrounded by the open marsh. Shaded by beeches, oaks, and maples, this spur is especially pretty in the fall. When you return to the loop and head west, you'll make your way by and between the remaining ponds.

As you head north, the trail straightens out and, for the most part, it dries out as well. The railroad tracks are on your left, and the trail returns you to the intersection of Lonesome Pond Trail. With footsteps cushioned by the pine needles, you'll exit as quietly as you came in, slipping past the trailhead sign and crossing Old Mill Road.

Nearby Activities

If watching the waterfowl dive and splash made you want to drop a line in the water, go around the corner to the Tinkers Creek Area of Liberty Park (formerly Tinkers Creek State Park). There, just off Aurora Hudson Road, you'll find plenty of fish-friendly spots and a completely different set of trails. Serious bird-watchers will want to visit Aurora Sanctuary State Nature Preserve, a 164-acre property owned by the Audubon Society of Greater Cleveland. Access is available off East Pioneer Trail. For more information, contact the local Audubon Society at 216-556-5441, or visit **naturepreserves.ohiodnr.gov /aurorasanctuary.**

GPS TRAILHEAD COORDINATES

N41° 17.089' W81° 23.498'

From Cleveland, follow I-480 E 8.9 miles; keep right at the fork to continue on I-480 E for another 5.5 miles. Keep right at another fork to stay on I-480 E/OH 14 for another 9.7 miles, and take Exit 36 (OH 82/Aurora Road). Turn left (east) onto OH 82/Aurora Road, and go 0.8 mile. Make a slight right onto OH 82, and go 2.6 miles. Turn left (east) onto Old Mill Road, and go 0.8 mile to the small parking lot on the left (north) side of the road.

38 Tom S. Cooperrider-Kent Bog State Nature Preserve

The boardwalk is made of recycled plastic.

In Brief

Kent Bog is one of a handful of places in Ohio where small cranberries (on the state's list of threatened plants) make a stand. It is also home to what is probably the largest, southernmost stand of tamarack trees in the continental United States. Ancient history and modern ecology are both on display here: Visitors can see what's left of this 12,000-year-old bog from a boardwalk made of recycled plastic.

Description

Long, long ago, a retreating glacier left behind a giant ice cube. It was buried with silt, clay, and gravel. Eventually, the ice melted, forming a glacial kettle lake. Over the next few

DISTANCE & CONFIGURATION: 0.5-mile loop	**ACCESS:** Daily, sunrise–sunset; pets, bikes, and skates are prohibited.
DIFFICULTY: Easy	**WHEELCHAIR TRAVERSABLE:** Yes, the entire boardwalk is ADA compliant.
SCENERY: Rare bog plants and the birds and animals that relish them	
EXPOSURE: About half shaded	**MAPS:** USGS *Kent;* also at trailhead kiosk and preserve website
TRAFFIC: Moderate	**FACILITIES:** None
TRAIL SURFACE: Boardwalk	**CONTACT:** 330-527-5118; naturepreserves.ohiodnr.gov /cooperriderkentbog
HIKING TIME: 30 minutes	
DRIVING DISTANCE: 33 miles from I-77/I-480 exchange	

thousand years or so, the lake was covered by boreal plants and then completely filled in with peat. Today, in what is left of that ice cube, a tiny bog hosts rare plants, including sphagnum moss, Virginia chain ferns, small cranberries, and tamarack trees. It is a bog full of history, firsts, and rarities.

In 1985 the Tom S. Cooperrider–Kent Bog State Nature Preserve was the first state nature preserve purchased with money donated by Ohioans through a state income tax refund program. This state nature preserve, often called Kent Bog, was named to honor Tom S. Cooperrider, PhD, a nationally recognized botanist who played an instrumental role in discovering and protecting this unusual and important area.

The boardwalk was added in 1993, which also was a first. Paid for in part by a grant from the Division of Litter Prevention and Recycling of the Ohio Department of Natural Resources, the walkway is made of recycled milk jugs and water bottles. (See? What you recycle at home today, you may find underfoot tomorrow!)

A bog is a harsh environment; its climatic conditions are called limiting factors. Extremes in temperature, wetness, nutrient levels, and acidity significantly limit the plants that can survive in a bog. During summer, root level temperatures in the peat can be as much as 40° cooler than the surface temperature. Bogs favor plants that can thrive in an acidic, mineral-poor environment because nutrients from dead plants are tied up in peat and therefore not available to nourish the plants. That's one reason carnivorous plants tend to show up in bogs. Many other unusual species thrive here as well.

Sphagnum moss is one. This moss continually grows from the top while dying at the bottom. Sphagnum moss can hold up to 20 times its own dry weight in water, is more than twice as absorbent as cotton, and has antiseptic properties. Where it grows, it lowers root temperatures and oxygen levels. Its peculiar properties have earned it at least two footnotes in history: American Indians used sphagnum to diaper their babies; during the Civil War and World War I, doctors used the moss as emergency field dressings.

Small cranberries also grow here—one of the very few spots in Ohio they call home. Most people are surprised to see that cranberries are not so much trees as viny, woody shrubs that creep over the ground. Poison sumac is here too. Like its mean, nasty cousin

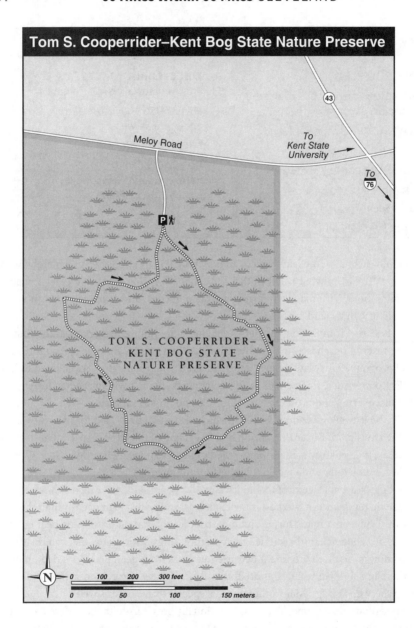

poison ivy, poison sumac has white berries. (Several other sumac species, which sport red berries, are harmless.)

If you visit the bog in the fall—October is your best bet—you'll notice that the needles on the tamarack trees have changed from green to yellow, and they may be falling off. They're not dying! Tamaracks are deciduous conifers, so they shed needles like other trees shed leaves. Tamarack trees love the cold; they grow as far north as trees can grow in

Canada. This far south, however, they are rare. Walk through the bog in the winter, when the tamaracks are nearly bare, and you'll be able to spot catberry, a bog holly identified by its bright-red berries.

To see all these and many other bog oddities, step onto the boardwalk trail from the south end of the parking lot. Turn left, following the loop clockwise. The walkway circles a sedge meadow and runs northeast through a marsh and wooded stretch of land. As you stroll through, you can stop along the way to read many educational plaques describing some of the bog's unusual conditions and inhabitants.

Six park benches placed along the boardwalk provide good places to observe wildlife. Birders will watch for rufous-sided towhees and berry-loving waxwings. The bog is also home to deer, foxes, and cottontail rabbits. Rare spotted turtles also live here, but it's unlikely that you'll see one. The spotted turtle is palm-sized, with brilliant yellow spots on its shell. To protect these slow bog residents, turtle tunnels were built into the boardwalk's underside. They allow the turtles to move freely about the bog, out of sight of most visitors as they walk over the boardwalk.

As you are leaving the bog, you'll cross a dry moatlike depression that surrounds it. The adjacent upland trees provide excessive shade and leaf litter to this trough around the bog. That—and the well-oxygenated runoff that enters here—allows other species to creep into the bog. The main peat mass, with its limiting factors that control bog ecology, is reduced and threatened by the invaders. Eventually, the bog will naturally go the way of the glacier, and its long history will be, finally, just history. Visit now, so you can say you were here when.

Nearby Activities

Head north from Kent on OH 43 to visit the bog's nearest relative, an alkaline fen. Herrick Fen (see page 136) in Streetsboro is about a 15-minute drive from here. Or head east to Ravenna to peer into pitcher plants (and other bog dwellers) at nearby Triangle Lake Bog. See **naturepreserves.ohiodnr.gov/trianglelakebog** for directions.

Wonder how these "relics from the ice age" relate to our modern way of life? Look to Portage Lakes State Park (see page 151) for a little perspective. While our Great Lake to the north and abundant rivers throughout Ohio get a lot of attention, the state has surprisingly few natural lakes and ponds. Many of those that once existed here have dried up and become bogs and fens. The Portage Lakes are a prime example of several natural lakes that survive and thrive. So why not go enjoy them before they evolve away?

GPS TRAILHEAD COORDINATES

N41° 7.760' W81° 21.225'

From Cleveland, take I-77 S about 30 miles to I-76 E. In 9.5 miles, take Exit 33 (OH 43). Turn left (north) onto OH 43, and go 1.7 miles. Turn left (west) onto Meloy Road. The bog's entrance is just 0.1 mile west of OH 43 in Kent.

39 Towner's Woods

The cross-country ski trails at Towner's Woods are well-used in the winter months.

In Brief

The 234-acre Towner's Woods is home to an ancient American Indian mound, as well as a number of creatures that require a variety of habitats: Woodpeckers, owls, and deer claim the forest, while eagles like to perch high above Lake Pippen, which is closed to recreation. The grassy fields along the southern perimeter of Towner's Woods provide the perfect spot for the rare American woodcocks, or timberdoodles, who perform their unusual mating dance on early spring evenings.

Description

Tucked away, unassuming Towner's Woods park, established in the mid-1970s, has evolved in its first four decades. Visitors enjoy its riches in many different ways. When the trails are snow-covered, sledding and cross-country skiing make the park a popular destination. During the summer months, it's a cool and shady spot to hike (or bike along the rail-trail), and fall draws folks who admire the forest's flurry of color, as well as many young runners who use the cross-country ski trails to train.

DISTANCE & CONFIGURATION:
5.8-mile balloon

DIFFICULTY: Easy, with a few hills

SCENERY: Fields, forests, wetlands, remnant prairie, lake views, a Hopewell American Indian mound

EXPOSURE: Mostly shaded

TRAFFIC: Light–moderate

TRAIL SURFACE: Dirt and grass

HIKING TIME: 1.5 hours

DRIVING DISTANCE: 31 miles from I-77/I-480 exchange

ACCESS: Daily, sunrise–sunset. Lake Pippen, part of the city of Akron's watershed, abuts the park and is off-limits to all but City of Akron Water Department workers.

WHEELCHAIR TRAVERSABLE: No

MAPS: USGS *Kent;* also at park website

FACILITIES: Restrooms and water in parking lot near trailhead; sledding hill, picnic tables, shelters, gazebo, benches. A portion of The Portage Hike & Bike Trail runs through Towner's Woods, extending west to Kent and east into Ravenna.

CONTACT: 330-297-7728; **portagepark district.org/parks-trails/towners-woods** and **portageparkdistrict.org/parks-trails /the-portage-hike-bike-trail**

In spite of all those visitors, the park somehow maintains its peaceful demeanor, inviting those who just want to enjoy a bit of nature's refreshing tranquility.

This hike explores two distinct areas: the rail-trail known as The Portage Hike & Bike Trail and Towner's Woods park. Trailheads for both sit on the eastern side of the parking lot. The park's wooded, hilly trails lead off to the left, but this hike begins to the right of a large park bulletin board, where you'll see a sign for The Portage. Tall oak and hickory trees stand on your left; a railroad track lies to the right. Follow the rail-trail about 100 yards into the trail where it forks. Turn right and follow the Butterfly Trail into the former farmland, strolling along a gentle, grassy hill. Birds and flying insects abound here, and it's a good spot to imagine how wide expanses of Portage County looked before trains and people rolled through in ever-increasing numbers. The Butterfly Trail is only about 0.5-mile long, so you'll soon return to the harder, flatter trail.

From there, you can continue east on The Portage, which is mostly shaded (at least until it crosses Red Brush Road), into the city of Ravenna and beyond. It's a great trail for cyclists and pedestrians too, but if you're here to hike forested trails, you'll want to return to the Towner's Woods trailhead. So instead, turn left onto the rail-trail, returning to the parking lot and the main trailhead.

Most of the trails through Towner's Woods wind through thick forests of oaks, maples, and pines to find shady and strikingly beautiful views of Lake Pippen on the west. More than 4 miles of interconnected trails are located throughout the park; all are well marked. My favorite route goes like this.

Follow Forest Path and then Meadow Loop to the east, past the sledding hill. Turn left to join the Brigham Ski Trail. Follow it north, over lots of hills. Soon after the cross-country ski trail turns left, heading west toward the lake, it intersects the aptly named Lakeside Trail. Tall oaks and pines run alongside, reaching heights of 50 feet or more.

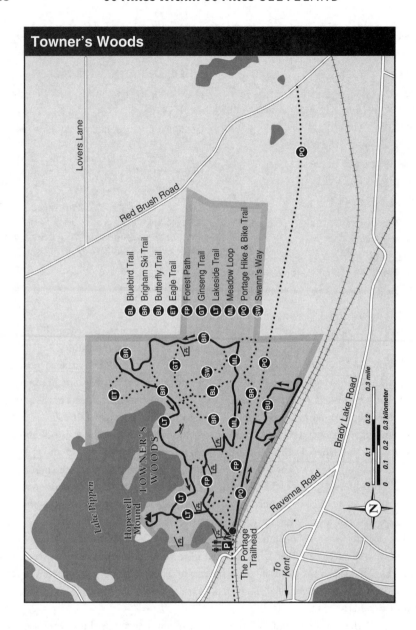

Towner's Woods

BL Bluebird Trail
BR Brigham Ski Trail
BU Butterfly Trail
ET Eagle Trail
FP Forest Path
GT Ginseng Trail
LT Lakeside Trail
ML Meadow Loop
PO Portage Hike & Bike Trail
SW Swann's Way

Lakeside Trail is skinny and rather sharply banked in some places. It drops down several railroad-tie steps to the lowest point in the park, just a couple of feet above the water level. Soon after, Lakeside leads you north onto a small peninsula, where you'll find the Hopewell American Indian mound.

The Hopewell people (and the mound) date to between 100 BC and AD 500. The mound was excavated in 1932, and 11 burials were found inside. The Hopewell culture had an extensive trading network that included communities from the Atlantic coast to the Rocky Mountains.

Unfortunately, the excavations weren't conducted as carefully as most are today, and some artifacts were undoubtedly lost in the process.

Whatever its prehistoric significance, the mound sits rather artfully on the top of a sandy knoll overlooking the lake. It's probably safe to say, at least, that long ago, the Hopewell found this spot as beautiful as we do today. Once you're done exploring the mound, head south to return to the trailhead.

Nearby Activities

In the middle of Towner's Woods, you'll find a sizable sledding hill and two large picnic areas with grills. Beckwith Orchards (**beckwithorchards.com**) is just around the corner from Towner's Woods. The orchard is open seasonally, and the Beckwith family is usually happy to allow visitors to wander through its gardens—a nice extra hike in itself.

Officials from the Portage Park District, the cities of Ravenna and Kent, and Kent State University (**kent.edu**) have worked together to connect Towner's Woods with other recreational venues via The Portage. The path is paved as it goes west from Lake Rockwell about 2.5 miles into the city of Kent; heading east, the trail extends from Red Brush Road to Peck Road in Ravenna. (Paving of that section was underway as this edition went to print.)

Though there's no access to the lovely Lake Pippen, just north of Towner's entrance on Ravenna Road is an access point and small parking lot where canoe and kayak enthusiasts can put in and paddle away.

Special thanks to Christine Craycroft, executive director of Portage Park District, for reviewing this section.

GPS TRAILHEAD COORDINATES

N41° 10.329' W81° 18.703'

From I-77, take Exit 156 and merge onto I-480, heading east. In 6.6 miles, keep right to stay on I-480 E, and in another 5.5 miles, keep right again to stay on I-480. Continue to follow I-480 E another 10.6 miles to OH 14 in Streetsboro. Follow OH 14 E 1.7 miles, and turn right onto OH 43, heading south about 3.9 miles to pass through Twin Lakes. Turn left (southeast) onto Ravenna Road, following it 2.1 miles to the well-marked park entrance.

40 Walborn Reservoir

Fishing is popular at Walborn Reservoir.

In Brief

Wander through a lush, fertile landscape typical of Stark County farmland in this park. The reservoir offers excellent opportunities for bird-watching; an active eagle nest has contributed to the growing local population.

Description

In northern Stark County, near Alliance, Stark County Park employees are busy. Not only do they host many activities and classes at Walborn Reservoir, but the marina is also popular with serious anglers as well as recreational boaters.

DISTANCE & CONFIGURATION:
2.6-mile figure eight and out-and-back
(parking is in the middle, so do either side
as a separate loop if you choose)

DIFFICULTY: Easy

SCENERY: Bluebirds, wildflowers, ospreys,
eagles, loons, possibly signs of beavers

EXPOSURE: Mostly shaded

TRAFFIC: Marina, busy; trails, lightly
used

TRAIL SURFACE: Dirt and grass

HIKING TIME: 1 hour

DRIVING DISTANCE: 53 miles from
I-77/I-480 exchange

ACCESS: Park: April–September: Daily,
sunrise–9 p.m. October–March: Daily,
sunrise–7 p.m.; marina open April–
September

WHEELCHAIR TRAVERSABLE: No

MAPS: USGS *Limaville;* also at park kiosk
and park website

FACILITIES: Restrooms, water, concession, and phone at marina

CONTACT: 330-935-0367; **starkparks
.com/park.asp?park=5**

From the northeast end of the parking lot, head east and follow along the edge of the farm field, drinking in the fresh smells that only good growing soil can provide. As you wind right (south), you'll eventually head into the woods, quite possibly meeting up with some horses out hiking (with their riders). Continue following the Shoreline Trail as it heads west to reach the shore, where you'll be able to see the dam to your left. You'll soon join up with the Loop Trail as the path continues to crank clockwise. Be still and listen—few things are as peaceful and calming as water lapping gently on a shore. The going is relatively easy, as long as you don't mind a bit of slogging through the sandy soil.

While visiting here in the summer, you'll probably see bright-yellow cloudless sulphur butterflies along this stretch. Spring–fall, keep an eye out for herons, a pair of bald eagles, and the occasional ospreys, especially in August and September, when the low water beckons waterfowl with tasty surprises. The work of the Ohio Department of Natural Resources to repopulate this area with ospreys has paid off, and you may see one circling overhead. The birds resemble gulls, but if you see what you think is a gull dive feet-first into the water, then you've spotted an osprey.

As you make your way along the shore, you'll find yourself crawling over fallen tree branches and creeping over the carcasses of expired crayfish. Ohio has about 20 species of crayfish. Many varieties burrow in the mud and are active only at night. That's fine with the owls, which like to eat the little crustaceans. Live crayfish also make good bait, but when you fish here (or anywhere!), it's important to use only native species. Bait that swims away can establish itself in the new habitat, and some species, such as the rusty crayfish, are so aggressive that they can wipe out native varieties and wreak havoc on a delicate ecosystem.

As you skirt the shore, you'll have to be nimble to stay dry, clambering over trees and tree roots that hug the bank. With roots half in water, half in soil, some of the roots appear to have grown into thin air when the water is low. Also, when the water is low, especially along the western shore, you'll appreciate displays of driftwood and rock art. Over the years, water and wind mold unique shapes and etch unusual patterns in both media. The

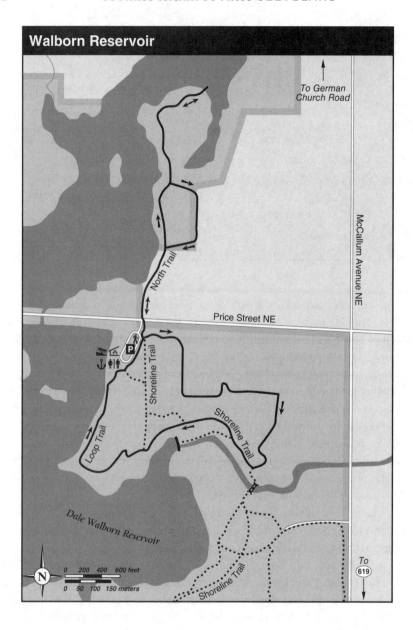

pieces are displayed against a background of variegated dirt and clay. Take a flat rock and skip it into the lapping water before you return to the marina, at about 0.7 mile. Follow the boardwalk around the dock, and then cut across the parking lot (northeast) to return to your starting point.

This time, cross Price Street and head north to visit the typically quieter side of Walborn. You'll go up a slight hill and find yourself amid tall maple, chestnut, hickory, and pine trees. The soft dirt path wiggles through the woods, turning slightly away from the water before bending left to offer you another look at Walborn's wet playground. A barely noticeable fork in the trail gives you an option to veer to the right and west. Depending on the season and recent weather, you may choose the west side of this mini-loop, as it tends to be drier. Regardless, the two paths merge back into one in a very short distance. The west portion of the loop leads you away from the shore ever so briefly, and then returns to the water's edge again where it ends. If you have a fishing pole, this is a good place to drop a line.

Fish and frogs keep the insect population hopping; ducks, herons, and other birds let their voices be heard. Near the water's edge (and all along the short North Trail), you might see some evidence that beavers are working here; park employees are working just as diligently to keep them from creating their own dam here. Time will tell who will win. Flip a coin, place your bets, and (unless you want to stay and fish) turn around to follow your path back to Price Street and the parking lot.

Nearby Activities

There's a 10-horsepower limit on the reservoir, making Walborn a good place to bring small sailboats or canoes. The marina also rents kayaks by the half hour. Fishing is good here year-round; bass is a common catch.

For more hiking and boating nearby, follow Price Street east about 3 miles to Deer Creek Reservoir, another Stark County Park with a lake loop trail. A trail that connects the two parks is in the planning stages. For information about interpretive programs or about the status of connecting trails, go to **starkparks.com/park.asp?park=6** or call 330-477-3552.

GPS TRAILHEAD COORDINATES
N40° 58.662' W81° 10.805'

Follow I-77 S toward Akron, taking Exit 129 to I-76 W. In 1.7 miles, take Exit 18 to I-277/US 224 E toward Canton. In 3.9 miles, continue onto US 224 E, and go another 13.8 miles. Turn right (south) onto OH 44 S/Ravenna Louisville Road, and turn go 3.1 miles. At Pontius Street NE, turn left (east). In 1.9 miles, veer right onto Price Street NE. Trailhead parking is on the east side of the reservoir in 1.7 miles.

41 West Branch State Park

Michael J. Kirwan Dam—the reason West Branch State Park is here

In Brief

If you can ignore all the fun that massive West Branch State Park has to offer and make it to the business end of the park—the dam—you'll find a place where time almost seems to stand still.

Description

With so much to explore in West Branch State Park, you might want to stay a few days. (No kidding—the campground is very popular; see the key info for contact information.) The park sprawls over more than 5,300 acres; the lake comprises another 2,650 acres. The dam is on the far east end of the park. In fact, it's not part of the park at all. Rather, the park is part of it.

Micheal J. Kirwan Dam and Reservoir is a recreational area owned by the U.S. Army Corps of Engineers. The adjacent land and reservoir is leased to the Ohio Department of Natural Resources, which manages it as a park. Boring details aside, here's why you'll want to go: The dam provides one of the most sweeping vistas in northeast Ohio, and one that stretches out a sunset to the delight of visitors.

From the parking lot, traipse up a short hill to the dam access road. It's closed to vehicular traffic but is as wide as a city street. Almost any time you go, you'll find other walkers, joggers, and cyclists here, but it never seems crowded at all.

DISTANCE & CONFIGURATION: 3-mile out-and-back	**DRIVING DISTANCE:** 35 miles from I-77/I-480 exchange
DIFFICULTY: Easy	**ACCESS:** Daily, 6 a.m.–11 p.m.
SCENERY: Heavily wooded beech-maple forest, a few stands of pine, lake views, overlook	**WHEELCHAIR TRAVERSABLE:** No
	MAPS: USGS *Ravenna* and USGS *Windham;* also at trailhead and park office (5708 Esworthy Road)
EXPOSURE: Mostly shaded	
TRAFFIC: Moderate on weekdays; heavy on weekends	**FACILITIES:** Restrooms, phone, picnic shelter, and grills by boat ramp
TRAIL SURFACE: Partially paved	**CONTACT:** Park office: 330-296-3239; **parks.ohiodnr.gov/westbranch;** U.S. Army Corps of Engineers: 330-358-2247
HIKING TIME: 1 hour	

The dam access road really deserves a better name, but it is what it is. A rose by any other name, right? From the minute you're on the dam roadway, you have a bird's-eye view of the reservoir, or at least the western end of it. You'll be heading northwest as you cross the dam, and while it's pretty anytime, I highly recommend timing your visit to late afternoon or early evening, so you can stroll as the sun begins to set.

As hikes go, this one is as straight and flat as it gets—you're walking over a dam, remember? The sun playing over the vast stretch of water to your left (as you head out) can play tricks on your mind. Let it. That's part of the magic of this hike—you don't have to pay attention to where you're going; there's absolutely no way to lose the trail.

The trail's unnatural straightness and unusual position, well above surrounding landmarks, can also mess with your perception. It's 2 miles from one side of the dam to the other. At times as you walk across, it will seem as though you're nearly there; at other points, as if you'll never get there. And when you get there—the other side of the dam, that is—you'll turn around only to find that the return trip plays the same tricks on your mind. Again, let it. Hiking is at least as good for your mind as it is for your body.

Because timing is important with sunset hikes, here's some advice: Don't underestimate the time you'll need to cross the dam and return. It's tempting to stop, savor a view, watch a water-skier in the distance, gawk at a deer or a hawk . . . so allow some extra time in your plan. And take your camera. The sunset views here make almost every photographer look like a professional.

Nearby Activities

West Branch State Park—named for the west branch of the Mahoning River, which was dammed in 1965—offers a variety of wet and dry activities for folks of all ages and interests. In addition to some popular snowmobile/bike trails, an 8-mile segment of the Buckeye Trail loops through the park's western end. Add to that about 20 miles of nature and

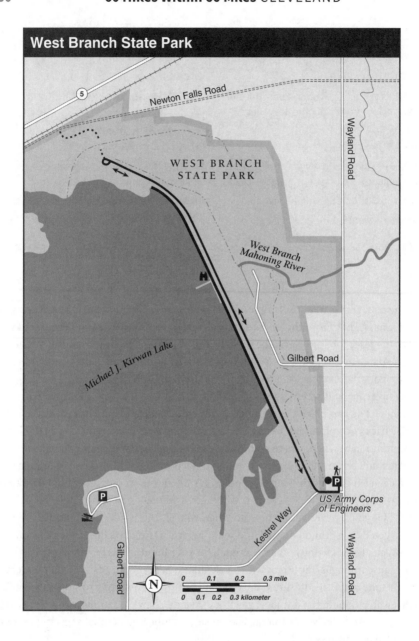

West Branch State Park

bridle trails, not to mention the paved path across the dam causeway, and there's enough day hiking here to keep you and your boots busy for a month.

The park's campground is extremely popular and hosts a variety of family-friendly events, including the extremely popular Christmas in July and the annual Halloween Campout in October.

A 700-foot swimming beach, complete with restrooms and a vending area, is located on the southeastern side of the reservoir. Admission is free. The marina rents boats, ranging from canoes and kayaks to ski boats and WaveRunners. Call the marina at 330-296-9209 or visit **westbranchmarina.com.**

GPS TRAILHEAD COORDINATES

N41° 9.433' W81° 4.636'

From I-77, take Exit 156 and merge onto I-480, heading east. In 6.6 miles, keep right to stay on I-480 E, and in another 5.5 miles, keep right again to stay on I-480. Continue to follow I-480 E another 10.6 miles to OH 14 in Streetsboro. Follow OH 14 E 11.6 miles, and exit onto OH 5. Merge onto OH 5 E, and in less than a mile, veer right to stay on OH 5. Follow OH 5 about 7 miles east of Ravenna and turn right (south) onto Wayland Road. Follow Wayland 1.3 miles, and turn right (west) onto Gilbert Road, where a small parking lot and the Corps office are located.

42 Wingfoot Lake State Park

This once-private park is now open to everyone.

In Brief

This property was operated as a recreation area for employees of the Goodyear Tire & Rubber Co. for several decades. When it opened (again) in 2010 as Ohio's 74th state park, interest in its history was revived, and the park began building a new generation of fans.

Description

It's a safe bet that most visitors to Wingfoot Lake State Park don't go just to hike the 800-plus-acre property. Land-based attractions here include a miniature golf course, a disc golf course, tennis courts, a fenced dog park, and several large and well-appointed picnic shelters. In addition, the 444-acre lake offers fishing and boating opportunities. And while hikers almost certainly won't find solitude here, they will find a wide and gently rolling paved path circling the park. From that path, visitors can enjoy plenty of people-watching opportunities as well as gain an interesting perspective on the Goodyear Airdock and its place in history.

From the northeast side of the main parking lot, you'll probably see some disc golf or sledding enthusiasts—depending on the season—before you reach the paved trail, near one of the large enclosed picnic shelters. The path heads slightly downhill under the

DISTANCE & CONFIGURATION: 1.5-mile loop	**DRIVING DISTANCE:** 41 miles from I-77/I-480 exchange
DIFFICULTY: Easy	**ACCESS:** Daily, 6 a.m.–11 p.m.
SCENERY: Lake and cultivated woodlands, unique view of the Goodyear Airdock	**WHEELCHAIR TRAVERSABLE:** Yes
	MAPS: USGS *Suffield*; also at kiosk
EXPOSURE: Mostly shaded	**FACILITIES:** Boat rental, disc golf, miniature golf, playgrounds, sledding hill, tennis and volleyball courts, several enclosed shelters, grills and picnic tables, and dog park
TRAFFIC: Moderate–heavy	
TRAIL SURFACE: Paved	
HIKING TIME: 35 minutes	**CONTACT:** 866-644-6727; **parks.ohiodnr .gov/wingfootlake**

shade of mature oaks, maples, and other deciduous trees. You'll soon come to the park's boat concession area, where visitors can rent pedal boats and small pontoon boats in the warmer months.

As you continue along the gently rolling path on the edge of Wingfoot Lake, you're likely to encounter a few anglers hoping to hook bass, bluegills, crappie, brown bullheads, walleyes, or yellow perch. But while the landscaped grounds and lake views are sure to please visitors, for most, those sights will take a backseat to the supersize structure on the southern edge of the lake: the Goodyear Airdock.

The massive blue-and-silver building where hundreds of airships have been erected is a rather obvious reminder that The Goodyear Tire & Rubber Co. makes more than tires. In fact, Wingfoot Lake Airship Base is the oldest airship base in the United States. In 1925 Goodyear built and operated the first US commercially licensed blimp flown using helium; it has sold several different airship models to the U.S. Navy. On clear days from late spring through early fall, visitors will often see (and hear!) the company's blimps take off and land across the lake.

Regardless of the activity in the air, there's plenty to see and do on the ground on the north side of the lake. Follow the path as it curves along the shore and then inland, and you'll see multiple structures enjoying new life in this park, from the canteen where Goodyear employees and their families once purchased candy and other items (now used primarily for office space) to three large enclosed picnic shelters, one with a built-in sound system. Approximately in the center of the park, you can stop to enjoy a game of miniature golf or watch younger visitors frolic on two large playgrounds.

As the paved path continues to loop around the park's perimeter and back to the main parking lot, you'll pass volleyball and boccie courts before reaching a dog park on the northwestern side of the property.

Returning to the main parking lot, you'll know just where you are: The historical stone sign featuring Goodyear's distinctive winged-foot logo marks the spot.

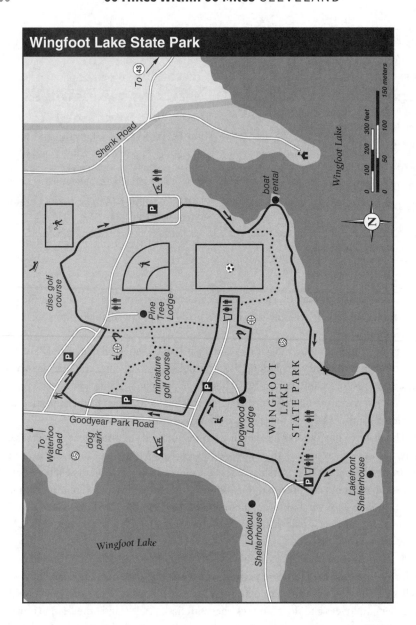

Nearby Activities

Wingfoot is situated near other popular Ohio state parks, including Quail Hollow to the south (see page 156). The more rustic, but also lovely, Mogadore Reservoir to the north is owned by the city of Akron (330-628-3343; **akronohio.gov/cms/Water/Watershed_ Mogadore**).

Great scenery—not all of it natural—can be found at Wingfoot Lake.

GPS TRAILHEAD COORDINATES

N41° 1.085' W81° 21.707'

Follow I-77 S toward Akron, taking Exit 129 to I-76 W. In 1.7 miles, take Exit 18 to I-277/US 224 E toward Canton. In 3.9 miles, continue onto US 224 E, and go another 6.7 miles. Turn right (south) onto Martin Road, and in 0.3 mile, turn left (east) onto Waterloo Road. Follow Waterloo about 1 mile east to the park entrance at Goodyear Park Boulevard.

SUMMIT (NORTH), LORAIN, AND MEDINA COUNTIES

Gorge Metro Park (see page 243)

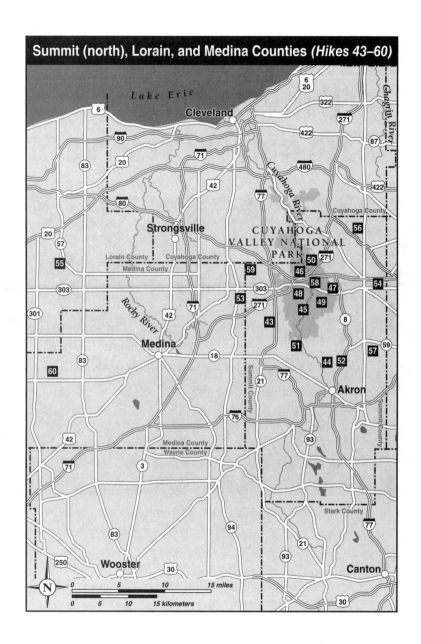

Summit (north), Lorain, and Medina Counties *(Hikes 43–60)*

43 Bath Community Activity Center & Bath Nature Preserve

Enjoy the shady spots in this preserve, as the trails are mostly exposed.

In Brief

This Summit County nature preserve looms just up the hill from an unassuming community park. Take a tour of the smaller park, and then sneak into the vast preserve through a tunnel.

Description

When you pull into the parking lot off busy North Cleveland–Massillon Road, you may not be expecting much. An oversize wood statue of Mingo Chief Logan greets you by the trail kiosk, and his imposing figure might distract you for a moment. After you've introduced yourself to the chief, visit the trail kiosk to get the lay of the land, and then head toward the trailhead—just to your right—to wander through a small stand of trees.

DISTANCE & CONFIGURATION: 1.25-mile balloon and 3-mile figure eight	**DRIVING DISTANCE:** 21 miles from I-77/I-480 exchange
DIFFICULTY: Moderate with some steep sections	**ACCESS:** Daily, 7 a.m.–sunset
SCENERY: Deer and hawks in the oak-maple-hickory forest, frogs and other aquatic life in the ponds, bog-loving tamaracks, broad prairie hillsides	**WHEELCHAIR TRAVERSABLE:** No; though a long stretch of trail is paved, most of it is very steep.
	MAPS: USGS *West Richfield;* also at the trail kiosk at Bath Community Activity Center off North Cleveland–Massillon Road
EXPOSURE: Mostly exposed	
TRAFFIC: Moderate	
TRAIL SURFACE: North Fork Trail, crushed limestone and pavement; King, South Woods, and Creekside Trails, dirt and grass	**FACILITIES:** Restrooms and water fountain at trail kiosk and at picnic shelters found at either end of trail
	CONTACT: 330-666-4007; **bathtownship .org/Parks%20folder/BNP%20page%20 parks.htm**
HIKING TIME: 1.5–2 hours	

The well-shaded path brings you quickly to a pretty, working water pump ready to cool you off; not far east of there, you arrive at the tennis courts. Follow the footpath beyond the tennis courts and you'll soon find two soccer fields and a picnic area.

Traipse by the soccer fields and peer into the woods: You've found King Trail, just a short jaunt through the woods.

The path rolls along under the shade of oak and shagbark hickory trees. Squirrels scurry about, picking up their nuts. When you reach a fork, follow the trail as it veers west to the shelter, where a picnic might be under way; if it's a weekend, chances are that you'll catch a ball game of some sort in progress. Alternatively, continue a little farther south before the trail loops back to the playground. Retracing your steps back to where you began, you might shrug and say, "Well, it's just your average community park." But wait—there's more. Much more.

Turn your back to Chief Logan and walk to the north end of the parking lot, where a tunnel invites you to slip away from the community park to the nature preserve. Follow the crushed limestone path through the tunnel, and keep going. The trees give way to wide-open sky, and soon you're climbing, climbing, climbing to meet it. Just as you're thinking, "I could use a bench to rest," one appears. When you continue on (and up) the path, it takes a few turns to maneuver around a long sledding hill. At about this point, you have a choice to make: Stay on the exposed gravel trail, or take a stroll on a shadier path (Hillside Trail) for hikers only. (Bicycle traffic is permitted on the limestone North Fork Trail, but it's not heavily used.) I suggest staying on the long, clear path, North Fork Trail, until you reach the Round Top, near Ira Road. Along the way, you'll probably see a few trail riders (one trail here is reserved for equestrians only), and you'll also find the entrances to South Woods and Creekside Trails, for hikers only. Don't go there—yet.

Bath Community Activity Center & Bath Nature Preserve

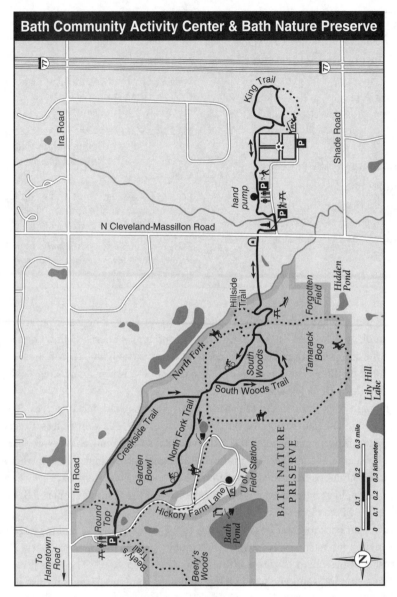

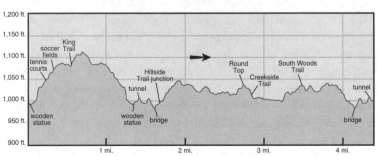

By the time you reach the northern end of North Fork Trail, you will have passed two small ponds and quite possibly a few folks dropping a line in one or the other. (Catch and release is mandated in the preserve, and fishing is allowed only April–November.) At the top of the trail, you'll note a few residential developments along Ira Road. The North Fork Trail has been extended into several of those developments, but once it crosses the road, the trail ventures into private property. From the top of the hill, you can appreciate a sweeping view—and understand why your legs might need a rest.

Once your energy returns, start back down North Fork, but this time, give in to your wanderlust and veer off the wide-open path to the northeast and enjoy the shadier Creek-side Trail as it skirts North Fork Creek. Soon after it returns you to the limestone path, follow South Woods Trail to the south for a 0.4-mile sojourn from North Fork's oh-so-uniform surface. While butterflies love the wide-open, prairielike fields along North Fork, you'll hear woodland insects on the two more rugged trails, providing welcome variety in this expansive preserve.

The 410-acre Bath Nature Preserve was once part of the Raymond Firestone Estate. The township purchased the land in 1997, and the preserve opened for public use in 2001. Students from the University of Akron are permitted to use part of the land for biology and ecology field studies. In 2005 the North Fork Trail was completed and connected to Bath Community Activity Center. And it has been waiting here for you, on the other side of the tunnel, ever since.

Once you've finished exploring the various plant communities—bog, old-growth forest, wetlands, and grasslands—return to the trailhead and nod to the chief. Now you understand why he's looking up the hill.

Nearby Activities

If you forgot your sled, fishing pole, tennis racket, bicycle, and soccer ball and are looking for something else to do, consider taking North Cleveland–Massillon Road south to OH 18, and then follow Smith Road to Sand Run Metro Park for some more hiking.

GPS TRAILHEAD COORDINATES
N41° 10.746' W81° 38.163'

Follow I-77 S toward Akron and take Exit 143 for OH 176 (toward I-271). Turn right (west) onto Wheatley Road/OH 176 and take a quick left onto Brecksville Road, which becomes North Cleveland–Massillon Road. In 2.9 miles, the Bath Community Activity Center and trailhead parking will be on your left, at 1615 N. Cleveland–Massillon Road.

44 Cascade Valley Park: Oxbow & Overlook Trails

The Cuyahoga River is home to countless creatures.

In Brief

Oxbow Trail winds through the Cuyahoga River Valley, north of Akron. From the burbling rapids of the Cuyahoga River to a cardiac climb to a fabulous vista, this hike offers variety over a short haul. Though a steep sledding hill and several ball fields are nearby, hikers can get away from the action in the center of the park to enjoy this remote wooded trail and great views of the surrounding valley.

Description

If Oxbow Trail were a book—well, it would be a novella—you'd describe it to your friends by saying, "It started a bit slow, but before I was halfway through, I hoped it wouldn't end." In fact, Oxbow packs so much scenery in its little loop that you'll be glad you picked it up. It's also a great casual dining spot. Oxbow's many picnic tables are placed to provide comfortable space between diners. It's entirely possible to enjoy a picnic supper here,

DISTANCE & CONFIGURATION: 1.7-mile loop	**DRIVING DISTANCE:** 35 miles from I-77/I-480 exchange
DIFFICULTY: Moderate, with all the climbing at once; not for weak knees	**ACCESS:** Daily, 6 a.m.–11 p.m.; leashed dogs allowed
SCENERY: Marsh, river, woodlands, rumbling rapids of Cuyahoga River	**WHEELCHAIR TRAVERSABLE:** No
EXPOSURE: Shady throughout, except for exposed steps	**MAPS:** USGS *Peninsula* and USGS *Akron West;* also at park website
TRAFFIC: Moderate most days; bustling on evenings and weekends	**FACILITIES:** Restrooms (may be closed in winter) and water; emergency phone at southernmost entrance
TRAIL SURFACE: Dirt carpeted with leaves; first leg can be muddy; steps and bridge slippery when wet	**CONTACT:** 330-867-5511; **summit metroparks.org/ParksAndTrails /CascadeValleySouth.aspx**
HIKING TIME: 45 minutes	

with the lilting of the Cuyahoga to entertain you, and never catch wind of the dinner conversation at another table.

Because the trail is damp along the river and shady throughout, it's a great place for insects to hang out, so it's advisable to apply some bug repellent when visiting. The insects attract birds, of course, and you're likely to hear, if not see, woodpeckers at work on some of the 60-foot-tall (and taller) trees along the way. Mostly deciduous varieties—tall oaks and black cherries—shade the trail.

Head south-southwest (counterclockwise) from the trailhead to meander through several marshy turns (in dry weather) or large puddles (in wetter times). In the spring, you'll be met by white trilliums (Ohio's official state wildflower) and a variety of violets that like the wet ground along the river.

About 0.2 mile into the trail, the path turns sharply left, heading north, and meets up with the Cuyahoga River. Traveling along the river's edge, you'll soon hear several rapids providing a musical accompaniment to the sound of your feet on the dirt and leaves. Approach very quietly and you may see great blue or green-backed herons fishing for dinner. Crouch down to look into the clear water and you'll probably notice a handful of empty freshwater shells.

Soon you'll pass a small clearing with several picnic tables. (Here you can also see the parking lot to your left.) Continue past the tables along the main trail. It remains flat and almost entirely shaded until you come to a railroad-tie staircase. Take a deep breath— you're about to climb up 98 (or so) steps. At the top, pause, take another deep breath, and turn around. The view is worth it.

Once you've caught your breath, you're faced with a decision: to do the Overlook Trail extension or not. It's just 0.5 mile—do it! (If you skip the extension, you'll take several smaller stairways down the hill and encounter a small footbridge that may be slippery when snowy or wet. You'll also find a few more picnic tables along the way. The Overlook extension rejoins the main trail before too long.)

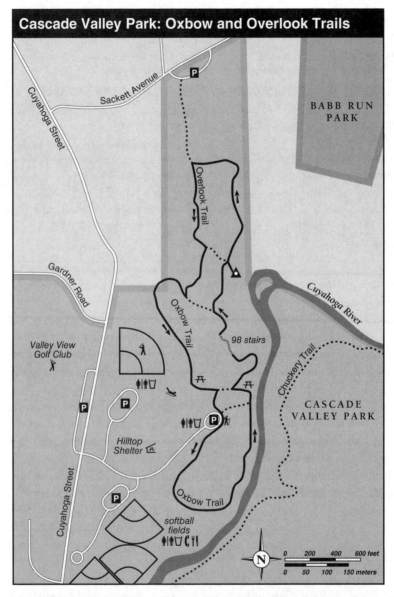

Cascade Valley Park: Oxbow and Overlook Trails

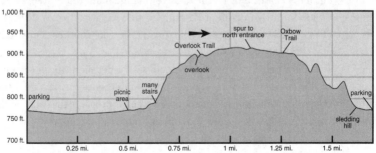

The Overlook Trail heads to the right a bit, up a bit more, to the right a bit, and up a bit, and you soon realize how great the view is going to be from the overlook. (*Note:* The overlook deck has been closed for long stretches in the past so crews could secure its position on the eroding hillside. At the time of this writing, it was open again. Whether the deck overlook is open or not, the view from this ridge is worth the extra hike.) The trail itself ventures close enough to the side of the cliff that you can see for miles, with feet planted safely on terra firma. After a few minutes admiring the view, amble on along the path, which veers to the left and then proceeds to work its way down the trail, with a few stairs here and a handrail there.

As you descend, the sledding hill comes into view. During the winter and early spring, thanks to the lay of the land, you'll be able to keep an eye on the sledding hill—and your car in the parking lot—during most of the final third of the loop. In the summer, you'll have less of a view but will continue to enjoy the trees' air-conditioning effect.

When there's no snow and no ball game, you won't have much company on the trail. Hilltop Shelter, above the sledding hill, is available for free on a first-come, first-serve basis. The shelter, which holds about 40 people, can also be reserved for a fee.

Nearby Activities

Oxbow is popular in winter, thanks to its sledding hill and in-ground toboggan runs. The hill is lighted for night use, and cross-country skiers frequent the trail when it's snow-covered. The park service maintains a 24-hour seasonal information line at 330-865-8060.

While you're here in the south end of Cascade Valley Park, stop and see the Signal Tree, so you can say you did. Local lore says that American Indians purposefully formed the lowest branches of the burr oak tree, which has grown here for at least three centuries, so the branches would grow at right angles to signal the way to an important trail. The tree isn't talking, but it's quite a topic of local conversation.

Within a couple of miles, you'll find plenty of other hiking trails. Visitors can hike from the Oxbow Trailhead to Gorge Metro Park (see page 243) via the Highbridge Trail (3-plus miles) or head over to Babb Run Bird and Wildlife Sanctuary, a Cuyahoga Falls city park about 2 miles north that can be seen from the overlook.

GPS TRAILHEAD COORDINATES
N41° 7.321' W81° 31.229'

Cascade Valley Park: Chuckery/Oxbow Area is located off Cuyahoga Street, between Uhler and Sackett Avenues, in north Akron. From Cleveland, follow I-480 E to I-271 S. From I-271, in 3.4 miles, take Exit 18A (OH 8). Merge onto OH 8 S, and go 11.3 miles. Exit at Broad Boulevard. Turn right (west) to follow Broad for 1.7 miles, and then turn left (south) onto 26th Street. In 0.2 mile, turn right (southwest) onto Sackett Avenue. In 0.6 mile, turn left (southeast) onto Cuyahoga Street. Follow Cuyahoga Street about 0.5 mile; the park sign will be on your left. (*Note:* There are two entrances to the Chuckery/Oxbow Area on Cuyahoga Street; take the northernmost entrance. An alternate entrance is also available on Sackett Avenue.)

45 Cuyahoga Valley National Park: Beaver Marsh Boardwalk & Indigo Lake

Indigo Lake

In Brief

Once a (real) dump, this area was transformed by some enterprising beavers into a viable habitat, and not only for themselves. Today more than 50 bird species nest here each year. Since the National Park Service (NPS) built a wooden boardwalk across the marsh and connected it to the popular Towpath Trail, humans can enjoy its serene beauty too.

Description

Can you say "extreme makeover"? In the early 1980s, this stretch of land was a soggy dumping ground, full of junk from a nearby car repair shop and assorted other trash. Even before volunteers from the Portage Trail Group, Sierra Club, and NPS could reclaim the land, a couple of beavers took matters into their own, um, paws. Park volunteers and employees helped the beavers by clearing out the debris, and the NPS opened a stretch of boardwalk across the marsh. From a single dam to a community of beavers, muskrats,

DISTANCE & CONFIGURATION: 3.5-mile out-and-back

DIFFICULTY: Easy

SCENERY: Beaver marsh and pond, more than 500 types of plants and animals

EXPOSURE: Boardwalk, almost entirely exposed; southernmost section of hike, shaded

TRAFFIC: Moderate–heavy (expect some bikes)

TRAIL SURFACE: Towpath Trail, wooden boardwalk and paved; trail connector and Indigo Lake, dirt and grass

HIKING TIME: 2.25 hours for walking and watching; an additional 30 minutes for Hale Farm

DRIVING DISTANCE: 17 miles from I-77/I-480 exchange

ACCESS: Daily, 7 a.m.–11 p.m.

WHEELCHAIR TRAVERSABLE: Boardwalk, yes; Indigo Lake connector and Hale Farm, no

MAPS: USGS *Peninsula;* also at **nps.gov /cuva/upload/HuntFarm_WEB2009.pdf**

FACILITIES: Restrooms at Hunt Farm Visitor Center, Indigo Lake, and Ira Road trailhead

CONTACT: 330-657-2752; **nps.gov/cuva**

mink, and many other animals and birds, the marsh and its adjacent land constitute one of the most diverse spots in the 33,000-acre Cuyahoga Valley National Park (CVNP), a reclaimed habitat for more than 500 types of plants.

The marsh's diversity and its accessibility (wheelchairs and strollers can easily navigate the wide, 530-foot-long boardwalk via the hard-packed, crushed limestone surface of the Towpath Trail) have earned it a spot on the Ohio Division of Wildlife's list of 80 official Watchable Wildlife sites. It's also an extremely popular spot with photographers, so don't be surprised if you have to dodge a tripod here and there as you walk along.

As you follow the Towpath Trail south from Bolanz Road, you'll pass by private farmland usually sporting cornstalks. During the summer growing season, the loud shots of corn cannons sound periodically in an effort to scare away the crows and other animals that enjoy the corn. (Take home some corn to enjoy without the noise when you purchase it at the nearby farm market—it really is some of the best in northeast Ohio.)

As you make your way toward the boardwalk, you'll see signs pointing to Hale Farm Trail. Note that it leads to Indigo Lake, and it's worth the extra mile it will add to your hike. But for now, you're on your way to this hike's namesake attraction.

When you reach Beaver Marsh, you're sure to notice the cattails. They are an important food source for many animals; when this area was first settled, they were also a staple in the diets of the American Indians and early settlers, who made meal from their long stems. (Speaking of diets, this might make you grateful for your next salad.)

Now that you've reached Beaver Marsh, you want to see beavers, right? Here are some basic tips: First, beavers are nocturnal. That means they do most of their home building and repair work in the evening. Visit near dusk and look for them as they swim. Watch for a wake, the V-shaped disturbance in the water created by a beaver's tail as it

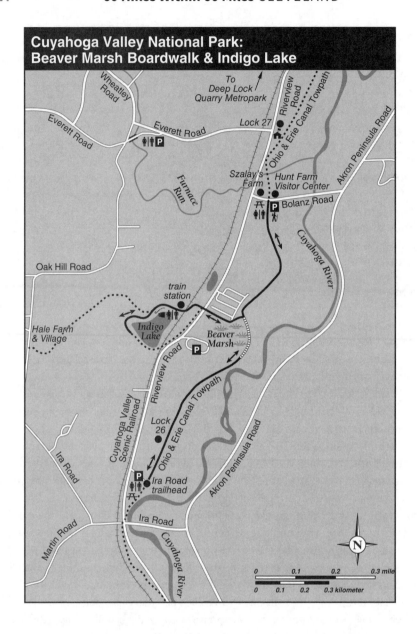

Cuyahoga Valley National Park:
Beaver Marsh Boardwalk & Indigo Lake

swims. Keep an eye on the water lilies, and you may see a hungry beaver grab a leaf to eat. He will roll the leaf and hold it in his paw like a green cigar as he nibbles on it. Also look for mink and muskrats that live in and around the water. Muskrats build their homes along the banks of ponds and streams and occasionally on top of beaver lodges.

Even if you don't see beaver, you're almost certain to see herons, a variety of ducks, and numerous smaller birds—active almost any time, in any season, on this stretch of the Towpath. Many benches dot the boardwalk, offering places to sit and watch.

The boardwalk offers such beautiful scenery, and so much to see, that you may not want to leave at all. And as you head south from the boardwalk, Ira Road trailhead (just past Lock 26) makes a natural turnaround point, giving you a chance to revisit the boardwalk. (Of course, if you don't turn around, you can follow the Towpath Trail into Akron, south into Zoar, and beyond.) But turn around you must to return to your car.

As you cross back over the boardwalk, even on a second (or third or fourth) look, it's still hard to imagine that this spot was once a dump. Clearly, this was a successful makeover. The beautiful result: a safe haven for hundreds of animals and plants and a great escape for the humans who make their homes on either side of the valley.

Just north of the boardwalk, you can take a pleasant excursion to Indigo Lake by following the signs to Hale Farm and Indigo Lake Station. The Cuyahoga Valley Scenic Railroad train stop is less than 0.5 mile due west. But you're not here to catch the train; you're here to admire the lake.

Indigo Lake is small but lovely; its name was inspired by its deep-blue hue. I am often surprised when I talk with frequent visitors to CVNP who are not familiar with Indigo Lake. In my opinion, it's one of the prettiest, most tranquil spots in the park. So let's just keep that between you and me, OK?

Walking around the lake will add about a mile to your Towpath trek. Follow the limestone path and signs pointing to Hale Farm & Village until the path is paved as it heads uphill. Before you reach the top, the path splits. (The paved portion rolls on to Hale Farm.) Follow the grassy trail as it bends to the left, rising above the lake. The trail continues, curving to the east, and begins rolling downhill, depositing you to a broad, open field and a wide-open view of the southern end of Indigo Lake. As picturesque as it is now, it's hard to believe that this lake started life as a gravel pit and quarry. Today, it's another successful makeover story, and a spot that provides satisfying views for park visitors, as well as a home for many birds, butterflies, and insects.

Once you've soaked up the loveliness of Indigo Lake, retrace your steps up the hill and back to the train station and Towpath. (The grass-and-dirt trail heads into the woods and then crosses the railroad track and Riverview Road, providing an alternate route if you'd prefer to complete the lake loop, but it will require you to walk north on the berm of Riverview Road a few hundred feet to return to the Towpath Trail.)

Once back on the Towpath, head north to return to the lot.

Nearby Activities

If you choose to visit Hale Farm & Village, you'll find yourself way, way back in time. The working museum is owned and operated by the Western Reserve Historical Society. It offers an accurate representation of life in the Western Reserve, circa 1826. Candle-making, glassblowing, and pottery demonstrations are regular fare; special seasonal events, such as the annual Maple Sugar Festival and Civil War reenactments, draw large crowds. For hours, admission rates, and an events schedule, call 877-4253-3276 or visit **wrhs.org.**

Hunt Farm, just north of the parking lot along Bolanz Road, is a visitor center that doubles as a museum. It highlights the role of the small family farm as a force in the valley's development. Just a long stone's throw from the visitor center, Szalay's Farm (4563 Riverview Road) sells fresh produce, from spring strawberries and summer sweet corn and apples to fall pumpkins and other squash.

CVNP offers hundreds of educational and recreational events throughout the year. Pick up a free calendar of activities at a park visitor center or check the online calendar at **nps.gov/cuva.**

GPS TRAILHEAD COORDINATES

N41° 12.018' W81° 34.326'

Follow I-77 S toward Akron and take Exit 143 for OH 176 (toward I-271). Turn left (east) onto Wheatley Road/OH 176. Go about 2.9 miles toward Riverview Road. Veer left onto Everett Road, and then in 0.6 mile turn right onto Riverview Road, heading south. In 0.3 mile, turn left onto Bolanz Road. Find trailhead parking on the south side of Bolanz Road.

46 Cuyahoga Valley National Park: Blue Hen Falls Trail to Buttermilk Falls

Pretty Blue Hen Falls is just the beginning of this hike.

In Brief

Sure-footed trekkers can follow the creek past quiet Blue Hen Falls down to the bottom of 20-foot-tall Buttermilk Falls.

Description

"Now I'm a *real* hiker!" my 5-year-old said, soon after we started out for her first time on the trail. Her brother earned similar bragging rights a few years later. This short but steep trail offers kids an introduction to "real" hiking, while its beauty appeals to explorers of all ages.

DISTANCE & CONFIGURATION:
1.3-mile out-and-back

DIFFICULTY: Moderate

SCENERY: Two waterfalls, meandering creek, deep ravine, deciduous forest, really big rocks

EXPOSURE: Completely shaded

TRAFFIC: Moderate

TRAIL SURFACE: Dirt trail: rooty, rocky, and steeply banked in places

HIKING TIME: 45 minutes for hiking; allow extra dawdle time at the falls

DRIVING DISTANCE: 15 miles from I-77/I-480 exchange

ACCESS: 24/7, but best done during daylight hours; tread carefully when wet or icy

WHEELCHAIR TRAVERSABLE: No

MAPS: USGS *Northfield;* also at park visitor centers and park website

FACILITIES: None

CONTACT: Boston Store Visitor Center, just east of Riverview Road at 1548 Boston Mills Rd.: 330-657-2752; **nps.gov/cuva**

Enter the trail at the north end of the parking lot. It was paved long ago, so gravel and dirt are more apparent than asphalt. Gradually, you'll descend about 30 feet as you follow the path; then the ground levels out and the trail turns sharply right.

The trail to Blue Hen Falls continues gently sloping toward a sturdy bridge and wooden bench facing the quiet falls. This picturesque point is an ideal conversation spot and about the only place to sit along the trail.

Blue Hen Falls is pretty, without a doubt. It tumbles 15 feet over the edge of a massive hunk of sandstone, landing in Spring Creek—and, if you keep going to the next (I believe, more exciting) waterfall, you'll soon find your feet in that creek. Continue on the trail past the bench to a narrow wooden bridge. Follow it across Spring Creek and you'll see the blue blazes of the Buckeye Trail rising to the left. Rather than following those blazes, continue on the path as it veers right, descending through the deep, thickly forested ravine.

During the spring, the pockmarked limestone and shale seem to glow with a green hue; in the fall, they appear to blush a bit under the reddening leaves. Many of the national park's moss and fern varieties thrive in this cool, moist hollow.

The path winds as it descends 50 feet or so. Fallen trees can make it somewhat challenging to stay on the trail, which twists and bumps over the hunks of fallen trees and along the edge of the ravine. The trail is narrow in places. You'll have to jump or splash your way across the creek at least three times, and you may cross trickles and runoff water several other times, depending on recent rainfall. The widest points you'll cross are 15–20 feet across, but don't worry—a slip here will land you in just a few inches of water. At the first wide crossing, look to your right (east) to see where layers of Bedford shale and Berea sandstone slammed into each other, forming the geological equivalent of a layer cake in the hillside. In the winter, when trickles of water freeze in place while falling down the wall, it's easy to imagine that the cake has been recently frosted and is awaiting a giant's first bite.

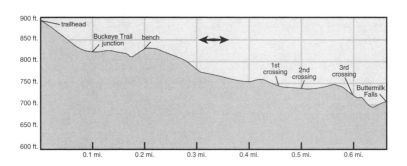

Cuyahoga Valley National Park: Blue Hen Falls Trail to Buttermilk Falls

Ohio & Erie Canal Towpath Trail

Riverview Road

Buckeye Trail

CUYAHOGA VALLEY NATIONAL PARK

Cuyahoga River

Boston Mills/ Brandywine Ski Resort

Boston Store Visitor Center

Buttermilk Falls

train station

Spring Creek

Boston Mills Road

Buckeye Trail

271

Blue Hen Falls

Blue Hen Falls Trailhead

P
P

271

80

80

N

0   0.1   0.2   0.3 mile

0   0.1   0.2   0.3 kilometer

Elevation profile:

900 ft. — trailhead
850 ft. — Buckeye Trail junction — bench
800 ft.
750 ft. — 1st crossing / 2nd crossing / 3rd crossing
700 ft. — Buttermilk Falls
650 ft.
600 ft.

0.1 mi.   0.2 mi.   0.3 mi.   0.4 mi.   0.5 mi.   0.6 mi.

Because the trail forms a crescent around the top and bottom of the falls, you can hear Buttermilk Falls before you can see it. Follow the trail as it bends right after the second wide creek crossing. The trail then heads down a final, sharp decline and a hairpin turn to the left before reaching the pool at the bottom of the falls. The pool at the point closest to the falls is several feet deep, so it is not safe for children to be unsupervised there. Whether or not you're willing to wade in, let your eyes adjust to the shadowy world under a few inches of water, and you are likely to see a small toad or tiny crayfish playing hide-and-seek among the large, flat shale stones.

On your way back up, stop about 20 feet above the second creek crossing. If you didn't notice on the way down, pause on your climb to appreciate your avian companions—the creek has created a popular corridor for woodland birds.

After passing the bench near the top of the trail, pause again to take in Blue Hen Falls. After viewing her louder, longer sister at the opposite end of the trail, you're likely to appreciate Blue Hen's unique, quiet beauty from a different perspective.

Nearby Activities

If you want a snack, more hiking, or both, take Boston Mills Road about 0.3 mile east of Riverview Road to the Boston Store Visitor Center. On the south side of the road sits the old company store, dating back to 1836. It has been given new life as a visitor center in the national park. In addition to the maps and information you'll find there, you can cross the street to a small snack shop where ice cream, beverages, and other trail essentials await, next to the Towpath Trailhead.

Just around the corner on Riverview Road you'll find Boston Mills/Brandywine Ski Resort (800-875-4241; **bmbw.com**), which has tubing runs in addition to several slopes for skiers.

GPS TRAILHEAD COORDINATES
N41° 15.384' W81° 34.360'

Take I-77 S to Exit 146 (Richfield/Brecksville). Keep right and then turn right (south) onto Brecksville Road/OH 21. In 0.5 mile, turn left (east) onto Boston Mills Road. In 1.1 miles, turn left (north) onto Black Road, and then make an immediate right (east) onto West Boston Mills Road. The entrance and parking areas are 2 miles east of Black Road. The small parking lot on the north side of Boston Mills Road holds just a few vehicles; additional spots are located in the overflow lot on the south side of the road.

47 Cuyahoga Valley National Park: Haskell Run, Ledges, & Pine Grove Trails

The ledges are naturally air-conditioned.

In Brief

This hilly combination of three trails visits some of my favorite spots in Cuyahoga Valley National Park, including a pioneer cemetery, awe-inspiring caves and ledges, and arguably the best spot in the valley to watch a sunset. For beginning hikers, especially little ones, start with the Haskell Run Trail. You can also shorten this hike by taking Ledges Trail to return to Happy Days Lodge.

DISTANCE & CONFIGURATION: 4-mile figure eight	**DRIVING DISTANCE:** 23 miles from I-77/I-480 exchange
DIFFICULTY: Moderate, with difficult sections	**ACCESS:** Daily, sunrise–sunset
SCENERY: Large rock outcrops, cave, valley overlook, forest, streams	**WHEELCHAIR TRAVERSABLE:** No
	MAPS: USGS *Peninsula;* also at park visitor centers and park website
EXPOSURE: Mostly shaded	**FACILITIES:** Portable restrooms located in Happy Days parking lot; restrooms and water available at Ledges and Octagon Shelters
TRAFFIC: Moderate–heavy near the cave on Ledges Trail; lighter traffic on Pine Grove Trail	
TRAIL SURFACE: Mixed—from large stones to dirt and gravel	**CONTACT:** 330-657-2752; **nps.gov/cuva**
HIKING TIME: 2 hours	

Description

From the parking lot, you'll cross under OH 303 through a 200-foot-long lighted tunnel; emerge to find yourself on the edge of the Mater Dolorosa Cemetery, which dates to 1869. Its inhabitants include Civil War soldier Thomas Coady and his parents, who lived to be 93 and 83 years old. (We'll never know the secret to their longevity, but we can guess that they walked a lot.) Many of the cemetery's other souls rest in mystery, as their names have long since faded from their sandstone markers.

The short but steep Haskell Run Trail abuts the southern edge of the cemetery. Step onto it, and continue straight ahead. Soon the path veers left and then turns to the right and drops about 30 feet, crossing a short wooden footbridge over the meandering creek for which the trail is named. From here, the trail bends sharply left, working its way up toward the base of the Ledges Trail. Arriving at the top of 20 or so steps, turn left onto Ledges Trail and follow the signs to Ice Box Cave. While the destination sounds refreshing (and it is), getting there requires a bit of work. Footing can be challenging on Ledges Trail because you'll climb over too many rocks to count—some left by glaciers' work, others placed by human hands.

In the 1930s the Civilian Conservation Corps (CCC) carefully created stairways out of the indigenous stones to provide hikers with a safer path. You will appreciate their work for both its form and its function. The CCC's mission, in part, was stated in a 1918 report of the U.S. Department of the Interior, which declared that "particular attention must be devoted always to harmonizing of these improvements with the landscape." Along this trail (and many other places in the park), you'll see evidence of the CCC's adherence to this goal.

Before you reach Ice Box Cave, you'll be called into one of the skinny, cool crevices along the right side of the path. Giant walls of Sharon conglomerate (300-million-year-old rock formed of cemented sand and small quartz pebbles) seem to have been dropped like a giant child's blocks, scattered across the Ledges area, creating a playground of sorts for

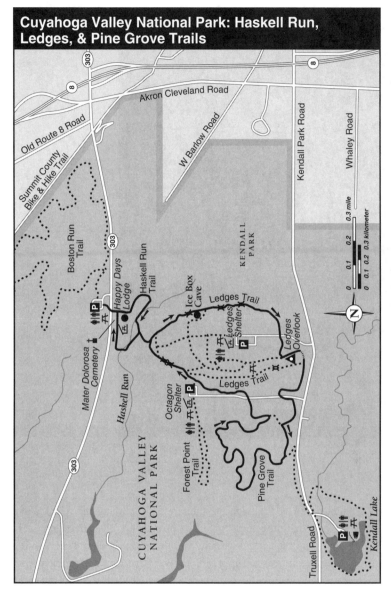

Cuyahoga Valley National Park: Haskell Run, Ledges, & Pine Grove Trails

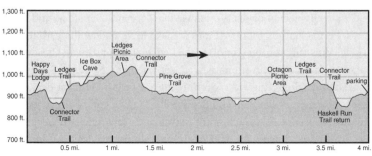

Another example of the Civilian Conservation Corps' hard work

average-size humans like us. Park signs prohibiting rock climbing and warning of the dangers of falling off the sometimes-slippery cliffs are posted here. Heed the signs, but have fun.

While the surrounding rocks naturally cool the entire Ledges Trail, you'll notice a distinct drop in temperature as you approach Ice Box Cave. South of the cave, you'll cross two tiny streams. Farther south, the trail veers right and leads you across the park's driveway to the Ledges Picnic Area. The trail rises a bit, revealing the south end of a large, open field where people on blankets often vie for space amid kite fliers and dogs chasing flying discs. Permanent restroom facilities are also here. Follow the path up another 30 yards to a sign directing you left (south) to the Ledges Trail or straight ahead to visit Octagon Ledges overlook. The overlook is a sunset-watcher's paradise. Sitting on the flat expanse of rock, you're facing west, overlooking the valley. On most days, you can see well past the communities of Bath and Brecksville. Many nights, a crowd gathers here to catch the short sunset performance, and I've watched a few times when viewers actually applauded as the sun slipped out of sight. It is an almost magical spot in this beautiful valley. Move on for now (you won't want to finish the hike without the benefit of daylight), and plan to come back another time to enjoy the nightly show.

The Ledges Trail continues just south of the overlook point, veering west and dropping down 41 wood-reinforced steps into the forest. A sign at the bottom of the steps points right (north) to complete the Ledges Trail loop, but you should continue straight through the cool forest, toward Pine Grove Trail. You'll cross the park road that leads to the Octagon Shelter and get a brief view of Truxell Road, about 200 yards to your left. Most days, the woodpeckers and the wind in the trees will distract you from any traffic noises that may come from the road.

Soon the trail turns right, heading north, where you'll notice a few pines amid the tall aspen, beech, and maple trees. About 2 miles into the trail, you'll see a sign noting the connector to Lake Trail, also part of the Virginia Kendall Unit of the park.

Midway through the climbing, twisting Pine Grove Trail, you'll find yourself overlooking a deep ravine and a small footbridge. Two sharp left turns and a 30-foot drop later, you'll cross that bridge and climb up again, this time ascending 66 wooden stairs. (As you huff and puff, remember to thank the Cuyahoga Valley Trails Council volunteers who built them.) As soon as you catch your breath, you leave Pine Grove on the connector, heading east to cross over the Octagon Shelter access road again. Follow the signs to the Ledges Trail and Happy Days Lodge, veering left to complete your clockwise jaunt around this rocky place.

Your final 0.25 mile is the second half of Haskell Run, so turn left at the junction with this trail. Your legs will get one more workout as you climb up a gravel trail and then a dozen stone steps to arrive on the western edge of the field adjacent to the lodge. Several grills and picnic tables here may seem rather inviting at this point, as you have likely worked up an appetite on the trail. Go back through the tunnel to return to your car.

Nearby Activities

Happy Days Lodge (formerly a visitor center) is open only for special events, including concerts and lyceum speakers often discussing topics related to the national parks. To find out what's going on at Happy Days Lodge and elsewhere in the park, call 330-657-2752, or visit **nps.gov/cuva.**

If you like, bring your bike and helmet. Trailhead parking for the Towpath Trail is off OH 303 about 2 miles to the west (in Peninsula), and parking for the paved Summit County Bike & Hike Trail is located just east of here, at the intersection of OH 303 and Olde Route 8 Road.

GPS TRAILHEAD COORDINATES
N41° 13.894' W81° 30.471'

From the I-77/I-480 exchange, take I-480 E to I-271 S. Take Exit 18 to take OH 8 south to OH 303. On OH 303, head west to find Happy Days Lodge parking lot, on the north side of OH 303, approximately 1 mile west of OH 8.

48 Cuyahoga Valley National Park: Plateau Trail

Chestnut Pond is a haven for green frogs.

In Brief

While Cuyahoga Valley National Park is full of great scenery, the Oak Hill area offers a special treat for the eyes. Here you'll encounter a series of S-curves that wiggle through the woods, following a ravine. A lovely change of scenery greets you at almost every turn on this loop trail.

Description

Enter the trailhead at the eastern end of the Oak Hill parking lot. A trail map is posted there on a park bulletin board. Both the shorter Oak Hill Trail and the outer loop of Plateau Trail begin to the left, or north, of the sign. A few grassy steps and a short wooden bridge later, the trails diverge. Oak Hill Trail turns to the right and loops around the highest point of the plateau in just 1.5 miles. But to do the shorter loop is to miss most of the hills, and much of the fun, of the longer and varied trail.

DISTANCE & CONFIGURATION:
4.8-mile loop

DIFFICULTY: Moderate

SCENERY: Pine and deciduous forests, three ponds, lush hemlock ravine

EXPOSURE: Mostly shaded

TRAFFIC: Light

TRAIL SURFACE: Dirt, with short stretches of grass and gravel

HIKING TIME: 2 hours

DRIVING DISTANCE: 16 miles from I-77/I-480 exchange

ACCESS: 24/7. Two restricted trails, one on either side of Meadowedge Pond, are clearly signed. They lead to the Cuyahoga Valley Environmental Education Center (CVEEC) and are authorized for CVEEC use only.

WHEELCHAIR TRAVERSABLE: No

MAPS: USGS *Peninsula;* also at trailhead kiosk, most park visitor centers, and park website

FACILITIES: Restrooms at trailhead

CONTACT: Cuyahoga Valley National Park: 330-657-2752; **nps.gov/cuva**; Cuyahoga Valley Environmental Education Center: **conservancyforcvnp.org/education?**

So stay on Plateau Trail, heading north, as the trail bends left and climbs gradually beneath the cover of hemlock trees. For a few paces, the old trees give way to meadow bushes and growth. This is one of the few stretches of trail where you'll be able to see the sky, as much of the way is completely shaded by hemlocks and deciduous trees. Half a mile into the trail, you'll cross another bridge and come to Chestnut Pond.

Small and easy to dismiss, the pond is a haven for amphibians who apparently take quite a bite out of the local insect population. (Translation: You can afford to stand on the pond's edge, looking and listening for frogs, without being bothered by mosquitoes.) As you turn and leave the pond, the trail turns sharply to the right. You're about to have one of those aha moments or, perhaps more accurately, an ooh-and-aah moment. Only a few steps from Chestnut Pond you'll find a long, long, long corridor of tall pines as visually stunning as they are fragrant. As you stroll through the hallway of pines, try to keep your feet on the ground while you gaze up at their tops, 60 feet or so above you.

At the western end of the pine corridor, the path veers right again. Gravel and grass work together to keep this stretch of trail nice and dry. Heading north, you'll begin to see evidence of the hard work put into this trail, which was completed in 1997. More than a dozen small culverts have been created alongside and underneath the trail. Designed and laid with care, they are both unobtrusive and necessary. As you round the loop and head east, the ravine is only a few feet from the trail. It's worth a few careful side steps to peer over the edge (beware, though—hearty poison ivy hides among the Virginia creeper and young oaks). The ravine is only about 10 feet deep here, but keep an eye on it; it grows wider and deeper as you continue on the trail.

At 1.5 miles, you'll pass a sign indicating a connector trail to Sylvan Pond. If you follow it, you'll also find the short (1.5-mile) inner loop, Oak Hill Trail. But for now, stay on the Plateau Trail; you have a lot to look forward to.

Cuyahoga Valley National Park: Plateau Trail

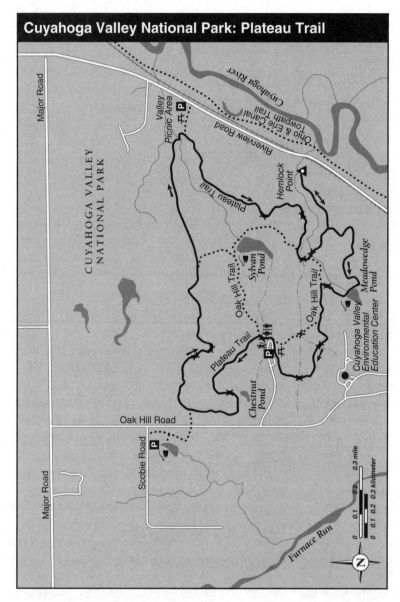

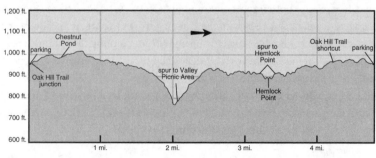

Plateau Trail is less used than many trails in this national park.

Less than 2 miles into the trail, tree buffs will find a section of the path loaded with multi-trunked trees. Is there a proper name for this? If there is, it's elusive, but children—who tend to name things more expediently than botanists—call them two-headed and three-headed trees. Call 'em what you will, but watching for them along this section may take your mind off the fact that you're heading uphill for most of the next 0.8 mile. As the trail bends to the right, you'll pass over a feeder stream to Sylvan Pond (unnoticeable during dry periods) and head south, easing downhill. Soon you'll cross another footbridge, this one high enough to warrant leaning over the railing for another look at the ravine.

Just past the 3-mile mark, you'll climb a bit more and veer left to Hemlock Ravine, where a sign directs you to a short side trip. The 0.2-mile, out-and-back trail to Hemlock Point is to your left. Unless you need to conserve your energy, you should take the opportunity to enjoy the overlook. Back on the main trail, you'll follow a series of S-shaped curves. In fact, the trail turns you this way and that, barely righting itself (and you) between the crooks as it slopes up slightly, and then takes you down a few feet, to the right. Here you'll see that the twisting served a purpose: Directly in front of you is the beautiful Meadowedge Pond—and you didn't even see it coming.

To arrive at Meadowedge Pond in the late spring or summer is perhaps the hiker's equivalent of a carnival visitor leaving the midway's relatively constant panorama for a spectacular, if brief, sideshow. The pond vista is an oasis of color and song. Orioles, gold-finches, and yellow warblers spin colorful, dizzying circles around the pond. Frogs bound in with a splash as you walk by and then scold you for interrupting their day. Lily pads cover much of the pond's surface, and cattails stand like a stockade fence around much of the perimeter, as if protecting it from too-eager visitors.

Linger here and enjoy the show; the colors and sounds offer an amazing contrast to the quiet, forested trail behind you. When you're ready for yet another change of scenery, follow the wide, grassy trail to the right, heading north into the shade of pines and hemlocks. The trail unfurls again in a series of S-curves to reach a sign indicating the Oak Hill Trail straight ahead. You can follow it from here back to the parking lot, or continue on Plateau Trail by turning left. For the sake of finishing what you've started, stay on Plateau Trail.

The ravine is on your right at this point, and the trail is at its flattest. Still, it's not straight, snaking along the last 0.75 mile in the now familiar S pattern. Near the end of the trail, you'll ease down a gentle slope, in the company of young hemlock trees, to emerge in an open grassy area surrounded by picnic tables and—in the spring and summer, at least—a lovely show of wildflowers, including oxeye daisies, coltsfoots, and clovers. It's somehow fitting that Plateau Trail manages to get in this final change of scenery as the curtain goes down on your hike. The show is over and the parking lot is on your right; you can leave, but you probably can't forget what you've seen here.

Nearby Activities

Up for another hike with dazzling views? Nearby Salt Run (see next page) offers exactly that. Hungry? You're also within a 5- to 10-minute drive of the historical village of Penin-sula, which has a plethora of restaurants and several seasonal farmers markets.

GPS TRAILHEAD COORDINATES
N41° 13.177' W81° 34.563'

Follow I-77 S toward Akron and take Exit 143 for OH 176 (toward I-271). Turn left (east) onto Wheatley Road/OH 176. Go 2.8 miles, and turn left onto Oak Hill Road. Go north about 1 mile, and the entrance to Oak Hill Picnic Area is on your right. (East Siders may prefer to take OH 8 south to OH 303, heading west 3.5 miles to Riverview Road, and then following it 0.6 mile south to Major Road. Turn right, following Major Road west 1.5 miles; then turn left onto Oak Hill Road, and go about 1 mile.) The entrance to Oak Hill Picnic Area (and the trails) is on the eastern side of Oak Hill Road. Follow the driveway 0.2 mile east to the parking lot.

49 Cuyahoga Valley National Park: Salt Run Trail

Prettier than your average parking lot view

In Brief

Hikers get a hilly workout while traveling through the former farm and estate of Hayward Kendall. Rolling meadows; shady creek crossings; and layers of moss, pine needles, and ferns provide a feast for the eyes. An optional 1-mile loop encircles beautiful Kendall Lake, which was created by the Civilian Conservation Corps (CCC) in the 1930s.

Description

Five rolling hills come together to greet you in the Pine Hollow parking lot. There are picnic tables aplenty here, and the view is always grand. On snowy days, the hills are alive with the sounds of little folks on sleds. Fog nestles in the lower areas in the morning; on a sunny afternoon, you can see acres and acres of, well, pines and meadows. Frankly, the

DISTANCE & CONFIGURATION: 3.3-mile loop

DIFFICULTY: Moderate–difficult

SCENERY: Beech-oak forest with hemlocks and pines, rolling hills, meandering creek

EXPOSURE: Completely shaded

TRAFFIC: Moderate

TRAIL SURFACE: Dirt and clay, steeply banked in places

HIKING TIME: 90 minutes for Salt Run; allow 30 minutes more for Lake Trail

DRIVING DISTANCE: 20 miles from I-77/I-480 exchange

ACCESS: 24/7

WHEELCHAIR TRAVERSABLE: No

MAPS: USGS *Peninsula;* also at trailhead kiosk, park visitor centers, and park website

FACILITIES: First-aid station, restrooms, and picnic tables at trailhead parking

CONTACT: 330-657-2752; **nps.gov/cuva**

parking lot vista is so pretty that you may have to pull yourself down to the lot's western end, where you'll find the trailhead. Come on—this is only the beginning.

Follow trail signs from the western end of the parking lot, over the rolling hills, and down about 10 feet to enter a dirt path. Turn left at the Salt Run sign to follow the trail clockwise. Meandering downhill, you'll soon cross a short footbridge. A shortcut to your right is best ignored—you'd miss much. Follow the trail as it bends left and heads uphill. For much of this hike, the trail rolls up and down, 10–30 feet at a time. The surface is rooty and uneven in places; this is a trail for sturdy boots, not sneakers.

Another curve to the left brings Quick Road into view, about 30 yards to the left of the trail. The road and the trail grow closer, then nearly together. The trail is covered with gravel for this short stretch. It's over soon—the white arrow on a trail marker beckons you off the road as the path darts back into the forest. And what a path it is—about 3 feet wide, it is the only level surface along the significant slope of the ravine. The ravine falls sharply to your right; you're beginning your descent into the densest part of the forest. A fork in the trail is signed—the right turn will lead you home sooner, via the shortcut trail (a loop of about 2.2 miles). Go straight instead, and you'll be rewarded with more gentle curves and steep drops, until you reach the bottom of an old field.

Enjoy the lower area of the Salt Run floodplain here, with its cool air and thick mosses; soon enough, you'll be making up the difference with a series of short but steep climbs. Pine stands rise ahead of you, the flatland is below you, and you're in for another hill—this one, about a 30-foot climb.

Salt Run Trail is part of the former farm and estate of Hayward Kendall. He willed 430 acres to the state with the request that the land be used as a park and be named for his mother, Virginia. The CCC dammed and developed Kendall Lake in the late 1930s. The area was transferred to the National Park Service in 1978, becoming one of the first complete units in the Cuyahoga Valley National Recreation Area. Today the Pine Hollow and Salt Run area is a mix of successional forest and old meadow. You'll find a beech-oak forest with a hearty population of grapevines and the occasional spicebush (stop and smell

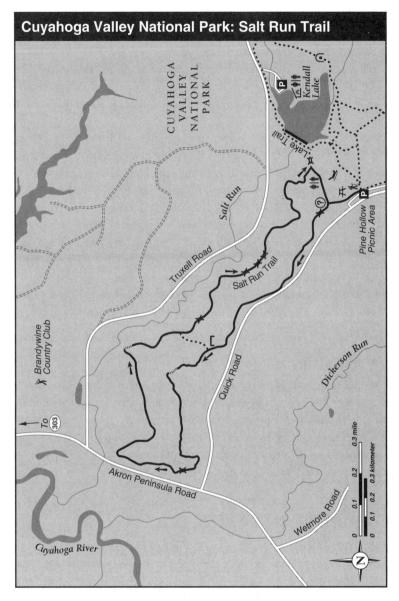

Cuyahoga Valley National Park: Salt Run Trail

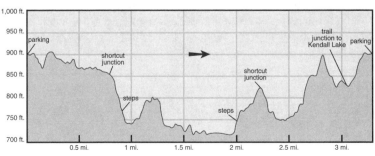

it; it's like lemon, nutmeg, and cloves in a single leaf). In the lower areas on the trail, you'll find a diverse population of ferns and mosses; in higher areas, where the sun can warm it a bit, you'll spot jewelweed.

There's also plenty of poison ivy in these parts. The general rule to avoid contact is "leaves of three, let it be." Poison ivy, similar to Virginia creeper, likes to climb trees. If you are sensitive to poison ivy and know you'll be in a dense forest, it's a good idea to wear long sleeves and pants.

As you rise up with the trail, you'll cross several long, wide footbridges. They can be extremely slippery when wet, so hang onto the railing as you go. Once you've landed back on the dirt trail, you'll probably notice that you're surrounded by skunk cabbages.

As the path veers right to head west, you'll see a sign for the connector trail to Kendall Lake. If you follow it (left), you'll circle the lake and return to this trail in just over a mile. It's a narrow but fairly flat trail, pretty anytime of year. To complete Salt Run from here, turn right. One more worthy climb awaits—punctuated by a half dozen railroad-tie steps notched into a steep hill of clay. Take special care here when the ground is wet.

Once you've reached the top, the remainder of Salt Run is relatively flat, and you'll finish your hike in the company of tall pines and hemlocks. Their needles lay a soft carpet on the trail, welcome after the harder trekking you've seen today. Take a deep whiff of pine and relax. You're finished.

Nearby Activities

Of course, there's no lack of things to do here in the heart of this 33,000-acre national park. Nearby Kendall Lake is a beautiful place anytime of year, so if you didn't take the extension trail to see it, consider driving over to have a look. Or head up to Peninsula and check out Deep Lock Quarry Metro Park.

If you'd prefer a different sort of walk, schedule a tee time at Brandywine Country Club, just a couple of miles north on Akron Peninsula Road.

GPS TRAILHEAD COORDINATES
N41° 12.891' W81° 31.917'

Follow I-77 S toward Akron and take Exit 143 for OH 176 (toward I-271). Turn left (east) onto Wheatley Road/OH 176. Go about 2.9 miles toward Riverview Road. Veer left onto Everett Road, and then in 0.6 mile turn right onto Riverview Road, heading south. In 0.3 mile, turn left onto Bolanz Road, following it 0.4 mile to Akron Peninsula Road. Turn left (north), and go 1.8 miles. Turn right onto Quick Road. Pine Hollow parking lot is 1 mile east of Akron Peninsula Road, off Quick Road.

50 Cuyahoga Valley National Park: Stanford & Brandywine Gorge Trails

The falls may be the namesake attraction, but there are other lovely views.

In Brief

This short trail packs a wallop in terms of scenery—and a respectable cardiovascular workout, thanks to an elevation change of more than 150 feet. Once you've completed this trail, you can say that you've seen firsthand what is possibly the most-talked-about feature of our local national park.

DISTANCE & CONFIGURATION: 1.5-mile loop	**DRIVING DISTANCE:** 13 miles from I-77/I-480 exchange
DIFFICULTY: Moderate	**ACCESS:** Daily, sunrise–sunset
SCENERY: 65-foot-high waterfall, ravine, great birding opportunities	**WHEELCHAIR TRAVERSABLE:** No
EXPOSURE: Mostly shaded	**MAPS:** USGS *Northfield;* also at trailhead, park visitor centers, and park website
TRAFFIC: Fairly busy	**FACILITIES:** Emergency phone, restrooms, and water at trailhead
TRAIL SURFACE: Wooden boardwalk and dirt trails	**CONTACT:** 330-657-2752; **nps.gov/cuva**
HIKING TIME: Allow at least an hour	

Brandywine Falls tumbles and dives 65 feet to crash into the otherwise mild-mannered Brandywine Creek below. The noise can cause you to raise your voice to converse on the boardwalk, but you'll have plenty of quiet time on the rest of the trail.

Start from the north end of the parking lot down the wide, sloping wooden boardwalk to visit the falls right away. No sense in waiting to see the main attraction.

Follow the boardwalk trail counterclockwise as the Brandywine Gorge Trail bends and approaches the top viewing platform—don't worry, the view gets much better from here. The stairs that take you down the next 300 feet or so get you close enough to the falls that they can properly impress you. Now that you've seen them—and probably taken a few pictures—move on to find out more about the falls.

The next stretch of boardwalk features a few interpretive signs explaining how the falls were put to work in the early 1800s. The first sawmill was built here in 1814, and the village of Brandywine Falls quickly grew up around the new industry provided by the falls.

The boardwalk deposits you on a grassy path that leads to a nondescript bridge crossing over the top of the falls. If you're tempted to take a more exciting path across the falls, perhaps through the water, don't. At least one hiker has died trying to cross at the top of the falls in recent years. Rushing water is stronger than you are, and you're wise to enjoy the falls from a safe distance. Back to the trail. On the north side of the landmark stands the iconic Inn at Brandywine Falls, a popular bed-and-breakfast. The inn is private property, but the trail on park property allows you a good look at the small farm the innkeepers operate.

Shortly after you wave good-bye to the chickens, the trail veers to the left and gets serious about going downhill. Not so serious that you'll lose your footing, but you can tell that you're on your way to the creek below. Tall hemlocks and oak trees are thick on the north side of the trail but sparse enough on the other side to allow you to enjoy a view of the creek below almost the entire length of the trail, until it bottoms out and crosses the creek on a narrow footbridge.

If you're returning to the trail for the first time in many years, you might think, "What footbridge?" Don't worry, your memory is right—a couple of decades ago, there was no

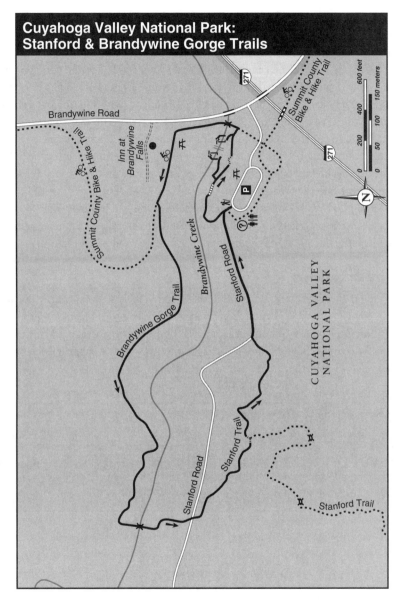

Cuyahoga Valley National Park: Stanford & Brandywine Gorge Trails

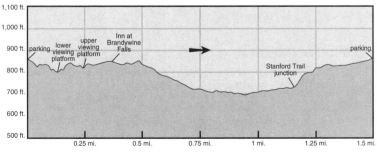

bridge here, and we all enjoyed crossing on several large, strategically placed rocks. But today, the footbridge takes us safely across instead.

From here the trail heads south and off into the woods far enough that you'll lose sight of the creek (though you can still hear it), and soon you'll have the option of leaving this trail to visit Stanford House, a little more than a mile away. (For lodging information, call 330-657-2909, ext. 119.) The Stanford Trail connects with the Towpath about 1.5 miles west of here, so if you're wanting a much longer hike, here's your chance.

When you're ready to return to the Brandywine Gorge Trailhead, follow the Stanford Trail back toward the falls. While you won't be able to see the creek or the falls until you've nearly reached the top of the gorge, the climb is very pretty, through thick woods sprinkled with a variety of wildflowers.

Returning to the parking lot, you may wish that you had brought your bike, as this trailhead also serves cyclists on the Summit Bike & Hike Trail, which essentially parallels the towpath here and through much of the Cuyahoga Valley National Park.

Nearby Activities

Want to bike? South of here, on the Summit County Bike & Hike Trail, you can ride alongside some tall rock ledges and then take the trail east into Hudson or south to Munroe Falls. Not interested in spinning your wheels? Stop at one of Cuyahoga Valley National Park's visitor centers (Boston Store is the closest to Brandywine Falls) and see what else you might find to do in this 33,000-acre wonder of nature.

GPS TRAILHEAD COORDINATES

N41° 16.597' W81° 32.399'

Follow I-271 S to Exit 19 (OH 82). Turn right (west) onto OH 82/East Aurora Road, and go 1.3 miles to Brandywine Road. Turn left (south) and follow it 2.6 miles to the trailhead parking lot on the right, immediately south of the Inn at Brandywine Falls.

51 F. A. Seiberling Nature Realm

In Brief

Inside the visitor center, you can learn as much about green building design as your brain can grasp—or handle a snake, or enjoy a puppet show. Outside, some of the gardens are as neatly buttoned-up as a Sunday school teacher—but when you reach the southern end of the nature trails, you'll find a bouncy suspension bridge sure to bring out your inner child.

Description

F. A. Seiberling cofounded The Goodyear Tire & Rubber Co.; if that was all he had done, you'd expect to find a park in Akron named after him. But Seiberling did much more. He served as an early member of the Board of Park Commissioners, and over the years he donated more than 400 acres to help establish the park system. In 1964 the park district purchased the 100-acre plot on which the nature realm now sits; Seiberling once owned the land, 1920–1948. Today the grounds of the nature realm offer the prettiest of plantings and well-groomed trails. Meticulous planning of the arboretum and surrounding trails provides constant changes of scenery—from the crab apples that bloom in the early spring to May and June's rhododendron blossoms to the rich explosion of fall perennials. You can always find color here.

When you enter the park from the southwest corner of the parking lot, wander into the herb and rock garden first. Like many of the 300 or so tree and shrub varieties here, most of the herbs are labeled for easy identification.

Once you've looped around on the stone walkway encircling fragrant herbs and medicinal plants, you'll find yourself looking down on the visitor center. You're looking down on it not because the hill is steep—it's more of a gentle slope—but because the building is partially underground. As you approach, you'll also notice some large solar panels near the building's entrance.

While the center was originally designed to be environmentally friendly, major renovations in 2009–2010 made the building a shining example of green building principles.

Go inside to learn more about those principles, and you'll also have an opportunity to meet a black rat snake and several more reptiles, amphibians, and other Ohio natives. Additional educational opportunities await inside—for children and adults—but don't stay too long; there's much to see outside.

Leave the building by the same door you entered, and head west toward the rather formal arboretum and garden area. When you follow either of the two wide, decorative brick-and-stone-patterned paths heading south, you'll see pines and crab apples. The paths wend through the arboretum, where you'll first see flowering, then weeping, and

DISTANCE & CONFIGURATION:
1.4-mile figure eight

DIFFICULTY: Easy

SCENERY: Fountain, small ponds, herb and flower garden, swingy suspension bridge

EXPOSURE: Mostly shaded

TRAFFIC: Moderate

TRAIL SURFACE: Paved or stone paths and mulched trails

HIKING TIME: 45 minutes

DRIVING DISTANCE: 21 miles from I-77/I-480 exchange

ACCESS: Grounds: Daily, 6 a.m.–11 p.m. Visitor Center: November–February: Tuesday–Saturday, 10 a.m.–5 p.m.; Sunday, noon–5 p.m. March–October: Tuesday–Saturday, 10 a.m.–7 p.m.; Sunday, noon–5 p.m. Closed holidays, but open most Monday holidays, 10 a.m.–5 p.m. Pets, bikes, and other recreational equipment not permitted.

WHEELCHAIR TRAVERSABLE: Yes, the visitor center and several trails

MAPS: USGS *Peninsula;* also inside visitor center

FACILITIES: Restrooms and water inside visitor center; restrooms also outside when building is closed

CONTACT: 330-865-8065; **summit metroparks.org/ParksAndTrails /FASeiberlingNatureRealm.aspx**

then vine tree varieties. Less than 0.2 mile from where you start, towering white trellises lure you to a small fountain; three great blue herons (made of wrought iron) bathe in it. (This is a popular place for wedding pictures, and amateur photography is encouraged. Commercial photographers, however, must obtain a special permit.)

Continue on the paved trail, veering south (right) at the fork in the path just a few paces south of the fountain. You'll follow a planting of pines and deciduous trees before turning east, leaving the paved path. (*Note:* Wheelchairs and strollers can continue on the paved path, heading northeast through the middle of the park.) The wide, flat, mulched trail continues south to Echo Pond. A covered observation deck sits on the pond's north side; a park bench on the south side of the pond is tucked near a stand of cattails—an excellent place to watch for birds, butterflies, frogs, and fish.

Leave the south end of the pond, and head east down a gentle incline. Turn right to follow Fernwood Trail (wooden trail markers display fern leaves). Fernwood winds its way south and then curves east through a thick deciduous forest, and you'll indeed find ferns here. This shady trail is farthest from the park entrance and where you're most likely to find solitude. The path straightens out at about 0.7 mile and then turns sharply to the left. From here, you wiggle your way northwest to arrive at the base of a bouncy suspension bridge.

The long wooden bridge supported by cables spans a 45-foot-deep ravine. You may find that you're torn between running across it to make it swing or stopping to take in the beauty of the ravine.

Once across the bridge, you'll find yourself on Cherry Lane Trail (signs marked with a carving of two cherries). Turn left and follow the path as it rises slightly to the west. Soon, the trail bends to the north, and the mulch surface is replaced by pavement.

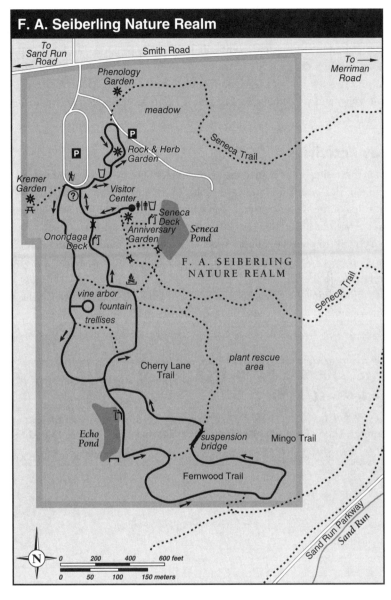

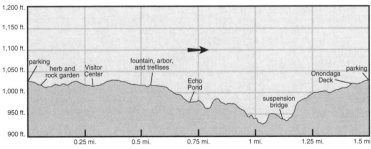

The western portion of Cherry Lane is as straight as the tall pines it borders. Soon, you'll come to a fork in the trail. Here you must decide whether to go left, taking the path through the rhododendrons and eventually back to the weeping and flowering trees, or to go right, through the planting of fruit and nut trees on your way to the Anniversary Garden, on the back side of the visitor center. For variety, go right. Either way, you'll enjoy the view, and you'll have logged about 1.5 miles when you arrive at the underground visitor center.

Nearby Activities

On the northern side of the nature realm, the longer Seneca Trail leads guests over more than a mile of the woodlands and open field, starting from the Anniversary Garden on the south side of the visitor center. If you'd like to learn more about Mr. Seiberling, you may want to visit beautiful Stan Hywet Hall at 714 N. Portage Path. The 65-room mansion with equally impressive grounds was the Seiberlings' home for many years. There is an admission fee to tour the house and grounds; call 330-836-5533 or visit **stanhywet .org** for details.

If it's more hiking you want, Sand Run Metro Park has it, just about 2 miles south of the nature realm.

GPS TRAILHEAD COORDINATES
N41° 8.360' W81° 34.546'

Follow I-77 S to Exit 138 (Ghent Road). Turn right (southwest) onto Ghent Road, and go 1.5 miles. Turn left onto Smith Road. Travel approximately 2 miles to find the park entrance (1828 Smith Road) on your right.

52 Gorge Metro Park: Gorge, Glens, & Highbridge Trails

Man-made and natural wonders await you at Gorge Metro Park.

In Brief

With pudding stones, lucky stones, waterfalls, caves, and an American Indian tale, Gorge Trail is irresistible to kids, and it's a great place to start a family hiking addiction. Don't be fooled by its fun nature, though—Gorge Trail offers enough up-and-down rock rambling to qualify as a serious hike. Two other trails here combine to provide nearly 7 miles of hiking just minutes from downtown Akron.

Description

The Cuyahoga River provides tremendous waterpower that has been put to good use here for well over a century. In the late 1870s High Bridge Glens Amusement Park opened on this spot, where patrons could enjoy a roller coaster and dance hall. Decades after the amusement park closed, the local electric company donated this 144-acre tract to the Metro Parks. Several educational signs along the trail offer history and geology lessons.

DISTANCE & CONFIGURATION: 4.5-mile figure eight, plus 2-mile out-and-back

DIFFICULTY: Moderately difficult, with a few steep sections and lots of steps

SCENERY: Two small caves, a waterfall, large rock passes, river views, an impressive bridge, 50-foot-high dam

EXPOSURE: Entirely shaded when trees have leaves

TRAFFIC: Moderate–heavy

TRAIL SURFACE: Dirt and rocks

HIKING TIME: At least an hour, so you can investigate the cave and enjoy the rock passes; 2–3 hours to enjoy all the trails here

DRIVING DISTANCE: 34 miles from I-77/I-480 exchange

ACCESS: Daily, 6 a.m.–sunset; avoid this trail when icy

MAPS: USGS *Akron East,* USGS *Akron West,* and USGS *Hudson;* also at trailhead

WHEELCHAIR TRAVERSABLE: No

FACILITIES: Restrooms at trailhead; water at picnic area

CONTACT: 330-865-8060; **summit metroparks.org/ParksAndTrails /Gorge.aspx**

Three distinct trails here can be combined for a total of about 7 miles. Let's start with the park's namesake, Gorge Trail.

From the northwest corner of the parking lot, head west on the wide dirt path. You'll follow the yellow circles on wooden signs that identify Gorge Trail. Pass three picnic shelters and the skating pond, all on your left, on your way to one of the area's great but unfortunately little-known historical sites.

About 0.4 mile into the trail, just beyond a small hill, you'll reach the Mary Campbell Cave, named for a young girl who was captured in Pennsylvania by Delaware American Indians. She lived in this cave with the tribe for five years before she was released at the end of the French and Indian War in 1764.

As the path goes downhill from the cave, it is studded with fist-size and larger rocks. The small ones are called lucky stones. These milky-white pebbles were smoothed by an ancient river, while other softer minerals eroded into mud. As a result of the way the sand and pebbles settled, layers of lucky stones can be seen in the Sharon conglomerate. *Pudding stones* refer to larger rocks that contain lucky stones of various shapes and sizes. The term probably came into use because the stones resemble British-style chunky pudding. Mind your lucky stones, and then cross over a footbridge and head uphill to another small cave. The trail becomes rocky here, and water tumbles over a 20-foot drop from above, sometimes spilling across the trail.

Continuing west, you'll notice at least three unmarked trails to the left. They are shortcuts, to be sure, but if you were to follow them, you'd miss some great sites, including a gigantic oak tree on the south side of the trail. About 0.9 mile west of your starting point, you'll find yourself between two boulders, each nearly 20 feet tall. Climb up a short but steep hill between the rock walls, and then turn left as the trail heads south through another rock pass.

Note that from this point, the trail is frequently rerouted and sometimes closed for maintenance, especially after storms. The sandy soil here is continuously eroding, so heed park signage and adapt your hike as necessary to preserve the sights here. This area is almost as fragile as it is beautiful.

As you continue through the narrow passageway (or around it, if you're claustrophobic), you'll see 22 stone stairs that have been laid inside the pass. At the top of the steps, turn around and watch as the hikers behind you emerge from what appears to be a tiny crack between the two rocks. As you continue west, you'll walk through a short "hallway" of dark gray and whitewashed shale; lucky stones decorate the walls on both sides.

A Gorge Trail marker indicates a sharp left turn, and from there you'll slip-slide down a sandy hill. The trail curves right again, heading west for the last time before dropping down a log staircase that is neatly stitched into the side of a sandy ravine. As the trail straightens out, you'll soon notice what looks like a root maze underfoot. From the large surface of exposed roots, you can overlook the shallow rapids of the Cuyahoga River. The trail earns its name here, providing beautiful views and sounds of the river gorge.

The trail bends left to cross over a long footbridge, and you may notice some fossil remains in the rock here. You'll cross another footbridge and roll over a few more small hills as you continue east. Once over the hills, a short log stairway takes you down to the dam overlook, where you can relax on a bench and enjoy the view.

Rested? Good. You'll climb up 105 wooden steps from the dam overlook before you veer right and east again. On your way back to the parking lot, you'll pass by a large wooden fishing pier. If you have time, hop onto it and enjoy a look at the water, so smooth here just above the dam. You'll pass by the south side of the picnic areas and a water fountain before returning to the trailhead where you began.

Ready for more? Head to Highbridge Trail, across the river. Once on the south side of the Cuyahoga, you'll stroll on a wide, grassy path for a while, thinking, "Is this all there is?" Don't despair—the scenery coming up is worth it. You'll bend away from the river until it's almost out of view and cross a short wooden footbridge. When you step off it, you'll notice that the ground to your right gently drops away. Keep going—you'll soon see how Highbridge Trail got its name.

At this point, the trail is wide and fairly flat with a gravel surface, and it ducks under a very high bridge (which carries traffic above on North Main Street to and from Akron). Stop and stare; it's an unusual vantage point.

Once you're in motion again, you'll soon reach the first of two steep stone staircases. They descend all the way to the river, where you have a couple of options.

You can cross the river and head up the other side to connect with the west end of Gorge Trail. *Note:* This is only an option when the river is low; at certain times, a couple of places allow for crossing where the water is just a few inches deep.

Another option is to head west on the south side of the river, following the trail to Cascade Valley Park (where you'll find Oxbow Trail; see page 208). And of course, there's always the turn-around-and-go-back option. That option offers a cardio boost, as those staircases are now heading up instead of down.

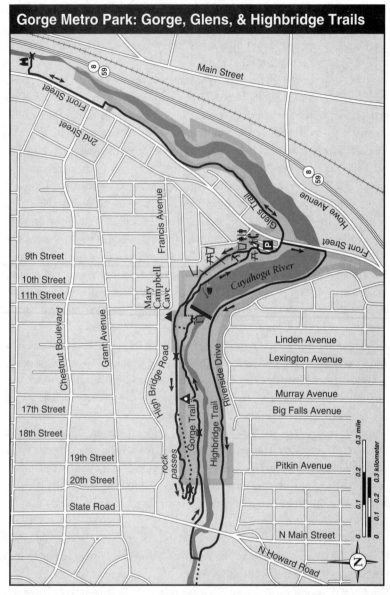

Gorge Metro Park: Gorge, Glens, & Highbridge Trails

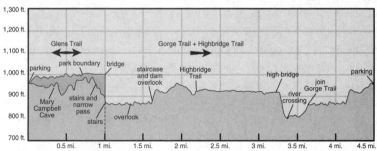

Combined, the Gorge and Highbridge Trails give you 5 miles of hiking pleasure. If you want a couple more, Glens Trail will accommodate you.

To reach Glens Trail from the main trailhead and Gorge Metro Park entrance, you'll have to cross to the east side of Front Street.

Glens Trail is narrow and hovers high above a stretch of the Cuyahoga known for bald eagle sightings and beautiful ice formations. The trail, also an out-and-back, ends on Front Street almost 2 miles north of the park's entrance, but you don't have to turn around there. Walking a few blocks north on the sidewalk will take you to yet another park, owned by the city of Cuyahoga Falls. There, a walkway and pedestrian bridge across the river provide more developed, but still stunning, views of this gorgeous gorge.

Nearby Activities

Summit Metro Parks hosts a wide variety of programs and events all year at Gorge Metro Park. In cold weather, the skating pond is open, conditions permitting. Watch the park website or call the seasonal information line at 330-865-8060 for skating conditions.

GPS TRAILHEAD COORDINATES
N41° 7.245' W81° 29.609'

Follow I-77 S to Exit 156 (I-480 E). Follow I-480 E for 5.6 miles toward I-271 S. Take Exit 1 to Miles Road, and in 1 mile, turn right to merge onto I-271 S. In 8.1 miles, take Exit 18A (OH 8). Merge onto OH 8 S, and go 12.5 miles. Take Exit 4 at Howe Avenue, turning right, and go 0.4 mile. Take the first right onto Front Street. The park entrance will be on your left immediately after crossing the river.

53 Hinckley Reservation: Whipp's Ledges

Climb with care.

In Brief

If you like to climb and gawk at great distances, Whipp's Ledges is for you. If buzzards are your bag, you'll want to visit this Medina County outpost of the Cleveland Metroparks in March.

You need to be cautious while climbing. To be blunt, a drop off the edge of one of these ledges could prove fatal—but with reasonable care, you'll enjoy the hike and the views tremendously.

Description

Hinckley Reservation has attained considerable fame as "the home of the buzzards," which are more specifically turkey vultures. Regardless, the raptors return to roost—quite predictably—in mid-March, and an annual party is held to celebrate the occasion. But all the fuss about the birds shouldn't suggest that they are the only ones who might be

DISTANCE & CONFIGURATION:
1-mile loop

DIFFICULTY: Short but difficult

SCENERY: Giant boulders and mini-caves of Sharon conglomerate, a spectacular view from the top

EXPOSURE: Mostly shaded

TRAFFIC: Moderate–heavy

TRAIL SURFACE: Dirt and rocks

HIKING TIME: 30 minutes, plus gawking time

DRIVING DISTANCE: 18 miles from I-77/I-480 exchange

ACCESS: Daily, 6 a.m.–11 p.m., except where otherwise posted

WHEELCHAIR TRAVERSABLE: No

MAPS: USGS *West Richfield;* also at ranger station on Bellus Road, boathouse, and park website

FACILITIES: Restrooms, water fountain, picnic shelter, and grills

CONTACT: 330-278-4544; **cleveland metroparks.com/Main/Reservations -Partners/Hinckley-Reservation-8.aspx**

attracted to the park year after year. Hinckley Reservation is full of reasons to return. Challenging hiking at Whipp's Ledges is one good reason. Start your steep climb on Whipp's Ledges Loop Trail from the eastern end of the parking lot. You'll huff and puff from the get-go, and the fact that you'll have some roots and a few stone stairs to aid your climb is a mixed blessing. These steps—from root to root and from step to step—require serious knee lifting. Keep going; the view is worth the climb.

A sign for the Buckeye Trail points right (southeast), but your trek continues to the northeast. Don't worry that your path isn't marked; your destination is impossible to miss. The ledges loom ahead of you almost from the moment you enter the trail. Up you go, huffing and puffing and rising along with the giant Sharon conglomerate outcrops. Your footing may be slippery, as the ground is sandy and pocked with lucky stones, small milky-white quartz pebbles that have fallen out of the larger conglomerate rock. Giant boulders—some 100 feet tall—loom straight ahead.

The trail bends to the left. Look at the massive stones on your right. Notice how the lichen grows in the indentations or pockmarks of the Sharon conglomerate, making an interesting play of light on the smoky dark rock.

Soon the massive stones to your left, 10–20 feet off the path at one point, begin to merge with those on your right, until you are squeezed into making a decision: Either crawl through a narrow tunnel or sidestep to the right, climbing up and on top of the boulders.

Whether you tunnel through or crawl up, don't miss the view from the top of the ledges—you'll stand about 350 feet above Hinckley Lake, and, looking west, you'll have a fantastic view of the valley.

As you ease down from the big rocks, you'll notice more blue blazes, but stay on your course. You'll probably need to use your hands as well as your feet to steady your descent. Loose gravel and leaf debris on top of the sandy soil make for slippery going, in both wet and dry conditions. The trail bottoms out just north of where you began, but before you

Hinckley Reservation: Whipp's Ledges

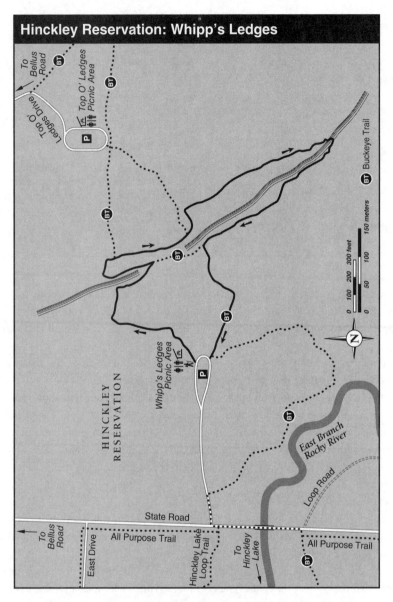

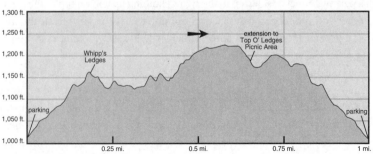

complete this short loop, you'll walk through a 4- to 6-foot-wide "hallway" created by two massive rocks, each about 20 feet tall. Though it's not a cave, you may feel quite boxed in.

From here, the path winds west a bit and then veers to the left to find its way back to the picnic shelter and the parking lot.

Nearby Activities

Though you've reached the end of this short trail, plenty of Hinckley Reservation remains to be investigated. The reservation covers 2,700 acres. Consider visiting Worden's Ledges to see the stone carvings there or head off for the lake. You'll find boaters there in summer, skaters in the winter, and ducks and other wildlife year-round.

While in Hinckley, don't be surprised if you see some rock climbers, but don't rush to join them. The reservation requires those who use top ropes to obtain a climbing permit before they start scaling the walls here. While visitors are not required to obtain permits for bouldering, caution is advised—climbing is considered an adventure sport for good reason.

Want to log some hilly miles without the climbing element? Hit the paved, accessible All Purpose Trail here for a 3.3-mile trek around Hinckley Lake. Also inside the reservation, you can rent various watercraft at the boathouse, located on the south end of the lake off West Drive. Swimming is another option. Take your pick of Ledge Lake (off Ledge Road at the southern end of the reservation), open seasonally (a day-use fee applies), or the lake swimming area (off Bellus Road at the northern end), where admission is free.

GPS TRAILHEAD COORDINATES

N41° 13.135' W81° 42.181'

Hinckley Reservation is located in Hinckley Township, just south of OH 303. From Cleveland, take I-77 S to Exit 146 (OH 21). Keep right on the exit ramp, following signs for OH 21. Turn right (south) onto OH 21/Brecksville Road, and go 2.2 miles. Turn right (west) onto OH 303. Follow OH 303 3.4 miles to State Road. Turn left (south). Whipp's Ledges parking lot is about 1.5 mile south of OH 303 on the left (east) side of State Road.

54 Hudson Springs Park

Have a seat, drop a line . . . or just relax.

In Brief

Bring the family: After circling the lake on the shady crushed-limestone trail, young hikers will be rewarded with a great view of a playground (including a hedge maze) on the northwest edge of this park. Those who've outgrown playgrounds can enjoy a picturesque sunset from one of many benches or decks on the lake's north side. And if your kids have paws, bring 'em along. A fenced dog run is on the northeast side of this city park.

DISTANCE & CONFIGURATION: 1.9-mile loop	**DRIVING DISTANCE:** 30 miles from I-77/I-480 exchange
DIFFICULTY: Easy	**ACCESS:** Daily, sunrise–sunset
SCENERY: Lake views, lush woods, a small island	**WHEELCHAIR TRAVERSABLE:** No
EXPOSURE: Three-quarters of the trail is shaded	**MAPS:** USGS *Hudson* and USGS *Twinsburg*
TRAFFIC: Moderate	**FACILITIES:** Restrooms in the parking lot; three picnic shelters within the park
TRAIL SURFACE: Crushed limestone	**CONTACT:** 330-653-5201; **hudson.oh.us /Facilities/Facility/Details/4**
HIKING TIME: 50 minutes	

Description

Hudson Springs Park spans 260 acres, including a 50-acre lake. Fishing and small (non-motorized) boats are allowed here. Hudson residents can rent space on the lakeshore to keep their canoes and rowboats handy; nonresidents may bring their own nonmotorized boats to enjoy the water for a small fee.

Though the lake is the park's largest feature, the trail seems to draw more visitors, and even though bicycles are allowed on the trail, you won't see many of them. The trail is well used, however, and you will certainly have company as you travel around the lake.

To follow the trail counterclockwise, head south from the parking lot, entering the trail just to the right of the shelter and boat launch area. The dirt-and-gravel path heads up a slight rise before it curves east. From here, you'll have a good view of the entire lake and its little island.

The trail is wide and relatively flat. On the eastern side of the lake, the trail rolls up and down over a few hills, 10 feet or so at a time.

On the south side of the lake, you'll cross over a well-disguised culvert; soon after, you'll notice an unmarked path on your right, leading east to a nearby residential neighborhood. It's one of several such footpaths here, most of which are unmarked. Just past this one, however, to the left of the trail, a sign points visitors to an overlook. The 0.3-mile or so detour off the main trail is well worth it.

Follow the fairly steep descent and you'll find a wooden deck with built-in benches overlooking the lake's calm waters. Returning to the main trail and rounding the eastern edge of the lake, you'll come to another observation deck, this one raised and facing west, making it perfect for sunset viewing. For a less direct but equally beautiful view of the sunset, follow the loop a little farther northeast to a second lower but slightly larger deck.

As you continue (now west) on the trail, you'll come to a dog run area (it is posted as such) and then to a disc golf course. Both are used frequently. Just a few steps from here, on the south side of the trail, two pieces of land jut into the lake. The park department wisely planted a couple of park benches and picnic tables here. They are situated so that

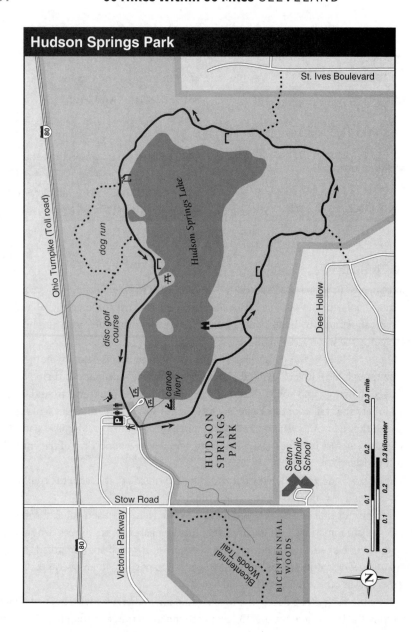

you can enjoy a peaceful lake view with your back to the action at the disc golf course and playground. Ah, but peaceful contemplation is only fun for so long. Heading west on the path again, you might find it hard to resist the playground's charm.

The northwestern corner of the park boasts play equipment for kids of all sizes. There's a small obstacle course, a tire swing, climbing equipment, and slides—and they're all fun. But perhaps most inspired is the little hedge maze, perfect for pint-size explorers.

The maze was dedicated in 1988 "To all children . . . from the Hudson preschool parents." It was a very thoughtful gift, from people who clearly know kids. The playground is adjacent to the parking lot, so when you're finished playing, you're free to leave. Bet you'll be back, though.

Nearby Activities

If the hedge maze, trails, bocce courts, disc golf course, and playgrounds don't tucker you out, cross Stow Road west to pick up the 0.5-mile hiking trail through Bicentennial Woods. Or, if you prefer a bit of history with your hike, drive into the heart of Hudson and admire its many well-preserved, century-old homes and other reminders of the city's Western Reserve heritage. Western Reserve College was established in Hudson in 1826. In 1882 the college moved to Cleveland, and Hudson took the loss hard. By 1906 Hudson had no water service, and the business district went bust. Then Hudson native James Ellsworth stepped in. He told local officials that he'd help out, provided they rescind all liquor licenses in town. The officials complied, and by 1912 Hudson was once again a thriving town.

GPS TRAILHEAD COORDINATES
N41° 15.089' W81° 24.465'

From Cleveland, take I-480 E to Exit 41 (Frost Road). Turn right (northwest) onto Aurora Hudson Road; in 1.8 miles turn left (south) onto Stow Road. The park entrance is on the eastern side of Stow Road, just south of the Ohio Turnpike, in less than a mile.

55 Indian Hollow Reservation

Before the large rock broke in two, it allegedly sheltered a boy from a tornado.

In Brief

Hikers can observe the effects of glaciers as well as spy herons and myriad birds enjoying this shady stretch of the Black River. A gravel loop provides a different experience away from the river, along land that was once quarried for stones used to build bridges and mills.

Description

About 30 miles southwest of Cleveland, Indian Hollow Reservation lies under the flight path of jets from Cleveland Hopkins International Airport. Watching them fly over, you can't help but feel sorry for the people in the sky, for whom the Black River is just a tiny line wending north to Lake Erie. For you, here on the ground, the river is the beautiful, dominant feature of this hike.

Begin at the trailhead map posted by the picnic shelter and restrooms. From here, a connector trail to your left leads you down a short hill and across a bridge over the East Branch of Black River to the Wayne Shipman Memorial Trail, a 1-mile loop. But before you follow that trail, take a few minutes to explore the banks of this beautiful river.

Take the Windfall Quarry Trail, a dirt path to your left, which will draw you into the woods and toward the river's edge. Follow the narrow dirt-and-rock trail north-northeast, and you'll be struck by the many shades of green and gray displayed by the lichen and moss on the rocks along the river. (Look for liverwort too.) In at least two spots on the

DISTANCE & CONFIGURATION: 2.5-mile balloons	**HIKING TIME:** 45 minutes–1 hour
DIFFICULTY: Easy	**DRIVING DISTANCE:** 30 miles from I-77/I-480 exchange
SCENERY: Black River, exposed sandstone walls, beech-maple forest, variety of wildflowers	**ACCESS:** Daily, 8 a.m.–sunset
	WHEELCHAIR TRAVERSABLE: No
EXPOSURE: Mostly shaded	**MAPS:** USGS *Grafton;* also at trailhead and park website
TRAFFIC: Moderate	**FACILITIES:** Two picnic shelters, grills, water, restrooms, and a small playground
TRAIL SURFACE: Windfall Quarry Trail and spurs, hard-packed dirt; Wayne Shipman Memorial Trail, crushed gravel	**CONTACT:** 440-458-5121; **metroparks .cc/indian_hollow_reservation.php**

Windfall Quarry Trail, the river appears easy to cross, and a path similar to this one calls enticingly from the other side of the river. Don't answer the call—the rocks are slippery, and the river runs several feet deep here. Continue on the dirt path on this side of the river, keeping an eye out for herons and other fishing birds.

You might also notice deep lines in the sandstone wall across the river. These lines were cut by a glacier during the Wisconsin Glaciation period, creating a wall that looks much like a layer cake. It is especially striking as you approach an old railroad bridge. Before you reach the bridge, however, you'll find a NO TRESPASSING sign—so if you want a good picture of the bridge, plan ahead and bring your long lens. Follow the trail as it bends left, looping into the woods and back on itself, to return to the base of the bridge. (A thick and fragrant stand of pines separates the trail from the private homes on your right.)

As you head to the trail across the river, you'll have time to consider this waterway's long history. Local authors Chris Smith and Paul Justy dug into the area's industrial past and uncovered more than a few fascinating stories about the Indian Hollow and Willow Park areas in Grafton. (Smith graciously shared some of those stories with me as he was writing *The Lost Quarry Industry of Indian Hollow and Willow Park—Grafton, Ohio.* His research was impeccable; the book is available at the Grafton Public Library.)

One of the large rocks placed just so in the river, for example, hasn't always been there. Apparently, it broke off around 1950. Prior to that, the rock jutted out a bit farther into the river—and saved a young boy's life. According to Smith:

"About the time of the Revolutionary War, a young Native American boy saw an approaching tornado coming up the river from the south. He was north of the rock and ran south, toward the tornado, because he knew his only chance to survive was to get under the rock. Luckily, a dry summer had reduced the river to a few inches of water, so he could easily run under the rock. Within seconds of reaching safety, the trees came crashing down. Not one tree on this bank of the river survived."

That's a pretty good legacy for a rock, but unfortunately, Smith found out that, later, the rock also marked the spot of several tragic events. Quarries were dangerous places to

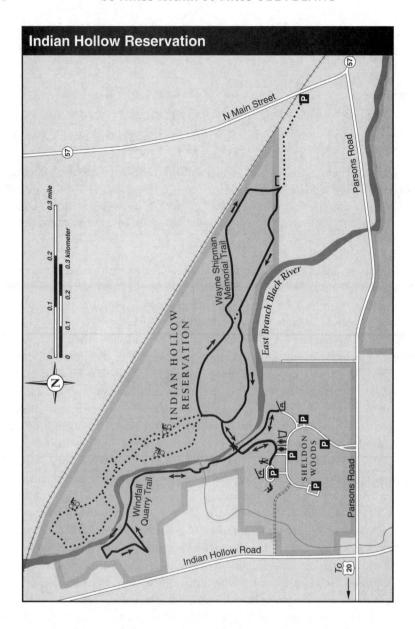

work, and snapping derrick cables injured and killed many quarry workers near the same rock. Smith also learned that, in 1899, a 14-year-old boy was hit by a quarry train and had to have an arm amputated.

While the rock has saved at least one life and been witness to many tragic events, it sits here quietly surrounded by great natural beauty; here, on this unmarked trail, so are you.

When you get back to the connector to the Wayne Shipman Memorial Trail, turn left and cross the bridge. As you do, you might appreciate the sandstone again for a different reason. Because the river bottom is sandstone, the water runs over it clear and bright. Crossing the bridge on a sunny day, the river fairly sparkles up at your shoes.

Across the bridge, the trail rises up a slight hill and splits. Veer left, following the gravel trail clockwise. The path is level and wide, with enough twists and turns to hold the interest of hikers and beginning mountain bikers. The trail lies under the shade of sugar maple and American beech trees. If you look closely, you may spot a tall cucumber tree. Indian Hollow is thought to be the only place in Lorain County where this particular member of the magnolia family grows.

Midway through the loop, a connector trail heads straight into the town of Grafton. In fact, you'll have to make a sharp right turn at a park bench to avoid going into town. After the turn, you're heading due west. This section is especially lovely in the late afternoon, when the sun bounces off the river and bleeds through the trees.

After completing the loop and returning across the bridge, head off the path again, this time to the left (south). Follow this unmarked, well-worn dirt trail to a large, flat rock. Perched just a few feet above the sparkling river, it seems custom-made for a picnic. Even if you're not packing a snack, stop, sit, and listen to the river rush by.

When you've heard enough, retrace your steps back to the paved connector trail; turn left and follow it back to the parking lot.

Nearby Activities

Bike trails rolling into Grafton give visitors a chance to see remnants of many quarries on their way into the historical town. Also, while you're here, you're not far from another great chapter in American history. In 1858 nearby Oberlin earned the nickname "the town that started the Civil War," after townspeople foiled an attempt by bounty hunters to return a fugitive slave to his owner. In addition to the town's rich history, the Oberlin College campus boasts beautiful gardens and landscaping and a fine legacy of its own. To reach Oberlin, follow Parsons Road west about 8 miles.

I sincerely thank Chris Smith, author and dedicated historian, for sharing his tremendous research and enthusiasm for Lorain County and Grafton in particular. His work has deepened our understanding of local history and will be appreciated by countless visitors to Indian Hollow as they gain a greater appreciation for the impact generations have had on this land and the role the river has played in the area's history. Thanks, Chris!

GPS TRAILHEAD COORDINATES

N41° 16.636' W82° 4.442'

From I-71 S, follow I-480 W 8.3 miles to OH 10 W. Keep left to continue on OH 10 W, and go 5.5 miles. Exit at OH 57 toward Medina. Turn left (south) onto OH 57/John F. Kennedy Memorial Highway, continuing about 4 miles before turning right (west) onto Parsons Road. Indian Hollow Reservation's Sheldon Woods entrance is on Parsons Road, just east of Indian Hollow Road, in less than a mile.

56 Liberty Park: Twinsburg Ledges

The park is very accessible, though some of the trails are challenging.

In Brief

Twinsburg Ledges has been a sweet and popular spot since it opened in 2011. And no wonder—a short but exciting trail makes the thrilling ledges more accessible than those at other area parks, such as Nelson-Kennedy Ledges State Park and Gorge Metro Park. And here, there's the added attraction of a resident black bear—figuratively and, quite probably, literally as well.

Description

Summit Metro Parks took "accessible" to heart in its design of the Nature Center, which opened in 2015. Inside, among the exhibits that pay homage to the site's former uses as an

DISTANCE & CONFIGURATION:
1.4-mile figure eight

DIFFICULTY: Moderate, with one steep hill and stretches of difficult footing

SCENERY: Ledges

EXPOSURE: Almost completely shaded

TRAFFIC: Fairly busy

TRAIL SURFACE: Limestone, dirt, wooden boardwalk

HIKING TIME: Allow at least an hour

DRIVING DISTANCE: 14 miles from I-77/I-480 exchange

ACCESS: Daily, 6 a.m.–11 p.m. Nature Center: Wednesday–Saturday, 10 a.m.–5 p.m.; Sunday, noon–5 p.m.

WHEELCHAIR TRAVERSABLE: 0.25-mile Maple Loop Trail, yes; Ledges Trail, no

MAPS: USGS *Twinsburg;* also at trailhead

FACILITIES: Emergency phone, restrooms, and water at nature center

CONTACT: 330-487-0493; **summit metroparks.org/ParksAndTrails /LibertyPark.aspx**

American Indian gathering spot and a maple sugaring operation, are several displays designed with help from the Cleveland Sight Center. The displays are specially created to be accessible to those with low vision. Other exhibits incorporate sensory elements that may improve the experience for visitors who are on the autism spectrum.

Another thing the nature center honors: black bears. Outside the entrance, visitors can see how they measure up to the impressive mammals that have certainly lived around here in the past and are very possibly living here now. Each spring, for the past several years, black bear sightings are reported in the Twinsburg area, particularly around the Ledges.

Ready to go for a hike now?

Just outside the nature center, the flat, 0.25-mile Maple Loop Trail gives visitors a look around from this relatively high vantage point in northern Summit County. Once you've looped around, it may be time to head down to the ledges to see what's below.

What you'll find after a shady and somewhat steep descent is a stunning wall of sandstone ledges and an invitation to wander into the small Glacier Cave. Don't worry if you're afraid of the dark; cracks overhead allow sunlight to peek through.

Once you've marveled at the cave's natural air conditioning, return to the trail and wander across the wetland via a long boardwalk. Metro Parks naturalists explain to visitors that the ferns, mosses, and lichens that grow here are a protective "living skin" and remind us that staying on the trail is required to protect the natural resources preserved here.

Once you've reached the end of the boardwalk, you'll return to the bottom of the hill and begin to climb back up to the trailhead.

Is this the best example of northeast Ohio's marvelous ledges? Well, they're as lovely as others, if not as extensive. That said, while I personally like my hikes a little longer and more challenging than this one, I realize that not everyone feels that way. And accessibility can be interpreted in many ways. Even if you're physically able to navigate more-difficult trails, such as those at Nelson-Kennedy or Whipp's Ledges (see pages 145 and 248, respectively), for example, this property is much closer to the folks who live in Akron

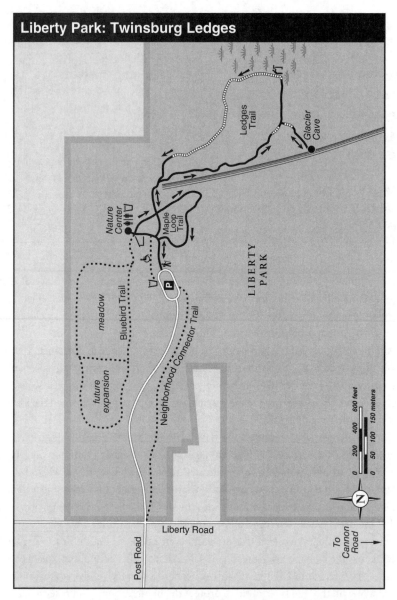

Liberty Park: Twinsburg Ledges

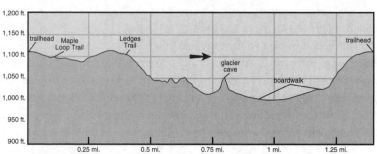

Near the entrance to Glacier Cave

and Cleveland. A shorter drive to reach this trailhead also makes the ledges more accessible to more people, and that's a very good thing.

Nearby Activities

The rest of Liberty Park, just a few blocks away at 9385 Liberty Road, is a vastly different (but very nice) park. It features several ball fields, a dog park, and a flat, exposed walking trail. Visit for a change of pace or to soak up some sun.

Also nearby: Twinsburg's historical city square. It has served as the center of town festivals since the early 1800s (including the internationally famous Twins Days celebration, held each August). A bandstand, historical church, and war memorial grace the square, located at the junction of OH 91, Ravenna Road, and Church Street. For information about the festivities, see **twinsdays.org.**

GPS TRAILHEAD COORDINATES

N41° 19.945' W81° 24.693'

Take I-480 E to Exit 36 (OH 82/Aurora), and turn left (east) onto OH 82, toward Twinsburg. In 1.7 miles turn left (north) onto Liberty Road. The park entrance will be on your right in 1.8 miles.

57 Munroe Falls Metro Park

A multifamily dwelling at Munroe Falls Metro Park

In Brief

This multifaceted park features a large swimming lake; during the summer, an admission fee is charged. Check the park website if you're planning a hike during the swim season; several free-admission days are planned throughout the summer. And of course, the trail is inviting all year.

Description

Indian Spring is one of those trails that feel longer than they are. Because of its rolling nature, you and your lungs and legs may feel as if you're getting a slightly better workout than you would on the average 2.2-mile trek. Don't fret; it's worth increasing your heart rate a bit.

From the parking lot, start off on the trail to the right to follow it counterclockwise. A short and fairly flat prelude takes you to Beaver Pond, where you may stop and take

DISTANCE & CONFIGURATION: 2.3-mile loop	**ACCESS:** Daily, 6 a.m.–11 p.m. Late May–mid-August: $4 for adults and teens; $3 for children ages 2–12
DIFFICULTY: Easy–moderate	
SCENERY: Swimming lake, beaver pond, mature shade trees, good birding opportunities	**WHEELCHAIR TRAVERSABLE:** No
	MAPS: USGS *Hudson* and USGS *Akron East;* also on trailhead bulletin board and at park website
EXPOSURE: Mostly shaded when trees have leaves	
	FACILITIES: Restrooms, water, concession stand (open June–August), and pay phone in main parking lot
TRAFFIC: Moderately busy	
TRAIL SURFACE: Dirt and grass	**CONTACT:** 330-867-5511; **summit metroparks.org/ParksAndTrails /MunroeFalls.aspx**
DRIVING DISTANCE: 26 miles from I-77/I-480 exchange	

advantage of a couple of benches to watch for signs of the industrious swimmers. Just past the pond, you'll head up a moderate climb and soon veer to the left.

Tall beech and maple trees comprise most of the woodlands here, though you may also spot black gum, sassafras, shagbark hickory, and tulip trees along the trail. As you continue to climb, notice the wetlands below. (You can see more of them if you visit the Tallmadge Meadows Area, located just south of here off OH 91. The trails there are flat and partially paved and provide still more birding opportunities.)

As you continue counterclockwise, the trail takes a sharp left and you'll begin heading down. You'll repeat this up-down pattern a few times, until you reach Heron Pond, on one of the most exposed portions of the trail. Until that point, however, you'll find that you're really in the thick of the woods.

While I don't advocate getting off the trail, if you were to step off the path just 10 or 15 feet and try to make your way parallel to the designated trail, you'd begin to get a sense of how densely wooded this area once was.

From Heron Pond, you'll duck back into the woods and continue slightly downward, getting a couple of nice peeks at the swimming lake in the process. The hike concludes with a descent via a charming natural stone staircase. At the bottom, you'll find yourself back in the trailhead parking lot.

Want to add a cardiovascular oomph to your hike? Try a few reps up the steep sledding hill that sits just west of the trailhead parking lot.

Nearby Activities

Munroe Falls Metro Park is a busy place, with plenty to do. A public swim lake draws locals in the summer, as does the sledding hill in the winter. In addition to the lovely trails, the park boasts several playgrounds as well as tennis and volleyball courts. Tallmadge Meadows, just a few miles south along OH 91, offers two flatter trails and great birding opportunities. Or you may want to bring your bike, as Brust Park (just north on OH 91) is a trailhead on the 34-mile-long Summit County Bike & Hike Trail.

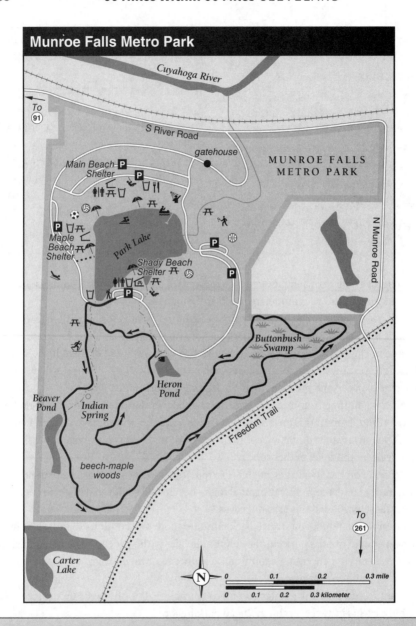

Munroe Falls Metro Park

Cuyahoga River

To 91

S River Road

gatehouse

Main Beach Shelter

MUNROE FALLS
METRO PARK

N Munroe Road

Maple Beach Shelter

Park Lake

Shady Beach Shelter

Buttonbush Swamp

Heron Pond

Beaver Pond

Indian Spring

Freedom Trail

beech-maple woods

To 261

Carter Lake

N

| 0 | 0.1 | 0.2 | 0.3 mile |
| 0 | 0.1 | 0.2 | 0.3 kilometer |

GPS TRAILHEAD COORDINATES
N41° 07.794' W81° 25.531'

From Cleveland, follow I-480 E to I-271 S. From I-271, in 3.4 miles, take Exit 18A (OH 8). Merge onto OH 8 S, and go 9.1 miles. Take the Graham Road exit (toward Silver Lake/Stow). Turn left (east) onto Graham, and in 1.8 miles turn right (south) onto Darrow Road/OH 91. In 2.3 miles, after crossing OH 59 (and then passing Brust Park), turn left (east) onto South River Road. The entrance to Munroe Falls Metro Park is about 1 mile east of OH 91, on the right.

58 Ohio & Erie Canal Towpath & Quarry Trails & Peninsula History

Quarry stones along the trail

In Brief

Peninsula displays the well-preserved vestiges of a canal-era and railroad town, while serving as a portal into the Cuyahoga Valley National Park. Some folks say Peninsula has a lock on history. Actually, it has two—and visitors will see both on this hike.

Description

Change steamed through Peninsula in the form of a canal in the 1820s and rolled through again in the 1880s when the railroad came to town. The changes kept coming, with the dedication of the Cuyahoga Valley National Recreation Area (now National Park) in 1975. And when the federal government comes to town to claim more than 30,000 acres, *change* is putting it mildly.

DISTANCE & CONFIGURATION: 3.1-mile balloons

DIFFICULTY: Moderate (Quarry, somewhat challenging; Towpath and village portions are easy)

SCENERY: Two canal locks, sandstone quarry, historical architecture, wildlife along the river

EXPOSURE: Trail, shady; sidewalks, exposed

TRAFFIC: Typically heavy in town, moderate on Towpath Trail, and light on Quarry Trail

TRAIL SURFACE: Asphalt, sand, dirt, crushed limestone, sidewalks in village

HIKING TIME: 1.5 hours

DRIVING DISTANCE: 16 miles from I-77/I-480 exchange

ACCESS: Towpath Trail, 24/7; Quarry Trail, 6 a.m.–11 p.m.

WHEELCHAIR TRAVERSABLE: Peninsula sidewalks, yes (most businesses, no); Quarry Trail, no

MAPS: USGS *Peninsula;* architectural tour guide at Peninsula Library & Historical Society, 6105 Riverview Road

FACILITIES: Restrooms, water, and drink machine at Lock 29 parking

CONTACT: Summit Metro Parks: 330-867-5511; **summitmetroparks.org /ParksAndTrails/DeepLockQuarry.aspx;** Cuyahoga Valley National Park: 330-657-2752; **nps.gov/cuva**

While other towns might buckle under the strain of being a gateway to a national park, Peninsula thrives. The town is well suited to serve as a portal back in time; in some ways, Peninsula also serves as an extension of the park. Lock 29 along the Ohio & Erie Towpath Trail literally deposits thru-hikers and bikers into the heart of Peninsula. The local bike shop is an icon to regular Towpath riders and a welcome beacon to folks with flats. Peninsula's restaurants are so popular with train riders that the Cuyahoga Valley Scenic Railroad features a layover lunch stop here.

Start your tour at the trailhead sign and map at Lock 29. Take the steps up to the bridge that literally and figuratively connects the relatively new Towpath Trail and national park to the historical town of Peninsula. An interpretive sign on the bridge highlights the building of the Ohio & Erie Canal. When construction began in 1825, workers had to devise it so that boats could negotiate the 395-foot elevation difference between Akron and Cleveland. Locks 29 and 28 were key to leveling the ride, and the canal was key to Ohio's economy.

Go below the bridge and walk into the now earth-filled lock. The mason's marks on some of the blocks are still visible, indicating the quarry and the work group from which the stone came.

Once over the bridge, continue south on the Towpath Trail and under OH 303, where the paved path gives way to crushed limestone. The river runs on your left; beyond it, railroad tracks carry passengers on the Cuyahoga Valley Scenic Line north into the park and south into Akron. About 0.5 mile into the trail, a sign points to Deep Lock Quarry. Take the cue and venture off the Towpath heading west. Cross a narrow, wooden footbridge and then head up a steep hill. A bench at the top may be a welcome sight after

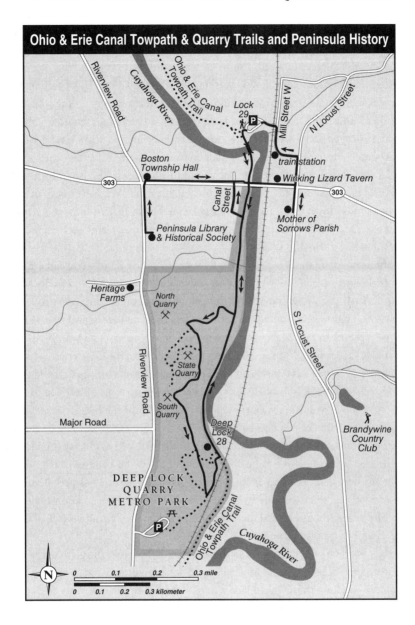

the climb. Follow the dirt path under tall pines and right over the rocky but now level ground. You'll reach the quarry shortly.

Sandstone dug here helped build many local homes and businesses, as well as several locks along the canal. Today, trees cover the quarry's floor, but the sheer stone walls leave no doubt where you are.

The adventurous may want to climb into the quarry, and it's allowed, but all should take care near the edges, as gravel and sand make for slippery footing. The trail skirts the eastern side of the quarry and heads south. As you go downhill, you'll see Summit County Metro Parks trail markers (in yellow), pointing west to the Quarry Trail parking lot, off Riverview Road. Unless you want to explore the park further, stay on the trail heading south and east to return to the Towpath. Before you do, you'll get another look at the quarry, and perhaps you'll wonder how many cars traveling on Riverview Road above realize how much history sits just below their commuting path.

Turn left (northeast) on the Towpath Trail to find Lock 28, also known as Deep Lock. As its name suggests, it is the deepest lock on the canal. While a typical lock would move a boat up or down 8 or 9 feet, Deep Lock could raise and lower boats 17 feet. For its hard work, Deep Lock was awarded a historic civil engineers landmark plaque, which is displayed inside the lock.

Continue north on the Towpath toward Peninsula. The calls of geese and other birds blend with the bubbling of the river, now on your right. As you head back to the center of this historical village, a few unmarked but well-used paths may entice you to leave the Towpath. If you follow one, you should soon find your feet on Riverview Road. Far easier, instead, is to return to OH 303 via the Towpath. There, you can end your hike, or continue on the village sidewalks to get a different perspective of the same era.

From OH 303, turn left (west) and head into the Peninsula Village Historic District, listed on the National Register of Historic Places. There's no sign to alert you to the history at 1749 Main Street, but it's worth a good look. Perhaps the biggest bargain on the block, this Vallonia model Sears Roebuck kit home sold for $2,076 in 1926. Its steep roof and white columns have been maintained so carefully that you might say it looks brand new or fresh out of the box. It's estimated that about 100,000 kit homes were built in the United States between 1908 and 1940. Most models came entirely as precut and numbered pieces of lumber. The homes were inexpensive but not inferior and were efficient to build. The Sears catalog boasted that a kit home could be built in about 60% of the time required to build a traditional home.

As you continue west and up a not-too-taxing hill, consider the girth of the maples that line the yards in Peninsula. Most of them were planted at or about the time of construction—making these granddaddy trees several times over.

Just before the intersection of Riverview Road and OH 303, you'll see the Boston Township Hall and its distinctive bell tower at 1775 Main. Built as a school in 1887, today it houses Boston Township offices, community meeting rooms, and the Cuyahoga Valley Historical Museum. Go south on Riverview to visit the Peninsula Library & Historical Society, where you can stop in to get an architectural tour guide or to learn more about the area (or visit **explorepeninsula.com/peninsula-historical-walking-tour**).

Turn around and head east along OH 303. Notice the building located at 1663 Main, built in 1820. Like many homes here, it is a good example of the Western Reserve Greek Revival style.

As you cross the bridge and the railroad tracks, you'll pass a variety of antiques shops, cafés, and galleries. The sign for the Old Peninsula Night Club hanging at 1615 Main Street has been around for many years; the building was a nightclub and a dance hall in the 1930s and '40s. Today, the restaurant is the Winking Lizard, but the owners still display the cool antique sign (along with their own).

About a block east of the Lizard, turn right and walk one block south on Akron-Peninsula Road to Mother of Sorrows Parish. Originally built in 1882, the church was enlarged in 1935 in a rather clever way. The building was literally cut in half, the west end was moved back, and the middle was filled in to enlarge the sanctuary. Now turn around and go north on Akron-Peninsula Road (also known as Locust Street). You'll pass Peninsula Town Hall, constructed with sandstone from the local quarry in 1851. Cost to the taxpayers? About $600. It's still used to house village services—talk about getting your money's worth.

Speaking of money, that concludes your nickel tour of Peninsula. You can continue north on Locust Street to Mill Street to return to the parking lot at Lock 29. Or continue to explore—you'll find plenty in Peninsula to pique your interest.

Nearby Activities

Peninsula hosts family-friendly events year-round; find the schedule at **explore peninsula.com.** To explore the national park from here, you can leave town on foot or by bike, either north or south, on the Towpath Trail.

Prefer to take the train? Get schedules and ticket information at 800-468-4070 or **cvsr.com.** Want to learn more about family farming in the valley? Operated by the same family since 1848, Heritage Farms, south of OH 303 on Riverview Road, operates year-round, holding a variety of annual events. It has a lovely herb garden, hosts a farmer's market on weekends, and sells Christmas trees, depending on the season. Find out more at **heritagefarms.com** or call 330-657-2330.

GPS TRAILHEAD COORDINATES
N41° 14.590' W81° 33.023'

From Cleveland, take I-77 S to Exit 146 (toward I-80) and keep right to OH 21/Richfield/ Brecksville. Turn right (south) onto OH 21/Brecksville Road. Go 2.2 miles, and turn left (east) onto OH 303/West Streetsboro Road. Go about 5 miles. Turn left (north) onto Akron-Peninsula Road/North Locust Street after crossing the river, and then immediately turn left again on Mill Street and into the lot. (A sign directs you to Lock 29 Trailhead Parking.)

59 Rising Valley Park

Rising Valley Park—a nice place for a walk. A prison, not so much.

In Brief

This 45-acre park located on the southern end of the Cuyahoga Valley was nearly turned into a prison. Fortunately, today's visitors can enjoy this beautiful area beside the East Branch of the Rocky River of their own free will. Look carefully and you might spy a variety of mosses, wildflowers, and "pieces of Canada."

Description

Parks come about in a variety of ways. Rising Valley was sort of a gift from the federal government. The land was originally part of the Cleveland Army Tank Plant proving grounds. In 1976, the United States government proposed that the area "be set aside for the construction of a minimum security youth prison." Residents and area officials' protests were heard—no one wants a prison built in their neighborhood, but it may have

DISTANCE & CONFIGURATION:
1.5-mile loop

DIFFICULTY: Easy–moderate

SCENERY: Broad expanse of valley, trickles of the East Branch of the Rocky River, thick young woodlands and wildflowers

EXPOSURE: About half exposed

TRAFFIC: Light

TRAIL SURFACE: Grass and dirt

HIKING TIME: 45 minutes

DRIVING DISTANCE: 15 miles from I-77/I-480 exchange

ACCESS: Daily, 6 a.m.–sunset

WHEELCHAIR TRAVERSABLE: No

Map: USGS *Broadview Heights*

FACILITIES: Restrooms at each picnic area, two picnic shelters with grills, water by northern picnic shelter, playground, ball diamond, soccer fields, and sledding hill

CONTACT: 330-659-4700; **richfield-twp .org/Parks.aspx**

seemed an especially ill-conceived location because the adjoining property was, at the time, a Girl Scout camp. This story had a happy ending: In 1977 the US government deeded the 227 acres to Hinckley and Richfield townships for the purpose of creating a public park and recreation area. Today, Richfield township manages a 45-acre portion of Rising Valley Park; the remaining acreage, located in Hinckley, is managed by Cleveland Metroparks as part of Hinckley Reservation.

As a condition of the transfer of land, a master plan had to be developed and implemented. The resulting Rising Valley Park Board committed itself to preserving this land and the adjacent East Branch of the Rocky River corridor for future generations.

There are no trail signs here, but a rather obvious path leads west from the parking lot and shelter at the north end of the park. The Ohio Operating Engineers, who run a training facility that abuts Rising Valley Park, have donated much time, labor, and materials to the park over the years. With a nod of thanks to the facility on the northern edge of the park, step onto the wide, grassy path and prepare to enjoy.

The path parallels a sledding hill, and the steep downhill slope offers fantastic views of the valley. At the end of the hill, the path veers left, heading south. Before you turn to follow it, take a few minutes to soak up the valley view.

As the path veers left, woods appear on your right. The wet woodlands and river are monitored by the Ohio Department of Natural Resources. You may spot jack-in-the-pulpits, skunk cabbages, or trilliums along the way. Wild turkeys, pileated woodpeckers, great horned owls, and red foxes call this area home. The path is easy to follow for 0.5 mile or so, reaching a few trickles of the river. Once you're finished exploring, return to the drier, grassy path.

As you continue to roll downhill and south on the wide grassy trail, an unmarked and little-used path cuts into the woods to your left. If you want a shorter hike, continue on this path as it curves east and then north again, depositing you by a ball field or picnic area. Otherwise, return to the more beaten path, continuing gently downhill and south.

Rising Valley Park

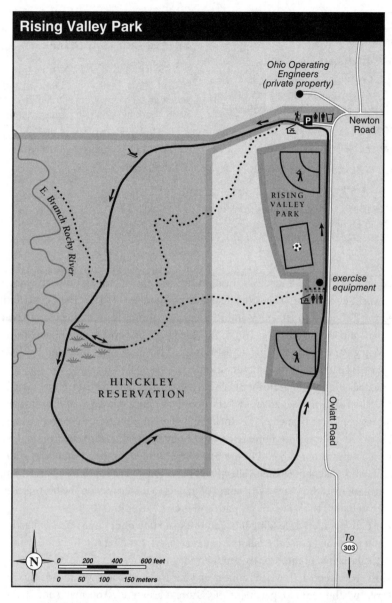

Ohio Operating Engineers (private property)

Newton Road

RISING VALLEY PARK

exercise equipment

HINCKLEY RESERVATION

E. Branch Rocky River

Oviatt Road

To 303

N

0 200 400 600 feet
0 50 100 150 meters

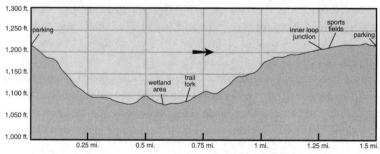

1,300 ft.
1,250 ft. — parking
1,200 ft.
1,150 ft.
1,100 ft. — wetland area / trail fork
1,050 ft.
1,000 ft.

inner loop junction — sports fields — parking

0.25 mi. 0.5 mi. 0.75 mi. 1 mi. 1.25 mi. 1.5 mi.

There you'll notice the woods on either side of the trail are littered with erratics, also known as pieces of Canada, or rocks that were imported by glacial ice sheets.

Continue through thick woods, where you'll find a variety of mosses. In the spring, daffodils pop up amid maple, oak, and beech trees.

As you near the southern end of the park property, the trail forks again. Bear left, going east and up a long, low-grade hill. (The other path, going straight and south, soon lands on private property in a residential development.) As you continue up the hill, it's easy to appreciate the delicate wildflowers here but not hard to imagine what a great run it must have been for tanks, plowing through the thick mud and rolling over assorted large rocks.

On your way back to the parking lot, you'll pass the ball fields and the picnic and play areas. Still, no matter how rowdy the ball games, no matter how many picnickers fill the shelters, don't you suppose it's an improvement on tank traffic, and far nicer than a prison ground?

Nearby Activities

Lengthen this hike with the 4.7-mile Medina section of the Buckeye Trail around Whipp's Ledges at Hinckley Reservation (see page 248). Take OH 303 west 1 mile and turn left on State Road. Follow State Road about 1.5 miles to Whipp's Ledges parking.

GPS TRAILHEAD COORDINATES

N41° 15.666' W81° 41.000'

Follow I-77 S to Exit 149B (OH 82/West/East Royalton Road toward Broadview Heights). Turn right (southwest) onto OH 82, and go 1.7 miles. Turn left (south) onto OH 176/ Broadview Road. In 3.8 miles, turn right (west) onto Newton Road, which veers left and becomes Oviatt Road. The parking lot for Rising Valley Park is located at this intersection. Alternatively, you can access the park from OH 303. Traveling west on OH 303, turn right (north) onto Oviatt Road. Follow Oviatt north about 1.5 miles—the park is not marked or signed until you reach the end of the residential drive. Continue to the parking lot, located at the north end of the park.

---

60 Spencer Lake Wildlife Area

In Brief

Want to get away from it all? Spencer Lake feels about as far away from it all as you can get, 40 miles from Cleveland. Once here, chances are fairly good that you won't meet another hiker on the trail. (But if the catfish are biting, you won't be alone.)

Description

From the parking area on the western side of the lake, head west on the park access road (Spencer Lake Road). About 0.1 mile west of the lot, turn left (south) into the woods, where the only marker is a blue blaze on a fence post. The wide, flat trail under the shade of tall oaks soon bends to the left because it has to—otherwise, it would lead you into the river.

The east branch of the Black River snakes by, about 20 feet below you and to your right. The edge of the trail is unforgiving here, but if you stay a foot or two back, you'll have lovely views of the shady river for the next 0.5 mile. The view is best enjoyed from a standstill, of course. While you're moving, you'll want to keep your eyes on the trail—you're likely to find a large log or a whole tree lying in your path. If you're quiet (and lucky), you may also catch a glimpse of some of the many songbirds that inhabit this area. The variety of food sources—tall oak trees, thistles, goldenrods, marshlands, and nearby open fields—makes this spot very attractive to a rich assortment of birds and mammals. Wild turkeys and a host of waterfowl frequent the area too. (So do mosquitoes and deerflies, in their respective seasons, so wearing insect repellent is a good idea.)

The trail bends left again and leads you by a field and some young-growth trees—their rustle entertains you as you continue east to the dam. This area can be quite wet during spring, but the wildflower display is worth getting a little bit of mud on your shoes.

If you don't like squishy trails, though, plan to come during a dry spell or, even better, in the winter, when you're likely to see people ice fishing on the lake. In the summer, when you emerge from the woods, you'll pass ironweed, goldenrods, milkweed, and other popular bird food before you land on the wide, grassy walkway to the dam.

You reach the earthen dam about 0.9 mile into the hike. This is my favorite stretch. I don't know why I like earth dams so much; I just do. The path continues east 100 feet or so and then turns right, crossing railroad tracks and ending at OH 162. Don't go there; instead, turn left, into the woods. Here the narrow path hugs the lakeshore and then darts into the woods, heading north. You'll roll up and down a few hills, rising slowly through bramble (and wildflowers, in the spring), until you reach a spot in the woods where it seems as if you might walk right into the lake. You don't, of course, but the view here is lovely.

DISTANCE & CONFIGURATION:
2-mile loop

DIFFICULTY: Easy

SCENERY: Lake, river, marsh, earthen dam, woods, foxes, muskrats, pheasants, waterfowl, possibly eagles or wild turkeys

EXPOSURE: Mostly exposed

TRAFFIC: Light

TRAIL SURFACE: Dirt and grass

HIKING TIME: 45 minutes

DRIVING DISTANCE: 41 miles from I-77/I-480 exchange

ACCESS: Spencer Lake is a popular public hunting area; hunting, fishing, and trapping are allowed by permit. This area is closed to all other activity September 1–May 1, 8 p.m.–6 a.m.; and May 2–August 31, 10 p.m.–6 a.m. Wear bright colors and avoid early-morning hours during hunting season.

WHEELCHAIR TRAVERSABLE: No

MAPS: USGS *Lodi;* also at **buckeyetrail.org/sections/sections .php?section=medina** and **wildlife.ohiodnr.gov/spencerlakewa**

FACILITIES: Two boat ramps and two fishing/observation decks (one wheelchair accessible)

CONTACT: 330-644-2293; **wildlife.ohiodnr.gov/spencerlakewa**

The path wiggles a bit through the woods, and in a couple of spots, you may need to climb over fallen trees to continue your hike. In one such spot, hikers beat out a secondary path around the fallen tree; then another tree landed on that path. Philosophers on the trail might consider this a good example of man versus nature; others will simply enjoy climbing over the tree. At various points around the lake, you may have to step around another visitor who is fishing. Channel catfish and largemouth bass are two varieties that anglers enjoy finding here.

About 0.5 mile from the southern dam, you'll reach the eastern parking lot and a newer, northern dam (a flood washed away the original in 1969; this dam was constructed in 1970). You'll also find the trailhead for the Buckeye Trail. Turn right if you're itching to go farther, but know before you follow the Buckeye Trail that it travels the entire state. Of course, you can follow the trail to the edge of the state wildlife area and turn around, adding less than a mile to your overall distance here. One particular part of the Buckeye Trail, dubbed the Medina section, travels from Findley State Park to the city of Medina, mostly on rail-trails and through other parks. Otherwise, turn left (west) to continue your walk here at Spencer Lake.

Cross the road and walk along the well-beaten path on the north side of the dam. It's a great spot to observe ducks and other migratory birds and catch a glimpse of some of the other animals here.

It's worth noting that this is a wildlife restoration area, actively managed for sport hunting and fishing. The state acquired the land in 1956 and built dams here in the 1960s. Fish and wildlife reclamation projects have been ongoing since. (Such projects are funded in part by hunting and fishing license sales, so everyone can enjoy more sporting opportunities.)

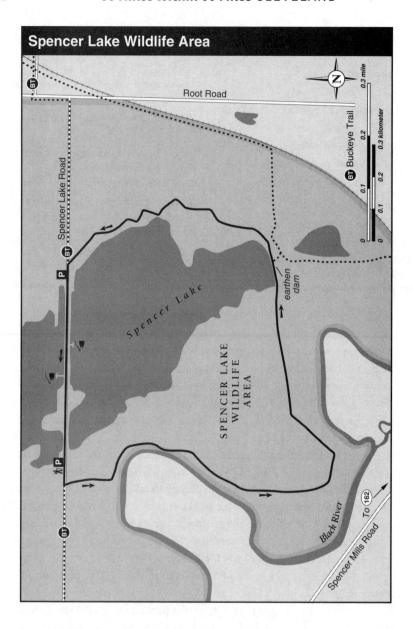

Over the years, grass carp have been stocked to control aquatic vegetation to improve the quality of fishing, and bass length limits and other measures are often in place. Heed any posted limits and work within program guidelines; they're created with all of Ohio's residents in mind. (*All* meaning the plants and animals, including *you*.) Sit quietly, and you may catch a glimpse of the mink and muskrat populations that attract sportsmen. Hang out until well after dark (hunting and fishing can go on here all night), and you'll also appreciate how dark the sky can be here, far enough away from major population centers that the stars can really shine.

To complete your hike, cross the causeway and return to the western parking lot for a round-trip of nearly 2 miles—or more, if you followed the Buckeye Trail for a bit. Before you go, you may also stop at one of the two fishing/observation decks for another perspective on the lake.

Nearby Activities

Looking for a long day hike? You can follow the Buckeye Trail west from Spencer Lake to Findley State Park, about 10 miles from here. For maps and more information about the Buckeye Trail, call 740-832-1282 or visit **buckeyetrail.org.** Just east of Spencer Lake Wildlife Area, off OH 162, you'll find two Medina County parks: Schleman Nature Preserve and Buckeye Woods, which offer more hiking trails, picnic facilities, and play equipment. To learn more about those facilities, visit **medinacountyparks.com.**

GPS TRAILHEAD COORDINATES
N41° 6.751' W82° 5.278'

From Cleveland, take I-71 S to Exit 222 (OH 3 toward Hinckley/Medina). Turn right (southwest) onto OH 3, and go 2 miles. Turn right (west) onto Fenn Road, and go 3.3 miles. Turn left (south) onto Marks Road, and then make an immediate right (east) onto Fenn Road again. Continue 11.4 miles as the road changes into OH 18. Turn left (south) onto Foster Road, and go 2.3 miles. Make a slight right (southwest) onto River Corners Road, and go 1.7 miles. Turn left (east) onto Spencer Lake Road. The parking area for Spencer Lake Wildlife Area is on your right in 0.3 mile.

Appendix A: Outdoor Shops

Appalachian Outfitters

60 Kendall Park Rd.
Peninsula, OH 44264
330-655-5444
appalachianoutfitters.com

The Backpackers Shop

5128 Colorado Ave./OH 611
Sheffield Village, OH 44054
440-934-5345
888-303-3307
backpackersshop.com

Gander Mountain

gandermountain.com
2695 Creekside Dr., Ste. 100
Twinsburg, OH 44087
330-405-2999

5244 Cobblestone Rd.
Sheffield Village, OH 44035
440-934-8222

9620 Diamond Centre Dr.
Mentor, OH 44060
440-639-8545

Appendix B: Places to Buy Maps

Also see the shops listed in Appendix A.

Cleveland Metroparks Nature Shops

clevelandmetroparks.com

North Chagrin Nature Center
3037 SOM Center Rd.
Willoughby Hills, OH 44094
440-449-0511

Rocky River Nature Center
24000 Valley Pkwy.
North Olmsted, OH 44070
440-734-7576

Hinckley Lake Boathouse & Store
1 West Dr.
Hinckley, OH 44233
330-278-2160

Cuyahoga Valley National Park

nps.gov/cuva

Boston Store Visitor Center
1550 Boston Mills Rd.
Peninsula, OH 44264
330-657-2752

Canal Exploration Center
7104 Canal Rd.
Valley View, OH 44125
216-524-1497

F. A. Seiberling Nature Realm

1828 Smith Rd.
Akron, OH 44313
330-865-8065
summitmetroparks.org/ParksAndTrails
/FASeiberlingNatureRealm.aspx

Appendix C: Hiking Clubs and Events

Akron Bicycle Club

(hikes off-season)

akronbike.org

Appalachian Outfitters

60 Kendall Park Rd.
Peninsula, OH 44264
330-655-5444
appalachianoutfitters.com

Cleveland Hiking Club

clevelandhikingclub.org

Portage Trail Walkers

330-673-6896

Appendix D: Other Resources

Ashtabula County Metroparks

440-576-0717

ashtabulacountymetroparks.org

Buckeye Trail Association

740-832-1282

buckeyetrail.org

Cleveland Metroparks

216-635-3200

clevelandmetroparks.com

Clinton Historical Society

clintonohiohistoricalsociety.org

Cuyahoga Valley National Park

330-657-2752

nps.gov/cuva

Geauga Park District

440-286-9516

geaugaparkdistrict.org

Lake Metroparks

440-639-7275

lakemetroparks.com

Lorain County Metro Parks

800-526-7275

metroparks.cc

Medina County Historical Society

330-722-1341

medinahistorical.com

Medina County Park District

330-722-9364

medinacountyparks.com

The Nature Conservancy

614-717-2770

nature.org

Ohio & Erie Canalway Coalition

330-374-5657

ohioeriecanal.org

Ohio Department of Natural Resources, Ohio State Parks

614-265-6561

parks.ohiodnr.com

Ohio Outdoor Sculpture Inventory

oosi.sculpturecenter.org

Portage County Historical Society

330-296-3523

portagecountyhistoricalsociety.org

Portage Park District

330-297-7728

portageparkdistrict.org

Stark County Park District

330-477-3552

starkparks.com

Summit County Historical Society

330-535-1120

summithistory.org

Summit Metro Parks

330-867-5511

summitmetroparks.org

Appendix E: Bibliography

Abercrombie, Jay. *Walks and Rambles in Ohio's Western Reserve.* Woodstock, VT: Backcountry Publications, 1996.

Bartsch, William W. "Lake View Cemetery Trail Guide." Eagle Scout project, Troop 656, Cleveland Heights, OH, 1988.

Bobel, Pat. *The Nature of the Towpath.* Akron, OH: Cuyahoga Valley Trails Council, Inc., 1998.

Cuyahoga Valley National Recreation Area Trail Guide Handbook. Akron, OH: Cuyahoga Valley Trails Council, 1996.

Directory of Ohio's State Nature Preserves. Columbus, OH: Ohio Department of Natural Resources, 1998–2000.

Gross, W. H. (Chip). *Ohio Wildlife Viewing Guide.* Helena, MT: Falcon Publishing, 1996.

Hallowell, Anna C. and Barbara G. *Fern Finder.* Rochester, NY: Nature Study Guild, 1981.

Hannibal, Joseph T. and Schmidt, Mark T. "Rocks of Ages." *Earth Science* 41, no. 1 (Spring 1998): 19–20.

Latimer, Jonathan P., and Nolting, Karen Stray. *Backyard Birds* (Peterson Field Guides for Young Naturalists). Boston: Houghton Mifflin Company, 1999.

Leedy, Walter C. Jr. "Cleveland's Terminal Tower—The Van Sweringens' Afterthought." *The Gamut,* no. 8 (Winter 1983): Cleveland State University Library, **web.ulib .csuohio.edu/speccoll/gamut/1983w/ctt.**

Manner, Barbara M. and Corbett, Robert G. *Environmental Atlas of the Cuyahoga Valley National Recreation Area.* Monroeville, PA: Surprise Valley Publications, 1990.

"Pathfinder—A Guide to Cleveland Metroparks." Cleveland, OH: Cleveland Metroparks, 1996.

"Peninsula Village Architectural Tour." Peninsula, OH: Peninsula Area Chamber of Commerce (n.d.).

Socha, Linda Hoy. "Area Cemeteries Rich in Historic Milestones of City," *Sun Newspapers,* 4 June 1998.

Towpath Companion. Akron, OH: Ohio & Erie Canal Corridor Coalition, 2001.

Watts, May Theilgaard. *Tree Finder.* Rochester, NY: Nature Study Guild, 1998.

Wright, Caryl. "Eccentric Russell 'caveman' was no hermit," *Russell Historical Society Newsletter* 1, iss. 9, 19 March 1990.

Zim, Herbert S. and Cottam, Clarence. *Insects.* New York: Golden Books, 1997.

Index

About the Author

DIANE STRESING grew up in Columbus, moved to the Cleveland area in 1989, and currently lives in Kent. A genuine Buckeye, Stresing received a bachelor of arts degree in journalism from Ohio State University. When she's not hiking, biking, or spending time with her family, Stresing works as a commercial freelance writer, providing B2B content to a variety of clients.

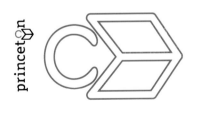

DEAR CUSTOMERS AND FRIENDS,

SUPPORTING YOUR INTEREST IN OUTDOOR ADVENTURE, travel, and an active lifestyle is central to our operations, from the authors we choose to the locations we detail to the way we design our books. Menasha Ridge Press was incorporated in 1982 by a group of veteran outdoorsmen and professional outfitters. For many years now, we've specialized in creating books that benefit the outdoors enthusiast.

Almost immediately, Menasha Ridge Press earned a reputation for revolutionizing outdoors- and travel-guidebook publishing. For such activities as canoeing, kayaking, hiking, backpacking, and mountain biking, we established new standards of quality that transformed the whole genre, resulting in outdoor-recreation guides of great sophistication and solid content. Menasha Ridge continues to be outdoor publishing's greatest innovator.

The folks at Menasha Ridge Press are as at home on a whitewater river or mountain trail as they are editing a manuscript. The books we build for you are the best they can be, because we're responding to your needs. Plus, we use and depend on them ourselves.

We look forward to seeing you on the river or the trail. If you'd like to contact us directly, join in at trekalong.com or visit us at menasharidge .com. We thank you for your interest in our books and the natural world around us all.

SAFE TRAVELS,

Bob Sehlinger

BOB SEHLINGER
PUBLISHER